Contents

Preface

What is marketing? This is a question asked not only by students and those who have newly entered the business world. All too frequently it is asked by many who have spent years in commercial and industrial activity.

Marketing is essentially an attitude of mind. Its principles apply to all forms of commercial enterprise. Although selling plays an essential part, the total marketing function is concerned with a much wider spectrum, embracing market research and analysis, product planning, coordination and pricing, advertising and promotion, as well as the study of distribution policies and methods.

This book seeks to explain in straightforward terms what is meant by the marketing concept.

1
What is marketing?

1.1 The historical background

At one time there was no such thing as marketing. Blacksmith, stonemason, saddler, carpenter, hosier and tailor all knew their customers personally. They were in a position to discuss the size, the shape, the design, the colour and the price of the goods they made with the people who bought and used them. A dialogue existed between producer and consumer.

With the coming of the Industrial Revolution this personal contact came to an end. Changes in production led to changes also in distribution. The greatly increased production of goods which resulted from mechanization required a mass market for their consumption, and distribution became a major undertaking. The manufacturer was no longer able to undertake the distribution of his products to the consumer. He invested his capital in premises, machinery and raw materials. He had neither the means nor the desire to distribute the product; nor was it necessary for him to do so. A distributive trade grew up to serve every industry. Wholesalers, with warehouses in major cities, purchased the manufacturer's products in bulk, stocked them and organized their distribution to retailers throughout the country. On the one hand, the wholesaler largely financed the manufacturing operation, while, on the other, by the extension of credit to retail shopkeepers, he financed much of the retail distribution of consumer products.

One of the major problems facing any manufacturer is to gauge the likely demand for the goods he proposes to make. Once the direct contact between producer and consumer had been broken, it was upon the distributive trade, in particular the wholesaler, that the producer relied for his market information. This function the wholesale houses performed exceedingly well. Through their teams of salesmen they served retailers in cities and towns throughout the country; the success of the retailer's business depended upon his knowing and anticipating the needs of his clientele, and this information was fed back via the 'travellers' to the buyers of the wholesale houses. These buyers therefore had a 'feel' of the market. They were generally greatly experienced in the various commercial aspects of the classes of goods in which they specialized. It was they who decided the particular 'lines' of goods which were to be bought from the manufacturers, the quantities which were to be stocked, subdivided into their natural categories according to the nature of the goods, such as size or width, colour, design and quality. It was they who decided the price at which the goods would be bought from the manufacturer and the price at which they would be sold to the retailer. By so doing, they effectively set the general price level at which goods would be sold to the consumer. Wholesale buyers were therefore, in some respects, the first practitioners of marketing.

The heyday of the wholesale distributor was the latter part of the nineteenth century and the early twentieth century. During this period there were of course considerable changes in consumer requirements. Apart from the more obvious changes brought about by fashion, all classes of merchandise underwent gradual change as the social habits of the population altered. Such changes were, however, often barely perceptible. The pace of life was very much slower than it is today. Furthermore, goods were usually made and bought to last: 'built-in obsolescence' had no meaning in the 1890s.

It was in the 1950s, with the arrival of automation on a large scale, that conditions underwent a dramatic change. As mass-production processes were introduced into nearly every industry, outputs increased rapidly. The dream of vast quantities of cheaply made goods at a price within the reach of every man and woman in the country now seemed likely of fulfilment. The national policy of full productivity and full employment resulted in rising wages and, by the 1960s, the so-called affluent society had arrived. Ironically, however, it was at this stage that the creation of mass markets – essential to absorb these vast quantities of goods – coincided with a rapid rise in the cost of labour in the distributive trades. The savings achieved by mass production were now being eroded by the increased cost of distribution. Furthermore, production in many industries was at last catching up with demand. The shortages of the immediate post-war years were giving way to abundance. What had been a seller's market since the outbreak of the Second World War in 1939 became very much a buyer's market.

For the post-war generation of businessmen this was a novel experience. It was recognized that the scientific approach, which had brought about the revolution in production, must now be geared to devising ways and means of creating and maintaining new markets to absorb the output. A lead had already been given in this direction by a number of American producers for whom the marketing concept had dawned some decades earlier.

1.2   The meaning, function and scope of marketing

The truths that the pioneers of marketing had discovered may be summarized under two headings:

1   The need for high-volume sales.
2   The need to create a consumer.

First, in every highly industrialized society the degree of competition between one manufacturer and another is often such that only the most economic methods of production will ensure survival. To achieve this required economy of production, high-volume output is essential. To maintain high-volume output, one obviously needs high-volume sales. This constant demand for sales can only be met if the selling side of the organization is able to continue to obtain repeat orders from its existing customers and can gain new customers to replace those who, for a variety of reasons, may cease to use its products.

The second truth that had to be grasped was that, to make a profit, it was necessary to achieve a sale, and to achieve a sale it was necessary to find a consumer. At a time when automation was leading to less flexibility in the methods of production, it became apparent that the producer would have to look to the flexibility of his market in order to find opportunities for increased sales.

Living standards were rising throughout the world by the early 1960s. As a greater number of men and women acquired the means to satisfy more of their elementary wants, so market opportunities increased; and the creation of a consumer, rather than the creation of a product, was the point from which the manufacturer had to set out in his quest for a profit.

Thirty years before, some of the larger American manufacturing firms had begun to group certain functions, such as product development, packaging, warehousing and physical distribution, and link these with sales and advertising under one executive. The reason for this amalgamation was the growing realization that all those functions that had a bearing on the task of satisfying the consumer's needs should have unified control. The concept of marketing was not the result of a sudden flash of inspiration. It matured over some twenty or thirty years in the United States, and since its introduction into Britain and other countries, it has undergone further modification to meet changes in world markets that have taken place during the past half-century.

There are many definitions of the word marketing, none of which is universally accepted. One of the most straightforward says that marketing is getting the right goods (or services) in the right quantity to the right place at the right time, and making a profit out of the operation. This definition clearly distinguishes marketing from those other functions with which it is often confused.

Marketing is a comprehensive function. It is concerned with every aspect of the product from its inception – design, pricing, distribution, selling and promotion – until it finally reaches the hands of the consumer. Even then, marketing still has a job to do: it must ensure customer satisfaction by the provision of after-sales service, such as maintenance, repairs, instruction booklets, spare parts and quality guarantees.

Therefore marketing is not merely a question of selling the product. It is concerned with what is to be sold, how it is to be sold, when it is to be sold and where it is to be sold. Since marketing is not just a question of selling, it follows also that the accumulated knowledge and experience of the selling staff of an organization can no longer provide top management with adequate guidance on marketing decisions. Manufacturing companies require an intelligence service to provide management with assessments of the market and of the people who make up that market.

As a result of the revolutionary changes that have taken place in the physical distribution of goods, manufacturers can no longer rely upon the guidance of wholesalers for their market information. It has become inevitable that personal skill and flair on the part of individuals must play a lesser part than strategy based on scientifically prepared statistics in the creation of business profits.

Following the definition we have applied to marketing, it can be seen that the functions of the marketing organization are extensive. They cover a much wider field than that generally alloted to the sales department of a company. Among the most important functions of marketing is the assessment of the market to discover where the consumers of the product are to be found, how many there are of them, whether their number – which constitutes the market – shows a tendency to grow or to diminish. Enquiry must be made into the methods currently used to distribute and sell to that market, and if these methods are likely to remain effective in the future. The attributes and the shortcomings of competitors must be assessed to establish the degree of competitive merit each of them enjoys in the market. It is also a function of marketing to probe into the attitude of the consumer with regard to both current products and those products it is proposed to develop. What do consumers need? What is their attitude to current products and the prices they have to pay for them? Do they have marked preferences between one brand and another and, if so, what are they? Marketing must look into the likely future pattern of demand. It must establish forecasts to ensure the correct allocation of marketing resources and also to provide essential information, not only for the planning and production departments, but for the budget of the company.

The choice of the best methods of distribution – via the wholesaler, direct to the retail outlet or by mail order – must be considered. Changes occur from time to time in the accepted channels of distribution of particular products, and those responsible for the marketing function must keep in step with events. Marketing must concern itself with the promotion of the product both through advertising and through merchandising, with the provision of samples, demonstrations, free trials and other forms of physical presentation.

In discussing the scope of marketing, we enter an area of controversy. Marketing is often regarded with suspicion by other departments in an organization as a threat to their independence and authority. The fact is that if marketing is to do its job properly, it is inevitable that other departments, including research and development, production, sales, finance and distribution, must abdicate some of their sovereignty in the common interests of the organization. If the purpose of the business organization is to earn a profit and that profit is dependent upon a sale, then the total resources of the organization have to be directed towards the creation and satisfaction of the consumer. It is the purpose of marketing to relate the abilities of the organization to the needs of the consumer, on the one hand, and to the profitable provision of goods and services, on the other.

The ability of a business to exploit a discovered consumer need is heavily dependent upon its relative strengths and weaknesses. No two people share precisely the same degree of ability, and no two commercial organizations, which are merely aggregates of people, have abilities that are identical. A company's areas of relative weakness will result in constraints – things it cannot do – whereas its areas of relative strength will provide opportunity – things it can do well. Every firm has an accumulation of capabilities: the knowledge and experience of its management, the skills of its workforce, the capacity and performance of its plant and equipment, the financial resources and borrowing power at its command. Awareness by management of such strengths and weaknesses, and of the degree to which the company's ability equates with the needs of the consumers whom it is intended to serve, is a basic necessity for any business.

What consumers want is the means to improve whatever it is they currently have in life. They are looking for betterment. Theoretically therefore, consumers are receptive to the purchase of anything and everything that will enhance their lives. In practice of course they are constrained by what they can afford. In the primitive state their essential needs are for sustenance and shelter. As they progress up the scale of living standards, their perception of essential needs becomes increasingly complex. When they reach the advanced level achieved by what are called the developed nations of the modern world, they are likely to possess disposable income over and above that which is required to provide for their essential needs; this allows them to pick and choose among the vast array of luxury goods and services currently on offer. A natural desire for life improvement sustains their aspirations, whose realization is restricted only by the limit of their purchasing ability.

The complexity of the aspirations of today's consumers has been fueled by modern technology. Every year technological advance creates yet more potential for human betterment which it is the task of commerce to convert into practical applications. To do this satisfactorily, it must understand consumers, their needs and desires.

Profitability depends on producing goods or services for sale at a price the consumer is willing to pay and at a cost that will allow sufficient margin for an acceptable return on the capital invested in the business.

No firm exists in a vacuum. The environment in which it operates will have a profound effect on all its activities: the behaviour of competitors; changes in technology; governmental policies of a political, economic, legal and financial nature; the ever-changing pattern of national and international attitudes and events. All such elements affect constantly the ability of the business organization to maintain profitability.

The bringing together of the abilities of the company and the needs of the consumer to achieve mutual benefit in what is often a hostile climate requires an attitude of mind and a method of operating different from those tolerable in former times. Marketing eschews the intuitive approach to problem-solving, insisting that management decision-making should be based on sound understanding of the commercial environment supported by factual knowledge and reasoned assumption. This is the scientific approach.

1.3   What is meant by the marketing plan

The essence of marketing practice is planning. To plan simply means to arrange beforehand. It comprises gathering information upon which decisions can be made regarding objectives and how they may be achieved. The process may appear to be very simple. In fact the preparation of commercial plans can be extremely difficult and time-consuming. This is the reason why many small and not-so-small businesses often carry on, year after year, without any formalized planning process. Such managements believe that their knowledge of their markets and the world around them provides sufficient evidence upon which decisions can be made. The *ad hoc* methods that appear to have stood them in good stead in the past are perpetuated. It is only when things start to go seriously wrong – their markets decline, profitability plummets and their cashflow is in crisis – that belatedly they think in terms of planning to help solve their problems. Usually, it is too late. The time to start planning is when times are good, not when they are bad.

Even in situations where managers have the benefit of a thoroughly market-oriented company and properly structured planning based on adequate research, it is no easy task to arrive at major decisions in today's increasingly hostile and unpredictable environment. There is abundant evidence, however, to show that firms that have adopted structured policy-making fare far better than those that continue to rely on intuitive judgement.

The essential framework for implementation of the marketing concept is the marketing plan. Since one business organization differs from another, there is no such thing as a structure that can be universally applied. Each firm must devise a plan suited to its individual circumstances. There are, however, certain basic ingredients that will be applicable in virtually all situations and should be included.

The first ingredient for the preparation of a marketing plan (Figure 1.1) is what is known as the marketing audit. Its purpose is to answer the question: 'Where does the company stand at the present time?' It does so by collecting and analysing information drawn from the firm's external environment relating to the general state of the economy, the current situation in the firm's specific markets and the activities of competitors. To this will be added an assessment of the internal resources of the company: the know-how and skills of management and workforce, research and development capacity, the capability and capacity of production facilities and the current financial situation. The marketing audit is useful because it shows how the company relates to the commercial environment in which it operates. The fundamental cause of problems often becomes easier to discern when current policies are re-examined in the context of the current environmental situation.

The audit also will highlight the relative strengths and weaknesses of the organization. These can be related to possible opportunities for the company that the present environmental situation may offer and the possible threats it may pose. These factors constitute what is known in marketing parlance as the SWOT analysis (Strengths, Weaknesses, Opportunities, Threats). Based on the findings of the market audit and the SWOT analysis, management can make reasonably informed judgements about policies previously decided upon and the extent to which they may need revision for the future.

When we speak of a policy, we are talking about a proposed course of action. To be meaningful a policy must have an objective. In marketing terms, objectives relate solely to the selling of a product or service to a market. Their expression may be more precise, such as the achievement of a certain volume or a certain monetary value of sales into a market or a percentage share increase of a market.

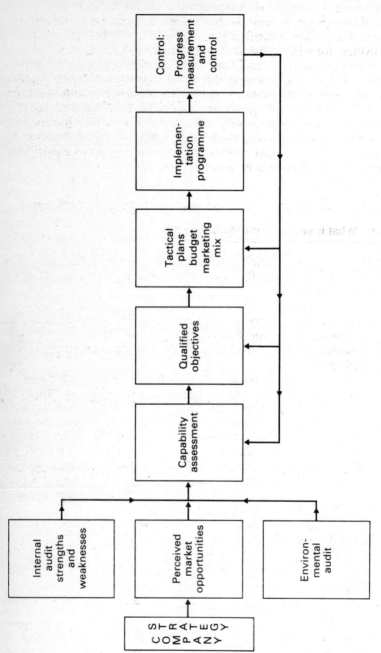

Figure 1.1   *Marketing planning process*

Objectives relating to such supportive activities as advertising or the establishment of distribution channels have no place in the marketing plan. They relate specifically to the company's policies for these activities, for which separate plans should be devised.

A further essential ingredient of the marketing plan is the formulation of strategies to achieve the stated objectives. Keeping in mind the fact that the capabilities of one organization will be different from those of another, strategies must be appropriate to the firm's specific situation. Furthermore, every sub-section of a market has its own characteristics. It is true, therefore, to say that every situation in which a particular supplier offers a particular product to a particular group of customers will be unique.

1.4   What is meant by the marketing mix

If we look at the various elements that constitute the offer of a product, we shall see that for convenience they can be classified under four headings:

1   *Product.* The quality of a product is capable of wide variation, according to the inputs specified for its production: e.g. how it is designed, choice of materials, method of manufacture, how it is packaged.
2   *Price.* The price at which a product may be sold is dependent on its production costs, plus distribution costs, plus the margin of profit that the organization requires to achieve an acceptable return on the capital invested in the business. By varying the price a firm will vary the profit margin per item of the product that is sold. However, a higher price may increase the profit margin per item yet cause a reduction in the volume of sales. Equally, a lower price, while reducing the margin per item, may cause a larger volume of items to be sold. Variations in sales volume can also affect the cost of manufacture.
3   *Place.* The place where the product should be made available must depend largely on what is considered to be most convenient to customers. The choice of channels for distribution of the product will vary widely (via wholesaler to retailer, direct to retailer, direct to customer via agents or mail order).
4   *Promotion.* The methods by which a firm may promote a product includes the various forms of advertising, sales promotion, the use of exhibitions, competitions, point-of-sale display and personal selling. The relative cost and effectiveness of these different forms of promotion vary considerably.

These four elements, known as the 'Four Ps', share two vital characteristics:

(*a*)   Each has an influence on attracting the customer to the product.
(*b*)   Each is capable of variation to suit the needs of the customer.

In order to employ these elements strategically for the achievement of a company's objectives, marketing has devised a concept called the marketing mix. Theoretically, it takes these four elements – product, price, place and promotion – and mixes them as one might mix physical substances to produce a compound. To continue the analogy, as one might vary the percentage of individual physical substances in a mix in order to achieve a specific set of properties in the resulting compound, so too does marketing formulate the marketing mix with varying percentages from each of the four Ps, to create a combination of benefits considered to be most suitable to meet the needs of the selected market.

This concept of a mix of customer-influencing elements – each of which offers a choice of variables – capable of being formulated to produce a compound of benefits specific to the needs of customer groups provides the link for matching the capabilities of the supplier organization to the wants of the consumer. The process has the further advantage of being extremely flexible. While the four Ps of product, price, place and promotion are the essential elements of the mix, other elements can be incorporated whenever necessary to take account of peculiarities either of the product or of the market. We shall return repeatedly to the marketing mix in subsequent chapters of this book because it is one of the fundamental concepts upon which the implementation of marketing principles is based.

Discussion questions

1   What is the marketing concept?
2   Name the basic functions of marketing in a business organization.
3   What is meant by a firm's strengths and weaknesses?
4   Define the SWOT analysis and its use in marketing planning.
5   Describe what is meant by the marketing mix and the essential elements it should contain.

2
Marketing and the product

Products are the means by which business organizations solve problems for their customers. What the housewife wants when she buys washing-up liquid is clean dishes. What the gardener wants when he buys an insecticide is insect-free rose bushes. A product is useless if it fails to provide a benefit to its user. The rule applies to all products, not merely articles of a utilitarian nature. For example, what we want when we buy an oil painting or a piece of sculpture is gratification of our aesthetic taste.

For the business organization, however, products have a further purpose. They exist to provide the source from which revenue is obtained to achieve the firm's objectives. It is a source in constant need of replenishment to permit the business operation to continue by recovering costs and providing profit from which to finance future activity. A company's products are therefore its most precious possessions, to be safeguarded always. Unfortunately, however, they are not immortal.

Consider the old-time candlemaker. What our ancestors wanted when they bought wax candles was light in their homes at night. The candlemaker sold his wares to a considerable market. He may well have had an excellent product, one that no home could do without. He doubtless believed that demand would remain high for all time and he need have no fear for the future of his product. What he failed to perceive was the development of fossil fuels to provide initially gas and subsequently electric lighting. Alas! He thought he was in the candle industry. It was only when his customers disappeared that he discovered his mistake: he was in the lighting industry and technology had offered his customers a better way to solve their problem.

2.1   The importance of the product range

Apart from the danger of market decline resulting from technological and other forms of change, to rely upon a single product is seldom wise and often is impractical. There are markets where the rate of demand fluctuates widely, owing to seasonal or other factors, yet the need of producers for revenue persists during lean trading periods. In these circumstances the possession of other products, selling into other markets where demand patterns are different, provides an obvious insurance. The needs of a market will often compel a producer to provide several product lines. In certain trades, for example, retailers traditionally enjoy quantity discounts based on the volume of their purchases from a single source, and have an understandable preference for dealing with a firm that offers a range of products.

Another advantage of profit multiplicity is that each product is a potential revenue-earner. In theory, at least, the more products a company has, the greater should be the aggregated revenue it will earn. It is of course not quite as simple as that. As we shall see later, products incur costs as well as contributing cash, and the careful balancing of products is an important aspect of marketing. Nevertheless, there are few companies that can afford to rely solely upon one product for their source of revenue.

As we have seen, products are the means by which the wants of groups of customers are satisfied. A customer group is what constitutes a market, so that products and their markets are inseparable. When a company seeks to increase its business, it is in fact seeking an increase in the sale of its products in their respective markets. This can be attempted in a number of ways. A greater effort can be made to sell more of an existing product into its existing market. But not all products necessarily are restricted to a single market. A manufacturer of processed cheese, for example, currently may be selling his product solely to the grocery trade via wholesale or retail outlets. He could opt to increase his sales by entering the catering trade, and sell direct, or through intermediaries, to hotels, restaurants, public houses as well as to hospitals, schools and industrial canteens. Although the same basic product would probably remain acceptable, it is likely that he would have to change the pack size and packaging. Certainly an entirely different marketing strategy would have to be devised.

An increase in company earnings may be achieved by the introduction of a new product into the firm's existing range. New product development is always speculative, but where the targeted market is one with which the organization is already familiar and has an established position, the element of risk is somewhat reduced. A far more adventurous step is taken when a company decides to embark on a new product aimed at a new market, which is always an extremely complex and hazardous undertaking.

2.2   The hazards of product innovation

Product innovation is hazardous because of the high research and development cost that often attaches to new products, and their enormously high failure rate. While estimates between markets vary, it is generally accepted that it can take up to fifty or more ideas to find one that becomes a successful product. It has been said that some twenty out of twenty-five new products failed during test marketing in the United States, and a world-wide food manufacturer states that only 8 per cent of new products are still on sale in the second year of their lives. Another such firm claims that two out of every three new products failed after introduction to the shops. See Figure 2.1.

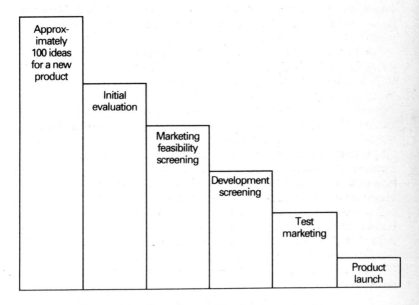

Figure 2.1   *Rate of mortality of new product ideas*

If new products are so precarious, one might well ask why do companies persist with innovation? Why should a firm that already has a range of good selling products spend time, effort and vast sums of money developing new ones, and thereby run the risk of expensive failure? The answer lies in what is called the product life cycle.

2.3   The product life cycle

The theory of the product life cycle is that, from the time it is launched on the market until finally it is withdrawn, a product passes through four main stages.

The first stage covers the period of introduction of the product to the market. Before initial sales can be achieved, stocks must be created, special advertising and other types of promotion launched and a high proportion of the time of the salesforce and senior management devoted to the new product. All this represents a considerable investment, whereas the profits likely to be derived from the product at this stage will be minimal.

Passing to the next stage, we shall probably find that sales are now growing rapidly in a market where there is perhaps little competition. It is during this stage of its life that the product can achieve its greatest penetration of the market and its greatest profitability.

By the third stage the fully established product undoubtedly will be faced with competition from other contenders for a share of the market. The market may continue to expand, owing to the effect of competitors' promotional effort. Sales may still rise, but so will costs. The presence of competition may necessitate a considerable increase in advertising to retain market share. Furthermore, a reduction in price is likely in the face of competitive pressure.

Finally, as more competitors, attracted by the profits being made, decide to enter the market, a stage is reached when the supply of goods outstrips demands. Competition becomes increasingly fierce, prices are further reduced and both sales and profit levels enter a decline. See Figure 2.2.

It must be emphasized that the time-scale within which products pass through these four stages is infinitely varied. We can all think of a variety of branded products that are at least as widely used today as they were 50 or more years ago. Their packaging may have changed, not to mention their price! But to all other intents and purposes they appear to remain the same. Yet the principle of the life cycle holds true. The continued survival of many famous brands is a tribute to the excellence of their composition and to the ability with which they have been marketed throughout the changing years. Most of them have been held in the third, or maturity, stage of their life cycles for a period of many decades. Any of them is liable, however, to slide into the fourth, or decline, stage of the cycle, unless its vulnerability is monitored constantly and appropriate marketing strategies continue to be applied.

There are of course circumstances in which the most excellent of products inevitably enter the fourth stage of their cycles, despite the best efforts their companies can make to prevent it. Throughout history, society has undergone change, but the speed of change

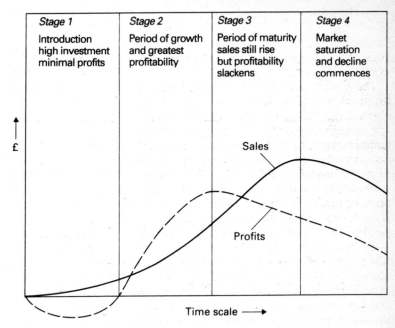

Stage 1	Stage 2	Stage 3	Stage 4
Introduction high investment minimal profits	Period of growth and greatest profitability	Period of maturity sales still rise but profitability slackens	Market saturation and decline commences

Figure 2.2   *Product life cycle*

during the lifetime of this, and the preceeding generation, has been excessive. The technological revolution of the 1960s, 1970s and 1980s has been accompanied by a revolution in social attitudes unsurpassed in any previous age. The changed attitude of consumers has led inevitably to changes in their needs and priorities. The effect upon products designed to satisfy such needs has been immense, and many types of product that once enjoyed a high demand are now outmoded and have been replaced. The process will undoubtedly continue and accelerate in coming years.

The benefit of the life-cycle concept is that it affords a view of the likely future sales pattern of the product if no action is taken to correct it. It is an extremely useful marketing tool. As soon as the sales growth shows signs of slackening, action can be undertaken. This may take the form of further development of the product by means of modification of the marketing mix, such as an up-date in its packaging, additional advertising or price adjustment. The traditional channels through which the product has been distributed may need review.

The life cycle provides an early warning system of dangers ahead in the marketplace. Reassessment of the market may indicate factors that will cause significant change in consumer needs, and that they

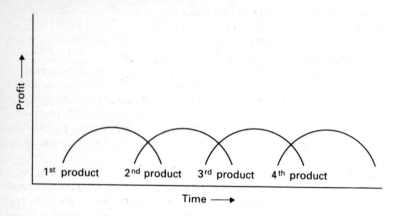

Figure 2.3   *How product sequence assists total profit*

will not be met adequately by the existing product. A replacement product may need urgent consideration.

It will be seen that the life-cycle concept has a vital strategic use in the achievement of a firm's longer-term objectives. Where there is a portfolio of products to provide a company's life-sustaining revenue, the ideal will be to have each product at a different stage of its cycle. In this situation, as the profitability of one product declines, that of another is rising to take its place. See Figure 2.3.

2.4   The importance of market share

We have already established that each product in a firm's range should be composed in such a way as to provide benefits that will satisfy the needs of specific groups of customers, and that these customer groups are what constitute markets. The fact that the continuing success of a product depends solely upon its ability to provide market satisfaction means that we must study the market constantly and be alive to its trends. We should also be aware that our product is not alone in the market. Our competitors, too, have products formulated to meet the market's needs, and the customer has a choice between their brands and ours. If we are to safeguard our product therefore, we need to know how he or she exercises this choice. In marketing terms we need to know the share of the market our product holds in comparison with those of our rivals. If our market share decreases, it will tell us that it is proving less attractive in satisfying customers' needs than competitive brands. If our market share increases, we can deduce that it offers benefits more closely related to customer requirements than those of other producers. Bear in mind that when we speak of the product in this context, we are in fact talking about the entire package of benefits offered to the customer that have been formulated in the marketing mix, including such elements as price, packaging, presentation and place of distribution.

Information on market share is far from being academic. Since a company's continued survival is dependent solely upon the success of its products in the marketplace, market share assumes prime importance. Every effort has to be made to maintain and increase market share. Where practical, the aim should be market leadership – the possession of greater market share than that of any single rival producer.

Market dominance does place extremely heavy demands on a company's resources in terms of capital utilization, research and development, advertising and the allocation of management time and effort. There is, however, conclusive evidence supporting the belief that unit cost of manufacture reduces as output rises. Based on the truism that the more one does something, the better one becomes at doing it, there is abundant proof that the greater the volume of production, the greater will be the productivity, in terms of working methods, labour efficiency and plant utilization. What this amounts to in terms of marketing is that the product that has achieved the greatest number of sales (and therefore the greatest volume of production), will be more profitable, relatively, than its competitors.

The advantages to be gained from being the biggest fish in the pond must, however, be related to the size of the pond. If the market in which our product leads is in sharp decline, the profitability we enjoy today could be gone tomorrow. So market growth, too, needs to be carefully monitored.

2.5   Market growth rate

If we keep in mind the fact that a market is merely an assembly of customers sharing similar wants, it will be apparent that markets are subject to constant movement. Very few remain static. The majority tend either to increase or decrease in accordance with consumer needs.

Markets whose products are basic essentials for modern living often tend to grow at a comparatively slow rate. Usually they are shared by a small number of long-established brands, usually in the third, or maturity stage, of their life cycles. In circumstances such as these the opportunity for any one producer to outstrip his rivals and gain a dominant position is slender. Price-cutting would be counter-productive, as would be any excessive promotional campaign. The temptation would be to relax and enjoy the profits one's current rate of turnover provides. The danger, however, is that the time must come, eventually, when the rate of market growth will begin to decline. Prices will come under pressure as competitors struggle to maintain their market share of a shrinking market. The product whose unit cost is high relative to that of its rivals will be one of the first to suffer.

Such a fate can only be averted if care is taken to ensure that the share of the market held by one's own product remains in accordance with the size of the market while market growth exists, however slight that may be.

Quite apart from the costs associated with its manufacture, a product incurs other costs that relate to its marketing: the cost of the sales force, the cost of advertising and other forms of promotion, and the cost of distribution from factory to consumer. These costs tend to escalate or diminish relative to the amount of marketing effort required to sustain the product during different stages of its life cycle. Whatever its situation, however, while it remains on the market, it has a cash requirement. On the other hand, a product is also a cash-earner. The amount of cash it can generate depends also on the stage it has reached of its life cycle.

The ability of a product to generate cash is also dependent upon its share of the market. The greater the rate at which the market grows, the greater must be the effort (marketing costs) the product will incur to keep up with that growth rate to maintain its market share. This means that market share is an indicator of the product's cash generation ability, whereas the market's rate of growth is an indicator of its cash usage.

2.6   The uses of a product matrix

If we apply the concept that these indicators suggest to each of the products in a company's range, a matrix similar to that illustrated in Figure 2.4 can be produced. Here four categories of product have been selected, and each category has been named in accordance with popular marketing jargon:

1   A *wildcat* (sometimes termed a 'problem child' or 'question mark') refers to a product that for various reasons has not as yet achieved its potential. It is in a growth market, which means it incurs a lot of marketing effort (high cash usage).

2   A *cash cow* is a market leader. The market has reached a stage of very limited growth and has become stabilized. This product is therefore a large cash-earner, but its cash requirement is small, because its marketing needs have become relatively minor. As its name suggests, it is suitable for constant milking.

3   A *star* is a product that has entered the range fairly recently. It

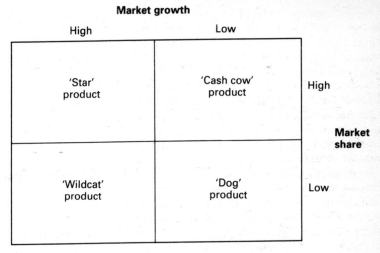

Figure 2.4   *Product portfolio matrix (as developed by the Boston Consulting Group)*

has already achieved a gratifyingly high market share. It is in a growth market, which means that its marketing requirements and therefore cash usage will be high, but this will be compensated for by its high earnings.

4   A *dog* is a product in a low growth market that has a low market share. Although its cash requirement may not be high, neither are its earnings. The company might well be better off without it.

Revenue generated by 'cash cow' products – after deduction of their marketing costs, which, as we have seen, are likely to be relatively low – is available to finance further marketing development of 'star' products in the company's range, as well as supporting some of the 'wildcat' products until their position in the market has become more stabilized.

Products that fall into the 'dog' category always pose problems. On purely economic grounds, there could be a clear-cut case for dropping them from the range. This can, however, provoke customer resistance, especially in industrial markets, where it is often the case that a customer may prefer to purchase the bulk of his requirements, covering a range of products, with a single supplier. If one of these products ceases to be available to him, he is not merely inconvenienced. He is forced to source it elsewhere, his regular buying habits are disturbed and the door is opened to a competitor. It is for this reason that many companies supplying into the industrial sector feel compelled to retain 'dog' products in their range for fear that once a rival producer is allowed through the customer's door to supply the missing product, it may only be a matter of time before he makes inroads into other, more profitable, business which they are not seeking to let go.

'Dog' type products are, however, a drain on resources that might be capable of better use. Part of the art of product portfolio management is to 'weed out' such no-hopers from the range as soon as it becomes expedient to do so.

The value to management of the product matrix is apparent. It expresses in a graphic form the life-cycle stage reached by each of its products, the market share held by each product and the growth rate of the respective markets, together with the use to which it may be put in balancing a portfolio of products. What should also be apparent is the imperative need for new product development. New products are required to replace those well-advanced in the maturity stage of their life cycles and which market research indicates may shortly enter the fourth, or decline, stage.

2.7   The need for a new product strategy

Although product innovation should be part of the everyday activities of a marketing department, the importance of the selection and development of new products means that a company should decide upon an agreed policy for its implementation. Concentrated effort is essential, and the task of devising and presenting new products should wherever possible be separated from routine activities and pressures. Sometimes new product development is undertaken by a committee. In this case it is desirable to include representatives of the design, finance and production departments, as well as the sales and marketing departments. Where a single person is given this responsibility, he or she should have sufficient authority to obtain advice and assistance from these sources. Whether a committee or an individual is appointed, the brief should include the collection, investigation and testing of ideas, and the screening of new products derived from them, to ensure that the whole operation is properly controlled and coordinated.

One cannot lay down a formula that will guarantee the success of a new product. Certain basic conditions do, however, apply to all successful product innovation. Adequate research is necessary to establish that there is in fact a market for the particular product, and that this market is ready to receive it. In the highly competitive field of consumer goods, accurate forecasts of the size of the market and the potential for sales of the product are essential. It is important, too, that the new product should harmonize with the firm's current production arrangements, and that the company's existing marketing knowledge and experience are capable of handling the proposed newcomer to the product range. A new product poses vital financial implications for an organization.

The time lapse between its inception and the stage where it begins to earn revenue can be lengthy and development, marketing and initial production costs may be considerable. Can the company support this burden or will the attention and care it devotes to its established product range be impaired? The same question should be directed to its management resources, which will be heavily stretched getting a new product developed, tested and launched.

The quality of a new brand must be at least equal to that of competitive brands already on the market, and should possess some additional benefit not to be found in currently available products. A new product should only be launched when all the necessary testing has been completed. It is a mistake to rush a new product on to the market to counter the activities of competitors without thorough market research and a full technical evaluation of the product itself.

A company operating in the consumer-goods field needs to be especially cautious in respect to new product launches. As soon as it becomes apparent a new product is likely to fail, it should be withdrawn. There are occasions indeed when it requires considerable courage to stop a new product 'in its tracks'. After many months of effort on the part of senior management and outside agencies, and a very considerable input of finance, it is inevitable that there should be pressure exerted to press on with the project in a vain hope that all will come right in the end. But if the product is flawed, either in design or composition, or in the method of its presentation, its chances of survival may be very slight indeed. The shelves and display areas of retailers are among their most important assets, and to fill them with a failed product can have a dangerous boomerang effect that can damage a supplier's image in the marketplace for a long period of time.

2.8   Market segmentation for new products

The inseparability of product and market means that the first step towards new product development begins with an examination of the market. A market is a group of customers sharing similar needs or problems. If our need is for a new dining room suite, we will go to a furniture store to discover what styles and qualities are available. If our problem is to find a venue for dinner for two, we will look for a suitable restaurant. In general terms, a furniture store belongs within the furniture market and a restaurant is broadly classified as part of the catering market. Yet there is all the difference in the world between hand-crafted furniture and furniture that is supplied in a flat pack for self-assembly. To eat a cheaply priced meal in a fast food establishment may be pleasant but it is a distinctly different experience to dining out at an exclusive restaurant. In other words, markets are composed of many subdivisions, or segments, whose customers exhibit approximately the same anticipated response to a particular product or service. Segmentation of a market is vital if we are to discover the needs of specific customer groups.

One obvious means of differentiating between the needs of one group of customers and another is to classify them according to age and sex. Thus the package-holiday market contains a segment that caters exclusively for members of the older generation, providing tour and holiday facilities geared to the interests and life-style of people aged 50-plus. Activity holiday packages, on the other hand, are designed to appeal to a younger age group of predominantly single people, and include water sports, rock and mountain climbing and horseriding among their attractions. Holiday camps, however, traditionally have set out to attract families with young children, with organized games for all the family by day and parent entertainment coupled with a chalet baby-listening service in the evening.

Segmentation in the clothing market can be seen in the specialized manufacture and retail distribution of garments such as babywear, female teenager fashions or industrial clothing for men. Segment-ation according to personal taste is another method, and we see examples of this in the production of speciality foodstuffs sold in health shops or served in vegetarian restaurants. The special needs and tastes of minority ethnic groups provide a further example of market segmentation, as do the many hobby and leisure-time interests of particular customer groups, such as golfing or sailing enthusiasts, craftworkers, gardeners or the owners of domestic pets.

It is among the multitudinous sectors of markets that many small and medium-sized businesses discover the opportunity for the exploitation of new products. This is where gaps may be discovered when social or technological change creates new consumer needs and problems that currently are not being fulfilled.

2.9   Creation of the basic product idea

One seldom encounters a completely original product idea. The vast majority of new products are adaptations of what has gone before. If one takes an existing product and examines it carefully, it is often possible to think of improvements or adaptations which might increase its utility or enhance its appearance. A study of the use to which an existing product is put may result in the discovery of hitherto undetected consumer needs not fully met by other products on the market. Thus an old product in a novel guise may be introduced to a newly found market.

Many of the apparently new products introduced during recent decades are really little more than up-dated versions of goods (and services) that were associated previously only with limited quality markets. Increased living standards generally have created entirely new markets for popular versions of what were once very exclusive product lines.

Ideas from research and development

We have said that new product ideas do not just 'happen'. They are not the result of flashes of inspiration. They are developed as the result of painstaking research.

One of the first places to look for new ideas is within the company's own research and development department. In order to carry out its day-to-day function, R & D of necessity keeps abreast of advances made nationally and internationally by competitive producers. R & D will also have an awareness of limitations in some of the company's existing products, culled from investigation of customer complaints. Ideas for the revamping of a current product – one that is perhaps about to enter the decline stage of its cycle – by means of redesign and technical improvement may well be forthcoming from R & D personnel.

Ideas from the production department

At first sight the production department of the company may not seem a particularly fruitful source for new product ideas. Production personnel are often thought to be obsessed solely with efficient plant utilization and the eradication of processes and procedures that conflict with this ideal. But the works manager and his staff must frequently exercise innovation when translating the efforts of the drawing office into feasible production items, and consequently will be able to bring their experience to bear upon the production-feasibility of new product ideas.

Ideas from the sales department

The salesforce of the company is an obvious source for product ideas. Both sales personnel and customers may be canvassed for their opinions with a view to establishing a consumer need – and therefore a market – not met adequately by existing products.

A fruitful field for investigation is the file of complaints, received either from distributors or from customers, with regard to the company's products. It will tend to highlight the shortcomings of those products and act as an indicator for modifications and improvements.

Ideas from the trade

The trade will be a major source of product ideas. All manufacturers examine with avid interest the new products of their competitors – not to copy the other firm's ideas slavishly but to study the trend being followed by competitive products. No product is entirely superlative, and a lot can be learned from an examination of the shortcomings of a competitive brand.

Ideas from consumers

Finally, we come to the consumers: the men and women (and children, too) upon whose decision the new product ultimately will either succeed or founder. They, above all, should be able to tell marketing what kind of new products are needed. Many of the most successful new product ideas have resulted from a study of novel applications to which current products are being put. The fact that a product is being used for a purpose for which it was not designed, or by groups of people for whom it was not intended, indicates a consumer need not being met adequately by any existing product.

'Brainstorming' techniques

A method of idea creation that has acquired a growing popularity is known as the 'brainstorming' technique. A number of people drawn perhaps from sales, R & D and marketing, are put together in one room and invited to come up with as many ideas as they can think of. There is no formal procedure. No minutes are taken. The whole atmosphere is kept as informal as possible with a view to creating an uninhibited exchange of ideas. To a limited extent some value can be derived from these sessions. In the end it is the quality of the minds thus brought to bear upon the problem that will decide whether or not the method is really productive.

2.10   Feasibility of the product idea

Once an idea has been arrived at, it is necessary to establish a method of finding out whether it is worth pursuing. Bearing in mind the high cost of new product failure, it is obvious that some organized method of screening is essential. See Figure 2.5.

One method is to gather views from various members of the

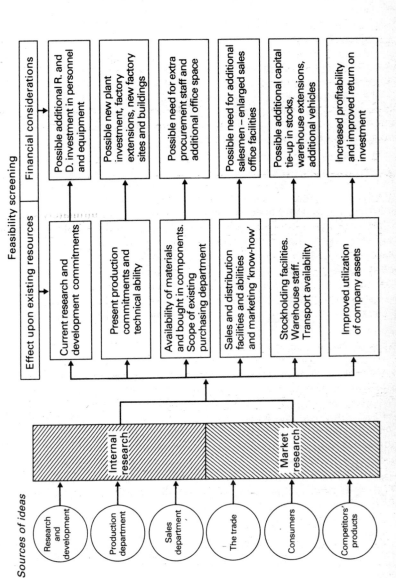

Figure 2.5 *New product ideas: feasibility and screening*

company's management, and opt for the major opinion. Again, the quality of this panel of judges will make or mar the value of the screening. Those taking part should try to take an objective approach. But how many people in an organization are likely to have an objective approach to a matter so closely affecting their own interests as a new product? Certainly not the production manager, upon whose plant it will be made, nor the sales manager, through whose distributors it will be sold.

A better approach is to examine each short-listed idea in relation to the resources that the company has at its disposal. Consider, for example, the capability of the research department to develop the proposed product. How will it relate to existing R & D programmes? Will it make use of knowledge which already exists within the department? Can development work that may be necessary for the new product be carried out on the present pilot plant? Are the right people to undertake this development work available? Do they know enough about the subject?

Similarly, one must question the extent of the company's market knowledge in relation to the new product. How will it fit into the company's present markets? In what ways will this new product affect, or be affected by, the company's image and reputation?

Is the market for which it is intended one that is subject to extreme fluctuation? Will it require special servicing? Can the company handle this? Will it be necessary to make various sizes or various styles of the new product? Will it be necessary to stock a range of replacement parts? If one is operating in the industrial goods field, will the new product in any way clash with the products of one's customers? These are just a few of the questions marketing must answer before deciding to proceed with a new product idea.

It must also investigate the available production capacity and discuss with those concerned the feasibility of making the new item with the company's existing resources. What about the supply of raw materials or bought-in components? Can these be obtained advantageously? Are there any particular advantages in bulk-buying? Can this new product be made on existing plant or will new investment be needed? If the existing plant is suitable, will the advent of the new product provide for better utilization than is the case with the company's current range of products?

On the other hand, it may be thought that the existing plant cannot accept any more work. In this event enquiries must be made into the possibilities for expansion. This will bring into question the availability of land and the possible limitations on its use imposed by local planning authorities.

Finally, one must ask whether the company has, in fact, any knowledge of the manufacture of this kind of product and whether its production management and its labour force possess the necessary skills to produce it.

The capacities of the sales department should also be considered. Can it cope with the anticipated sales of the new product with the existing salesforce? Will new sales personnel have to be recruited and trained? How about transport and warehousing facilities? Will new depots have to be established and additional vehicles put on the road? Does the company know anything about the selling of this kind of product? Has sufficient consideration been given to the possible special selling skills that may be required?

Before a final decision can be made, marketing must calculate the additional financial resources that the company will need to invest in the new product. Is the company financially strong enough to risk launching a new venture which may tie up capital resources for anything up to three years before the new product is established and begins to show a profitable return? Are there not better uses to which these resources can be directed? Can they be more profitably employed in an expansion of the firm's existing activities or in some alternative project which promises a better return?

2.11 The character of the product

It could be suggested that the type of market into which it is proposed to sell the product will depend on the type of product it is intended to produce. It is to be hoped, however, that what has been said in the preceeding pages of this book will show this to be antiquated thinking. On the contrary, it is of course the character of the product that will be determined by the market segment at which it is aimed. Marketing must decide to whom the new brand will be offered. Long before there is any investment of company resources, the size and growth rate of the market must be examined.

One must also decide who it is within the market that makes the buying decision. This applies whether one is promoting industrial products or consumer goods. In the industrial field not all buying decisions are made necessarily by the customer's purchasing department. According to the type of purchase, the ultimate decision may be made by individuals far removed from the buying department. The decision to buy a certain type of water pump may be made by the production manager. The decision to order a particular make of fork-lift truck may be made by the despatch manager. In the office the decision to order a certain brand of typewriter ribbons may be made by the office manager's secretary. Similarly, in the consumer field, the decision to ask for a certain brand of soft drink cordial may be made by the child, although it will be his mother who will purchase it at the supermarket.

The market for which it is intended

We have noted that markets are divided into segments, each of which has specific needs. We have the popular or mass sector, for example, with a number of quality or specialized sectors. In deciding the most suitable sector to enter, marketing must consider certain factors. The mass sector will obviously attract the larger suppliers. There is a hazard here for the small company, which may find itself jostled constantly by giant competitors, each seemingly intent upon depriving the others of any increase in market share. Selling prices in such circumstances are likely to be low. The opportunities for the small operator to increase his own market share in the face of such competition will be slender. In contrast, large producers often find that specialized segments of a market are too small to be attractive, and it is here that smaller organizations may find greater scope. Major manufacturing firms need to be careful when investing in new products to ensure that the market that has been targeted will be large enough to enable a worthwhile return to be made.

The personality or image of the product

The quality and utility of a product are insufficient to ensure its continued sale in a highly competitive market. Even if one were to build into a product improved features that enabled it to be in all respects superlative in comparison with those of competitors, this alone would still not be sufficient to guarantee that it could hold its own in the marketplace.

All product improvements cost money. However, if it were possible to place on the market a product superlative in quality and at no greater price than that of the competitive merchandise, it would still not necessarily succeed in holding its own without an artificially created personality to sustain it. Estimates vary widely between one product and another, but it may be accepted that for the vast majority of consumer goods at least 40 per cent of the price paid by the ultimate consumer has been spent on promotion. It is often this aspect of marketing that evokes the greatest popular criticism. One cannot eat the advertising, nor can one eat the package, yet to get at the breakfast food or the instant coffee we are compelled also to buy the promotion. Moreover, not only must the consumer pay for what he may consider to be fatuous drivel, he finds himself exposed to it on all sides through television, radio, the cinema, newspapers, magazines and street hoardings.

This is not the place to argue the merits of the international indoctrination of consumers with 'brand imagery'. It is sufficient to state that all major consumer marketing – and to an increasing extent the marketing of many industrial products – is based on the personalizing of the product by means of the establishment of a brand image.

One reaches a point in the development of a new product therefore when it is necessary to decide upon the personality it is to carry. However much it may excel in meeting consumer needs, without a distinctive personality created and maintained by advertising, it will fail. It will fail simply because competitors will copy it, and thereafter it will have nothing that belongs to itself alone to offer. This is the crux of the brand-image philosophy, namely, that although the product itself may be virtually indistinguishable from others as a product, the image or personality that it carries, and which is always associated with it, is unique.

2.12   The identity of the product

Selection of a name

To begin the personalization of the product we must give it a name. Arriving at a suitable name is almost as difficult as arriving at a suitable product. There are many hazards to be faced. The most important is the question of legal registration. Unless a brand name can be legally registered, not only in the home market but in overseas markets as well, it will be useless.

Names for brands which are appropriate and likely to have good appeal are not easily arrived at. Any name that is likely, however indirectly, to lead to possible association or confusion with an existing product name will invite objections. In the more fiercely contested markets of foodstuffs and toiletries it is not uncommon for several proposed names to be refused because of objections before a name is finally found that can be registered. When we come to choose a designation for our new product therefore, it will be as well to have a choice of several names.

Any names considered for products must be devoid of double meaning or of unpleasant associations. We must consider the display aspects of the name. The shorter it is the better. It must be easy to pronounce. In this connection one must consider overseas markets and the degree of facility with which the name can be pronounced by people to whom English is a foreign language.

Some manufacturers prefer to have a brand name to cover a range of products rather than a separate brand name for each of their lines. One of the advantages of an 'umbrella' arrangement of this kind is that only one brand name has to be promoted. All promotional expenditure is concentrated, and that one name can be more extensively promoted than would be the case with perhaps half a dozen individual product names. However, there is the danger that, if the nature of the products sheltering under this single 'umbrella' name differs widely, their association with the brand image may not be close enough.

There are many devices for getting names for new products. One can run a competition among consumers and invite their suggestions. It must be remembered of course that the replies will not constitute a true cross-section of the market. An alternative method is to invite a cross-section of consumers to suggest a name and to select the majority decision.

Selection of a package

Product packaging has become a highly specialized business. The wide range of materials, many of which are of a synthetic nature, and the special design techniques required not only to protect and promote the product but to enable the package to be mass-produced economically, recommend the use of packaging specialists.

In a very large organization that has its own design studios, there may be staff designers possessing adequate knowledge of the subject to undertake the package design for our new product. The majority of companies, however, will look to an independent industrial designer or to one of the firms of packaging manufacturers, who are likely to offer considerable expertise in the design of a package to suit both the product and the market for which it is intended. In practice, because the package is so much a part of the promotion of the product, marketing will want to consult the company's advertising agency and canvas its view before any final decision on package design is made.

There are certain fundamentals to the design of the package that must be appreciated if one is to work in harmony with packaging design specialists.

The pack should be appropriate to the kind of product it contains. It must fit the consumer's idea of the type of pack that is normal for this kind of merchandise. Although there is merit in some innovation, one must remember that the vast majority of consumers are conventional in their buying habits, and resistance will be encountered if the package appears to be incongruous for the product.

The pack should be distinctive. Some products have to fight for notice on the shelves of shops and supermarkets. Their packs must be eye-catching. Remember that some colours and colour combinations are aggressive, others recessive. The pack must establish the identity of the brand, even when its name is not visible. Too heavy a reliance on colour for identification can lead to problems: much newspaper advertising, for example, appears in black and white.

The pack should obviously have a pleasing appearance, encouraging the potential customer to form a favourable impression even before he or she has examined the goods. It should be well-constructed and durable and be easy to handle, particularly when the product has to be carried home in a shopping bag. It must keep the product in good condition in the home, be easy to store and, where applicable, provide for ease of dispensing. Packages for food and drink products have to comply with exacting health-care standards in many countries, must not taint the contents and must state the ingredients of which the product is composed. There is a considerable technology for the testing of synthetic packaging materials for toxicity, taste and odour. One must also bear in mind the point of view of the retailer who will more readily wish to stock a product that arrives in good condition and which it is easy for him to stack for display purposes.

When considering the size of the package, it is advisable to follow trade convention wherever possible. Consumer acceptance is easier to achieve with pack sizes that are familiar to the user, who is likely to be bewildered and suspicious of something outside his or her normal experience.

2.13   Test marketing the product

Once one has had an idea for a product that has been carefully screened for both manufacturing and marketing feasibility and which has been given a name, a pack and a personality, the time has come to consider testing it for public acceptability. The cost of launching a new consumer product on the national market is extremely high. As we have seen, it is at best a hazardous undertaking. At worst, it can bring ruin to the company concerned. Wisdom dictates that before the expense of a national launch is incurred, the product should be tested in a limited section of the market.

The principle of test marketing

Test marketing is a well-established device, used not only in the development of new products, but also to test the likely response to changes to existing products, to a new type of promotional offer or to a variation in price. Because the costs of test marketing may be only one tenth or even as low as one hundredth of the costs of a national campaign, this method provides a comparatively cheap way in which to detect faults in the product or its promotion, and to correct them.

There are certain disadvantages to test marketing. If the intention is to obtain a true pattern of demand for the product, it may take six or twelve months for this to be established. Furthermore, one must not accept all the results of a test-marketing operation as being indicative of the results one would get in a national campaign. No local area, however carefully selected, will mirror the national market accurately. There will be, for example, no national advertising in the local market. On the other hand, there may be a greater concentration of effort proportionately in the test area than would be likely, indeed, possible, in a national campaign.

The procedure for test marketing

Test marketing can be achieved in a number of ways. Samples of one's own product and those of competitors can be put into plain packs and given to a panel of consumers, selected on as representative a basis as possible, for their comments. It should be borne in mind that this method of testing will provide evidence only of the quality and utility of one's own product in relation to those of one's competitors. Because of the use of plain packs, the association between the product and its brand image will have been broken. In terms of practical market conditions therefore this form of test has only limited value.

The generally accepted method of test marketing is to introduce the product to the market through retailers in selected test towns. Once again the lack of association with a nationally advertised brand image must be taken into account when assessing the results.

A modification of this method is to supply the product through retailers in several test towns and, at the same time, to run an advertising campaign in one of these towns only, with a view to assessing the effect which this may have upon sales in that town. This will undoubtedly introduce a little more realism, but its effectiveness will depend upon the effectiveness of the local advertising media. In Britain and many other geographically small countries television, radio and press generally have a national, as distinct from local, coverage. Local press advertising restricted to individual towns or cities is likely to have a considerably limited effect upon the consumer compared with the effect of national advertising accompanying a national campaign. In markets where the main advertising media are locally based this method is more likely to be successful. A further modification is to market the product nationally through selected retailers and to devise a means of measuring the demand that occurs in those shops that do *not* stock the product.

The real purpose of test marketing is to find out if the marketing mix has been formulated correctly to match the features of the product to the needs of its potential customers. But the variables that arise when such a test is, of necessity, restricted to limited areas of the total market mean that its results will provide, at best, only a very general guide to the product's acceptance nationally. If the preliminary market research has been sufficiently thorough, its findings may provide a more reliable guide than that which may result from a localized test marketing. In situations where the life cycle of the product is expected to be fairly short, or where the financial cost of product failure may not be so far removed relatively from that of a series of inconsequential test-marketing exercises, producers frequently opt to go straight ahead with a national launch.

Discussion questions

1   Why is it considered advisable that a firm should have a range of products?
2   Describe the principal stages of the product life cycle and the value of the life cycle concept to the attainment of long-term company objectives.
3   What is meant by market share? Why is the market share that is achieved by its products of special concern to the company's management?
4   Discuss the effect that the market growth rate can have upon product profitability.
5   State some of the principal uses of a product matrix.
6   Indicate some important conditions applicable to the selection of new products.
7   Suggest possible sources for new product ideas and discuss methods by means of which their feasibility may be assessed.
8   List ten different consumer products and indicate who is most likely to make the buying decision that results in the purchase of each item.

3
Marketing and the consumer

We have seen how important it is to identify the needs of the consumer accurately. This does not begin and end with the launch of a new product. It is a continuous process, and a business organization should keep itself informed constantly of the pattern of such needs and the trends that may alter that pattern in the future. To provide this information is the task of an activity known as consumer research.

3.1   The meaning of consumer research

The basis of consumer research lies in the fact that mass production and consumption have brought about a standardization in the habits and the tastes of the vast majority of people. It has therefore become possible to examine the habits of a whole market by conducting tests upon small samples.

The uninitiated may be sceptical. It is an affront to our dignity and our belief in our own individuality to be informed that we are in fact just one of a herd, and that the habits by which we live our lives, and the urges which motivate us, are paralleled by those of the vast majority of our fellow citizens. Whether we like it or not, however, there is overwhelming evidence that this standardization of taste and living habits exists. It has been accentuated in the last half century by a blurring of the boundaries of what once were described as working and middle-class incomes.

It is unfortunate that the credibility of the methods used in the conduct of mass surveys should have been put in question by the apparent failure of some opinion polls to predict the outcome of political elections correctly. It should be realized, however, that opinion research differs considerably from consumer research. The opinion researcher, for example, will ask people their opinion on a topical controversial issue of the day, and direct questions seeking an opinion rather than a fact may not produce a truthful answer.

Respondents may offer an opinion regardless of whether they hold it or not, rather than admit to having no opinion at all. Similarly, when people are asked how they intend to vote, it is easy for a misleading set of answers to be obtained. There are those who will *say* that they intend voting for Mr A or Miss B, but when the time comes, their opinions may have altered or they may not even trouble to vote at all.

The consumer researcher, however, is dealing not with opinions but with behaviour. One of the factors that has been established by market research organizations over many years is the general honesty of ordinary people. When asked to provide facts about how and when and where they do their shopping and the uses to which they put the products they buy, the great majority tell the truth to the best of their knowledge. The main hazard for the researcher is not the deliberate lie but inaccuracies which can creep in owing to poor memory. Because this problem is recognized, however, steps are taken, in both the formulation of questions and in interviewing methods, to overcome the difficulty.

We can therefore forget the possible shortcomings of opinion polls, recognizing the additional hazards under which they must work. Our purpose is to consider the credibility of the results of consumer surveys where people are, in the main, invited to respond to a series of questions regarding their buying habits and the uses to which they put the various types of merchandise in which the survey is interested.

3.2 The uses of consumer research

Increasing sophistication of marketing methods generally has led to a more sophisticated approach to the question of consumer needs. Whereas consumer research was at one time solely concerned with establishing the how, why and when of the purchase of goods or services, it is now more interested in the use made of them by the ultimate customer. Indeed research now concentrates on people's composite activities, as distinct from a single activity or process.

We have already referred to the importance of identifying new consumer needs in order to formulate new products to satisfy them. It is by a study of the behavioural patterns of people that their unrecognized needs may be established. Modern research endeavours to discover how people live and work in their homes, the times of day at which they take their meals and the particular meals at which they eat certain foodstuffs. Efforts are made to find out how kitchen equipment is used and the part it plays in the general activity of, for example, the preparation of a meal or dealing with the family laundry. The findings of research of this nature are a guide not only to the future design of such equipment but also to suitable methods of promotion to the buying public.

Consumer research seeks to establish the total number of potential consumers for a given product, and to subdivide them by sex, age group, marital status, occupation, social class and geographical location. Bearing in mind that a consumer is not necessarily the same as a customer, consumer research has to find out who actually buys the product in question, and where it is bought: at the corner shop, at the cooperative store, at a chemist's shop, at a grocer's shop, or at a supermarket. Finally, it seeks to establish when the product is used and how it is used.

How consumer needs can be satisfied

Apart from identifying the consumer to whom we aim to sell our product, research should also tell us the *kind* of product the consumer is likely to want because it will more exactly satisfy her need.

The types of domestic equipment people have in their homes will affect their use of other products. The optimum size of food storage containers should relate to the size and shape of the storage area in the more popular sizes of domestic refrigerators. The market for humidifiers must relate to the number of homes that have central heating installed. The market for bathroom fittings is dependent on the number of homes with bathrooms. Such examples seem self-evident. What may be less evident are the factors that determine the extent of a market. Should one assume that the market for folding garden chairs is limited to the number of homes with gardens? What about the needs of caravan-owners? Is the market for facsimile machines limited to offices and factories? In Britain, at least, the number of people working from home increases annually. This is seen to be a considerable growth area for various types of business machines.

Consumer research can indicate to business the *preference* of consumers. Why is one brand of washing-up liquid preferred to another? Is it the quality of the product, its utility, the design of the package or its promotion – its 'brand image' – which evokes a favourable response? It can also alert the manufacturer to possible changes in the market likely to result from changing consumer needs. We have seen that no market remains static, and a product that is popular and in great demand today may be dead inside two years. Marketing must for ever be on the look-out for the advent of new consumer needs whose satisfaction may conflict with a current level of demand for an existing product or service. Thus the popularity and comparative cheapness of foreign travel creates and satisfies a demand, and in so doing tends to absorb some of the surplus purchasing power which might otherwise have been spent, for example, on new house furnishings.

3.3   Methods of consumer research

There are three main methods used in consumer research: desk research, field research, and motivation research. Each method plays a part in helping marketing to build a picture of the men and women who make up the market for the company's products or services.

Desk research

The starting point for any form of market research is that which can be done, as the name implies, seated at one's desk. There are masses of statistics prepared by government departments, trade associations and market research consultants readily available to the would-be researcher, and which he/she can consult without stepping outside his/her own office. Before we consider these, however, let us take a look at the information likely to be at the marketing department's elbow, namely, the records kept by the company itself. All trading organizations keep records of one form or another, such as customer's accounts, turnover figures, product sales totals, sales area turnover figures and salesforce commission records.

Company statistics
All this statistical information can provide useful guidance for the formulation of marketing decisions. It may require arranging and analysing. One may have to go back over five years or so and seek some relation between products and product groups in terms of volume and turnover. The company's sales figures should provide a barometer to indicate seasonal fluctuations. Indeed any major fluctuations in turnover must have a cause, and the discovery of that cause may well indicate some characteristic of fluctuating consumer needs or buying habits.

Customer research in the industrial-goods field can begin with a similar examination of company records. Since individual customers are identifiable, they can be categorized according to the products they use as well as the after-processes to which the products are put. Existing information, rearranged in this manner, can tell one a great deal about the market in which one is operating, as well as highlighting factors that hitherto may have been obscured.

Trade statistics
Statistics relating to the pattern of production and consumption in a particular trade or industry are usually available, in a classified form,

from the appropriate trade association. Trade directories, year books, trade periodicals and the financial press are additional sources of market information. In addition, there are in most industrialized countries firms that specialize in the provision of trade and technical information. They can provide market research services and will undertake to furnish to subscribers up-to-date information on market growth and trends.

Government statistics

Governments in most developed countries are anxious to promote both internal and external trade. Their trade departments are therefore an excellent source of statistical information for trade and industry.

Field research

Although desk research will provide marketing with a great deal of general information with regard to economic trends, it is unlikely to provide guidance as to the consumer's reaction to the company's specific range of products or to those of its competitors. This is the kind of knowledge one has to find for oneself.

Consumer sampling

The sample method in consumer research relies on two factors. The first, to which we have already referred, is that the vast majority of people interviewed in a survey will give answers which are true to the best of their knowledge. The second is that it is usually possible to establish that the sample is, within fairly acceptable limits, representative of the whole.

It is important that one should understand the importance of this second factor. Upon the degree of probability that exists in any survey will depend the credibility of its findings. If there is reasonable doubt that the sample that is being examined is not representative, then it will be better to abandon the project and start again. A wrong sample will produce wrong results, which could be disastrous for those who may decide to act upon them.

How certain can one be that any sample is truly representative of the whole?

Let us consider for a moment a typical example of sampling. You order a bottle of wine in a quality restaurant. Correctly, you should first be presented with the bottle, cork intact, in order that you may see the label, to be assured that its description corresponds with what you have ordered. Subsequently the wine waiter will uncork the bottle and pour a small sample of its contents into your glass to enable you to taste and test. This conventional method of approving wine is based on the overwhelming probability that the sample which is taken is representative of the whole of the contents of the bottle.

Few consumer surveys are quite so undeniable. Indeed, in an effort to minimize this problem, market researchers have developed a number of devices aimed to achieve the highest degree of representativeness compatible with reasonable economy.

We have already referred to the possibility that false statements made by respondents could have a detrimental effect upon the value of a survey. In practice, however, it has been found that a false statement in one direction is usually cancelled out by an equally false statement in the other. Where it is discovered that a high proportion of false answers have been given to a specific question in a survey, it is usually because that question has been badly phrased.

The obvious advantage of the sampling technique compared with a total survey of the whole market (even if this was possible) is that the cost is infinitely smaller. However, since the size of the survey will have a direct bearing on its cost, it will be dependent on the budget that has been allocated. The ideal sample is a microcosm of the entire population. It should be noted that the words *population* or *universe* refer, in marketing parlance, to the sub-section of the actual population which one is investigating. A *universe* therefore may be the total number of schoolteachers or the total number of families with two cars.

It is the composition of the sample that is more important than its size. It should be remembered that the researcher is not trying to establish a large or a small sample upon which to carry out the survey, but one of optimum size. For example, if one intends to survey a whole country, one would arrange about 2,000 interviews for the sample. This figure, however, would be equally applicable for countries with such divergent population sizes as, let us say, the United Kingdom, the USA, Germany or Holland. Where the universe is uniform, it is often possible to work with a smaller sample, but it must remain a true cross-section of the population.

Where the universe is not uniform, the researcher will probably divide it into sections, or strata, which are uniform. It will be appreciated that when this occurs the size of the sample that is decided upon will depend upon the size of the smallest sub-section, because no sub-section can contain too few respondents. However, this could lead to the necessity of interviewing such a large number of respondents that the entire survey would be hopelessly uneconomic.

Let us clarify this with an example. If we select a sample containing 2,000 interviews in order to study the buying habits of a universe of, say, 750,000 people, the situation is as follows: in order to represent the various categories of people that make up that universe adequately, 50 persons have to be included to represent those with an income in excess of, say, £50,000 per annum. Now it must be obvious that 50 is too few to reflect the variety of viewpoints, personal interests and buying habits of the highly paid sector of the universe.

The problem is that if we were to double the quantity of the £50,000 a year people, the whole sample would have to be doubled. That would be very expensive. The way round this problem is to double only the number of highly paid people and increase the sample to 2,050 interviews. A correction is made to the final results, when the figures that relate to the answers given by the more wealthy respondents are halved. Thus the proportions are maintained and the final results derived from the survey are not distorted. This device is known as *weighting* the results.

There are various methods of selecting samples for consumer surveys. Those most frequently employed are the probability, the random and the quota systems. In practice, researchers often use hybrid methods to suit the type of research in which they are engaged.

The probability system

Using the probability system, the researcher prepares a list of the names and addresses of the entire universe that he proposes to survey. These names are discovered in city and trade directories, telephone directories or professional lists. Copies of electoral rolls, obtainable from local authorities, are also used.

Once the list is complete, the researcher sets out to select a representative sample on a uniform basis. Thus, if he intends to work with a sample of 5 per cent of the universe, he will select one name in twenty. He will not merely select 5 per cent of the list of names, because to do so would fail to ensure that the spread of names was even.

The researcher must be careful lest bias should enter the sample. It has been found, for example, that people with the same initial letter to their names are not free from bias.

Since uniformity is the essence of this particular method, the interviewers employed to carry out the survey are not allowed to choose the people to be interviewed. Were they to do so, this could introduce bias, because, naturally, each interviewer will be biased to some extent in the kind of person he/she selects.

There are a number of difficulties with the probability system of surveying. Researchers have problems in getting a list of all the names and addresses which make up the universe, which is not surprising. Electoral rolls and other published lists of names quickly become out of date; also the time spent in selecting respondents from these lists is expensive.

A further problem is that, to maintain the uniformity of the survey, a person whose name has been selected *must* be interviewed. The pattern of uniformity will be broken if a neighbour is substituted. At first glance this may seem like pedantry carried to excess. On second thoughts, however, it will be seen that the way of life, and therefore the buying habits of a woman who is frequently out and difficult to get hold of, will be different from those of the woman next door, who, on the contrary, is readily available simply because she is nearly always at home.

The random system

The random system is a simplification of the above. It does not require a complete register of the population that is being surveyed. Small areas of the country are selected at random and in each of these districts one particular address is chosen, also at random, as the starting point of the interviewer's route. Calls are then made at every house in the street whose number ends in a randomly chosen unit. The interviewer then moves to the next street which has been chosen on a random basis, and the process is repeated.

A modification of this method is to list, in the first instance, all the districts in the country, urban and rural, and then to select, on a random basis, a limited number of districts for the conduct of interviews. Within those districts houses will be selected at random. Thus the geographical scatter of the homes that have been selected for interviewing is reduced without causing any reduction to the representativeness of the sample.

The quota system

A further modification and the method most frequently used for consumer surveys is known as the quota system. Here the first stage is to decide upon the size of the sample which will be taken and then to stratify the universe. This stratification, or dividing into sections, will be carried out on the basis of age, sex, marital status, income group, occupation and the size of the town, suburb or village in which respondents live.

When this has been completed, the entire sample is divided by the total number of interviewing days that are considered necessary to complete the survey. For example, if we assume that an interviewer can complete twenty interviews in a day and that the total number of questionnaires to be filled out numbers 2,000, the sample will be divided into 100 parts. Each interviewer is then given a quota, in this case twenty persons, whom she must find and interview. She is entrusted with the task of selecting her own respondents, but these must fit closely the various categories the researcher will stipulate, based on the stratification of the universe already carried out.

The quota system is considered to be not as representative as the probability or random methods, but it is much cheaper to operate. The costly listing of the entire universe is eliminated and the interviewer does not have to return to interview specific people not at home at the time of her first visit, as is the case with the other two methods.

The use of consumer panels

One of the major drawbacks to all the above methods of personal interview surveys is that they do not provide a means of supplying *continuous* information on the buying habits of the respondents. Marketing needs, in addition to research reports on specific consumer reaction, some form of permanent consumer audit by means of which it can monitor the buying habits of the respondents, their degree of loyalty to any particular brand, and the end of that loyalty and the change to a different brand. It also needs some means to gauge consumer reaction to advertising and promotion, not only of the company's product but of those of its competitors, as reflected in possible changes in buying patterns.

To provide this continuous information, panels of respondents are set up. The respondents are selected either randomly or by the quota method, and they are required to supply information on their shopping activities over a considerable period of time.

A housewife panel for consumer products would normally consist of about 2,000 respondents, representing as closely as possible a cross-section of the universe under scrutiny. They would be recruited usually by personal interview, and thereafter communicate with the market research organization by post. They would be supplied with a diary in which they would be asked to keep a record of all their purchases of certain branded goods. The information required usually is fairly simple, consisting of the name of the brand, the packet size (where this is applicable), the price paid and the name of the shop where the product was purchased. At the end of each week (or month) the housewife would return her diary to the market researcher and receive a new one for the subsequent period.

Consumer panels are seldom maintained by single business organizations. The cost of setting them up and maintaining them is very high. They are usually run by market research organizations to provide research data for a group of product manufacturers.

Cost is not the only problem. Researchers have constant difficulty in maintaining a panel once it is set up. The number of housewives prepared to undertake this work is limited, and many find it tedious. Too high a turnover of respondents, however, will reduce the very continuity which is the whole purpose of the panel. Furthermore, some housewives find that the task of writing the simple details of their purchases in a diary is difficult. However, those with a low degree of literacy cannot be eliminated from the sample, because the semi-literate members of the universe have to be represented.

Perhaps the greatest problem with regard to consumer panels is the danger of bias creeping in simply because the respondents, by undertaking panel membership, cease to be fully representative. They can no longer think and act in quite the same way as other housewives when they go shopping. The significance of their choice of purchases will introduce a degree of self-consciousness not experienced by the hundreds of thousands of other housewives whom they are intended to represent.

Interviewing methods

The basis for the sampling of respondents in a consumer research survey is to ask them to provide answers to a questionnaire. There are several methods of approaching respondents, including the personal interview, group interviews, the use of postal questionnaires and telephone interviews:

1 *The personal interview.* It is not surprising that the personal interviewer, approaching respondents at their homes, in the street or at work, achieves a much greater response than any other survey method. The interviewer can, by his/her presence, encourage the respondent to answer each question in the questionnaire, and can assist by explaining the reasons for the survey and the importance that attaches to the respondent's contribution. Mistakes made in answering questions or misunderstanding of the meaning of questions can be dealt with at the time, thus reducing considerably the number of spoiled questionnaires which would have to be disregarded at the editing stage.

 A good interviewer can add considerably to the response he/she obtains by assessment of the individual respondents. Often he/she is provided with a special form for comments of this nature.

 The drawback to the personal interview method is that it is expensive. Apart from remuneration, there is the question of travelling costs, which can be considerable, especially when the sampling method employed may call for the interviewer to make a number of recalls upon respondents. Even with the quota system, which avoids such recalls, the interviewer may have to devote considerable time to finding respondents who have the desired characteristics – age, sex, income bracket, occupation – to fit into the quota. The interviewers themselves must be carefully selected. Apart from all considerations of suitability, one must take account of the fact that the interviewer is a personality who will have his/her own ideas and opinions, which, however detached he/she may try to be, must create some bias.

2 *Group discussions.* Some researchers select a small group of respondents, representing a cross-section of the universe to be surveyed, and invite them to attend a group discussion. Such gatherings are usually chaired by an experienced interviewer,

who, instead of conducting interviews, puts a number of points to the meeting to provoke discussion.

The resulting conversation can be recorded on tape for subsequent examination by the research team. They are concerned not only with what the respondents have to say but the way in which they say it. By such means the broad opinions of a representative group of housewives may be considered. But the information gathered has of course no statistical use.

3 *Postal surveys.* The postal survey, which eliminates the need for trained interviewers, is obviously much cheaper than the systems previously discussed. There are, however, a number of problems.

The questionnaire sent out to respondents through the post cannot be as comprehensive as that used for a personal interview. Since there will be no interviewer at hand to explain the questions, they must be put in an elementary manner, and require as little writing as possible on the part of the respondent. The normal method is either to frame questions which require a simple 'yes' or 'no' answer, or to provide several alternative answers to each question, and respondents are asked to put a mark against the one they consider applicable.

One of the main difficulties with the use of postal questionnaires is that only about one person in ten will take the trouble to respond. Furthermore, the fact that they have taken this trouble, whereas the other nine out of ten have not, suggests they are not typical of the universe they are supposed to represent.

Various devices are employed to encourage respondents to respond. Sometimes a free gift is attached to the questionnaire, and the researcher hopes that the respondent will feel obliged to complete and return the form.

Like all unsolicited direct-mail approaches, of which this is but a specialized category, the accompanying letter of explanation must be concocted in such a manner that the respondent is urged to make the necessary effort to read and complete the questionnaire and post it back. This letter must explain the purpose of the survey in terms that the respondent will understand and, ideally, that will excite some interest on his or her part. This subject will be discussed in more detail in Section 6.6 on the subject of direct mail. It is sufficient to say here that postal surveys form an important part of mail-order trading and are frequently used to gain market reaction to new products and new selling techniques as well as the creation of mailing lists.

4 *Telephone surveys.* Market research by telephone is used to question consumers with regard to purchases of cars, domestic appliances and various types of household goods. It is extensively used by companies marketing double-glazing services. The method is comparatively cheap, response is immediate and the

interviewer can telephone a large number of respondents in a fraction of the time it would take to make personal visits to their homes.

There are drawbacks. The number of questions that can be put to respondents is limited. Attempts to establish their age and occupation are often met with a rebuff. Generally speaking, people do not like being telephoned by complete strangers asking them questions, and a semi-hostile response is often encountered.

Motivation research

In all the methods of consumer research we have so far considered, the researcher has been establishing ways and means of discovering how people behave in relation to certain products. The questions put to respondents in the probability, the random and the quota systems, and by means of the consumer panel, refer to the make of product they have purchased, the retail outlet from which the purchase has been made, the date and time of the purchase and the quantity of the product they have bought. Such information, reduced to statistical form, provides marketing with important guidelines on the state of the market and its likely trends and also on the situation of the company's own product and the products of its competitors within that market.

In spite of this abundance of information, however, one essential question is still left in the air. Why does the consumer behave in the way he/she does?

Upon reflection, it will be apparent that none of the research methods so far discussed can answer this question adequately. We have seen that ordinary people will, on the whole, provide truthful answers with regard to their purchasing habits for a wide range of the goods and services they buy. When it comes to the question of why they buy particular products from a particular retail outlet at a particular time, accurate answers are far more difficult to achieve. For one thing, the motives which prompt a considerable proportion of purchasing behaviour are entirely subjective, and it might be difficult for respondents themselves to offer any logical explanation. Secondly, people's motives for wanting to buy certain products, or to use certain products in certain ways, their preferences for one brand against another, are rooted in habits or mental attitudes which, even if they were recognized by the respondents, they might not wish to divulge to the research interviewer. If pressed to provide explanations for their actions, in all probability they would take refuge, consciously or subconsciously, in evasion or falsehood.

It has long been recognized that research into the motives of consumers – or, as it has come to be called, motivation research – is a specialized field and demands specialized methods of approach on the part of the researcher.

Motivation research originated in America. It was found that the purchasing behaviour of consumers resulted from influences that could be divided into two groups. The first of these was external influences, such as the size of the family being catered for, the social class to which it belonged, the appeal of the product in its physical form – its size, shape, taste or smell – and its emotive appeal by means of advertising and promotions. The second group consisted of internal influences, such as the customer's personality, acquired knowledge, moral standards, superstitions and religious beliefs.

To tap this subterranean flow of motives, the consumer researcher has turned to the field of clinical psychology and has adopted and adapted a number of its techniques. The methods used in motivation research are considerably more expensive than conventional methods of consumer research. Respondents are asked to submit themselves to various types of psychological test, such as word association, sentence completion and cartoon tests. These are all designed to establish subjective reactions to certain stimuli, as a result of which, it is claimed, the researcher can classify the pattern of their behaviour.

It is hardly surprising that a method of research intended for commercial purposes that relies upon methods still at a pioneering stage of medical research should not receive universal acceptance in the business world. Indeed considerable scepticism exists as to the value of motivation research. Apart from doubts as to the validity of its methods, a major drawback is that, in general, it does not lend itself to statistical treatment.

The construction of questionnaires

All forms of consumer sampling, with the exception of certain types of motivation research, have as their basis a list of questions which the respondent is invited to answer. The construction of the questionnaire is therefore a vital part of the research process. The success of a survey will depend as much upon the way in which the questionnaire has been prepared as upon all the other factors we have already considered. The market researcher will need to know what information marketing requires and how it wants that information presented. He will then be able to prepare a series of questions for respondents to answer which will be strictly relevant to the purpose of the survey.

In drawing up the questionnaire, the researcher will take account of four main considerations:

1   The general subject of the survey.
2   The classification of respondents.

3   The provision of control questions.
4   Questions designed to establish the information required.

When approached by an interviewer and asked to provide answers to a questionnaire, the majority of people will want to know something about the survey before they accept. They may ask for whom the survey is being conducted and what is its purpose. Although the respondent has a perfect right to request and to receive such information, disclosure of the name of the sponsor and the purpose for which the survey is being conducted can, on occasion, be undesirable from the sponsor's point of view. For example, if one is surveying a market in which one is not currently active but into which it is intended to enter as part of a diversification programme, such information is obviously highly confidential.

There are other reasons why a manufacturer may not wish to have his name disclosed to respondents. If the men and women who are being interviewed are aware that the survey is being conducted on behalf of the manufacturer of a certain brand, this is likely to cause some bias to enter into the way in which they answer the questions. According to the make-up of the individual, there could be a tendency not only to over- or under-criticize the product in question, but also to read into the questions interpretations that do not apply.

To overcome such difficulties, it is not uncommon for researchers to omit the name of the sponsor firm from the questionnaire. Alternatively, companies with unknown and therefore innocuous names are founded specially so that their names can be shown on questionnaires and cited to respondents on demand.

Similar problems can arise with the title of the survey. Here again, in the interests of security or to avoid introducing unnecessary bias into respondents' answers, it may be desirable to avoid an exact statement of purpose. This can be achieved by the use of a general rather than a specific title. But in the effort to avoid disclosure of confidential information regarding the client company, the researcher must be equally careful not to mislead the public by stating to respondents things that are not true.

To assist classification and to enable comparisons to be made from the answers of various sub-groups of respondents, it is normal for the first set of questions to establish facts about the person being interviewed, such as:

1   Sex.
2   Age.
3   Marital status.
4   Occupation.
5   Membership of professional organization, trade union, etc.
6   The occupation of the head of the household.

7   Does the family own the house it lives in?
8   Is it rented?
9   Is there a telephone?
10 At what age will the children in the household, if any, leave school?
11 What is the family income?

Some of these questions intrude deeply into the respondent's personal and financial affairs, and the problem of untruthful replies has to be faced. Sometimes researchers put such questions at the end of the questionnaire in the belief that by the time this stage has been reached, the interviewer will have succeeded in establishing friendly relations with the respondent, thus reducing his or her embarrassment or suspicion. Researchers often are divided on the question of whether or not the name of the respondent should be recorded. There is a strongly held opinion that a guarantee of anonymity allows the respondent to relax and generally produces more truthful replies.

The researcher's next consideration, before preparing questions on the general subject matter of the survey, is to decide the number and nature of the control questions to be incorporated in the questionnaire. Control questions aim to check the accuracy of the respondent's answers to the standard questions. Where the answer to a control question is at variance with the answer given to the standard question, it is apparent to the researcher that incorrect replies have been recorded. Where this occurs, the entire questionnaire will be eliminated from the survey.

Care needs to be taken in the wording of the control question. If it merely repeats the original question, it is likely to be answered in the same vein, and no control will have been achieved. To be effective it must broach the same subject as the standard question but from a different point of view.

In deciding upon the wording of questions and their sequence in the questionnaire, the researcher must bear in mind the mental attitude of the respondent. He or she has been approached by the interviewer, who has explained what the survey is about, that they have been selected by pure chance and are therefore representative of public opinion, and to invite their cooperation in providing answers to certain questions which will contribute to the success of the project. It is important that the confidence of the respondents should be gained as quickly as possible, as this will enable them to relax and cooperate with the interview.

The work of the interviewer to achieve this desirable situation will be assisted by the way in which questions are worded and the sequence in which they appear on the form. As soon as the introductory questions, which establish the respondent's characteristics, have been dealt with, it is important to move on to questions dealing with the substance of the survey, and which are likely to engage the respondent's interest. The sequence should be logical, because this enables the interest to be maintained and prevents the irritation that can occur when the respondent is asked to switch his mind from one topic to another to answer questions that may seem aimless in their intent.

One of the major problems of consumer surveys which are concerned with people's behaviour rather than their opinions is their dependence upon the memory of respondents. We have said before that, generally speaking, the public is prepared to cooperate in research of this nature, and wrong answers are seldom given intentionally. However, questions that relate to such mundane matters as the last time one purchased a certain brand of washing powder are hardly likely to stimulate the memories of most people, and the housewife may be forgiven if she cannot remember the price she paid for it or the shop where she bought it. Experience has shown that one should seek information about goods bought only the day before. Slightly less reliable results will be achieved from enquiries made into purchases of a week before. If one seeks to take the respondent back over a period of two weeks or more, answers of doubtful accuracy can be expected.

As to the type of questions used in questionnaires, these fall generally into three categories:

1 Dichotomous questions.
2 Multiple choice questions.
3 Open-ended questions.

Questions that can only be answered by the words 'yes' or 'no' are called dichotomous questions. Where these are used in a questionnaire, it is usual to state the alternatives and add spaces for 'don't know' and 'no answer'. Researchers like dichotomous questions. They make the work of interviewing much easier and also simplify the counting of results. An example of a dichotomous question is 'Did you go abroad for your holiday last year?'

A multiple choice question is one which admits several different answers. When these are used in a survey, the alternative answers are provided, and usually the respondent is invited to choose the answer with which she agrees. Again, statistical analysis is simplified. A multiple choice question may ask: 'If you went abroad for your holiday last year, did you travel by (1) scheduled airline, (2) charter flight, (3) boat and rail, (4) boat and car?'

The open-ended question provides greater latitude for the respondent's answer. He/she is invited to answer the question in his/her own words, and the interviewer enters that answer on the form. An open-ended question may ask: 'Why did you go abroad for your holiday?'

Care must be exercised in the use of words in questionnaires. They should be kept as simple as possible. It must be remembered that, in the majority of surveys, a cross-section of the population will be interviewed, and this must, of necessity, include people of the lowest intelligence or education as well as the highest. Every word that is used should have a precise meaning, because if the respondent is in any doubt as to the meaning of the question which is put, he/she is liable to give a genuinely mistaken answer. Unfortunately many of the words in the English language have more than one meaning, or a different meaning in different parts of the country.

That enemy of the researcher, namely bias, can be introduced unwittingly in a survey by the use of ill-advised questions. If you ask a housewife 'Do you give your children a cooked breakfast every morning?', she could imagine that to answer in the negative would suggest she was failing in her duty as a mother. A better approach would be to say: 'Some children like a cooked breakfast; others have no appetite first thing in the morning. Do your children like a cooked breakfast or do they not like a cooked breakfast?'

Once all the questionnaires in the sample have been completed, the researcher is faced with the task of processing the information obtained. The first step is to edit the questionnaires. The editor's job is to check every questionnaire to make sure that correct answers have been given. This is achieved by means of the control questions which have been inserted for this very purpose. Researchers refer to the Triangle Clause, which consists of three related questions within a questionnaire, each of which approaches the same subject from a slightly different angle. If it is found that one of the answers to these questions contradicts another, it can be assumed that the answer which has been given to the third question decides the issue.

Having ensured that the information which appears in the questionnaire is satisfactory, the editor applies code numbers to each answer. Where dichotomous and multiple choice questions are used throughout a questionnaire, these are usually coded in advance. The open-ended questions are usually more difficult to classify. They are often grouped and tabulated by hand, and those that do not fall into any convenient group are placed under a miscellaneous heading. Finally, the coded answers are tabulated by means of a computer to provide the information in statistical form that the client company requires.

In this chapter we have considered in some detail the methods employed generally in consumer research and, more particularly, the conduct of sample surveys. In the majority of small and medium-sized commercial firms it is unlikely that marketing will conduct consumer research itself. It is specialized work, and few companies have their own market research departments. Even where such departments do exist within the business organization, it is normal practice for the conduct of field research to be undertaken by outside agencies. These may be independent firms or the market research departments of advertising agencies. Independent organizations differ very considerably, according to their degree of experience and the nature of the work in which they specialize.

Market research departments of advertising agencies usually specialize in advertising research. There has been an increasing tendency, however, for the advertising agency to attempt to provide a complete marketing service to clients, and this has led them into various branches of consumer research. The general practice is to undertake the organization of a consumer survey but to sub-contract to outside agencies the work of interviewing, editing and tabulating. The final report on the survey is then presented by the advertising agency's own market research specialists.

Discussion questions

1 Discuss some of the ways in which consumer research can assist in the design, packaging and promotion of products.
2 How would you use desk research to obtain market information in respect to: (a) frozen foods; (b) lawnmowers; (c) dry cleaning services?
3 Explain the advantages and disadvantages that apply to the use of: (a) postal questionnaires; (b) telephone interviews; (c) personal interviews.
4 Describe how you would set about organizing a consumer research project within your local area to discover the number of people who, within the previous two weeks, have purchased a particular brand of instant coffee and why they chose this brand in preference to others.

4
Marketing and distribution

Distribution is the place element of the marketing mix of benefits that the producer offers to the consumer. It is the means by which a product is brought to the right place at the right time to satisfy customers' needs.

In the interests of clarity, however, we must distinguish between two separate aspects of distribution. The first is concerned with the *channels* through which the product flows in its journey from factory gate to customer. The second relates to the *physical movement* of goods from their source to their ultimate destination.

4.1 Distribution channels

A company has a choice of distribution channels:

1 It may elect to follow the traditional route: producer to wholesaler, wholesaler to retailer, retailer to final purchaser.
2 It may decide to omit the wholesaler from the chain and distribute direct to the retailer.
3 It may prefer to bypass intermediaries and sell direct to the public through its own retail outlet, by mail order, or by means of door-to-door or party-plan agents.

None of these methods is necessarily exclusive. Many organizations use more than one channel for the distribution of their products. See Figure 4.1.

4.2 Distribution via the wholesaler

The wholesaler justifies his existence in the distribution chain in the performance of three essential functions:

1 He buys in bulk.

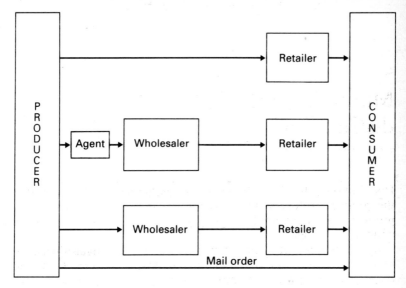

Figure 4.1 *Alternative distribution channels*

2 He bears risk.
3 He breaks bulk.

Where neither manufacturer nor retailer is in a position to assume these three responsibilities, the wholesaler provides a necessary service.

Let us examine these functions:

1 *Bulk-buying.* Because he buys goods in bulk, the wholesaler relieves the manufacturer of the cost of making a large number of small deliveries. Thus the cost of delivery to the manufacturer is greatly reduced. He requires a comparatively small salesforce in order to sell his product to a limited number of wholesalers.

2 *Risk-bearing.* If it were not for the existence of the wholesaler, the manufacturer would need to hold larger stocks of his product. He would tie up more capital in financing these stocks, and would incur increased costs through the need for greater storage space. The greatest risk in stockholding, however, is deterioration in the value of the merchandise before it is sold. When the wholesaler buys goods in bulk and holds them in stock to meet demand, he relieves the manufacturer of this risk, which can be very real in markets that are subject to fluctuation, or where the merchandise is perishable or vulnerable to sudden fashion change.

3   *Breaking bulk*. By breaking bulk the wholesaler offers a wide variety of goods in relatively small quantities to the retailer. Where a retailer carries a large selection of items, he has greater reliance on the wholesaler's services. Buying direct from the manufacturer in bulk would create problems of finance and storage. He would have to deal with a large number of manufacturers instead of a few wholesalers. He would need to see far too many salesmen and would be over-burdened with the necessary correspondence and accountancy work.

The unit cost of delivery incurred by a manufacturer making a large number of small deliveries to hundreds or thousands of retail outlets would be extremely high. For the wholesaler, however, who delivers an assortment of items to the retailer, the unit cost of delivery obviously is much smaller.

Since distribution via the wholesaler would appear to offer such advantage, why is it that so many manufacturing firms now omit the wholesaler and prefer to sell direct to the retailer? The answer to this question lies in the fundamental change that has occurred in the marketing of consumer goods.

The development of product branding has been accompanied by a dramatic increase in the adoption by manufacturers of the direct-to-retailer method of distribution. By going direct to the retail outlet, the manufacturer maintains a far greater control over the marketing of his product. He is able to coordinate better the efforts of his salesforce with advertising, promotion and in-store merchandising. He can sustain his marketing policy in the knowledge that it will not be frustrated by wholesalers with divergent marketing objectives or other opposing interests to serve. Because product branding demands heavy investment in advertising, the manufacturer must ensure adequate shop distribution for his product.

There are other factors that have played a part in accelerating the direct-to-retailer approach. Within the retail trade itself there have been major changes, with the gradual extinction of many small independent traders and the growth of large group concerns – variety chain stores, multiples and consumer cooperatives. In Britain there has been a movement of population away from the countryside and into the towns, which has helped the manufacturer to supply the more easily located urban retailers economically. The improvement in long-distance road haulage brought about by motorways has facilitated the movement of goods. These factors assist the producer to make direct deliveries from factory to retailer, and reduce his dependence on the depots and warehouses of the wholesale trade.

The cost of production also has a bearing on the choice of distribution method. The more sophisticated product manufacture becomes, the greater the need for investment in plant and equipment. This need for high capitalization limits the number of manufacturers producing any one class of product. Heavy investment in production compels each producer to ensure its fullest utilization, and this means controlled distribution.

In certain fields, however, wholesale distribution remains essential. Small-scale producers, such as farmers and market gardeners, are clearly not in a position to distribute their own products. There are certain types of product, of which tea is an example, that need blending or after-processing and depend upon the specialized technical and commercial 'know-how' of the wholesale trade. Furthermore, some highly perishable foodstuffs must be distributed rapidly before they deteriorate to a nil value. It requires highly organized and experienced wholesalers to provide this service.

There are indeed large numbers of medium to small production companies with a limited range of products that would find it totally uneconomic to supply direct to the retail trade. They need the services of the wholesale trade, which buys in bulk and distributes, in small quantities, to a scattered market.

When all the factors have been considered, manufacturers of non-branded products have to face the ultimate question. Could they sell as effectively as the wholesaler, based on the profit margin that the wholesaler demands, if they themselves were to undertake the distribution of their products directly to the retail trade? The wholesaler's costs are shared between a range of merchandise. The costs of a salesforce supported by adequate warehousing and despatch services are often prohibitive for the distribution of a narrow range of products to widely dispersed outlets.

The wholesale trade is very diverse. There are firms that cover the whole country with depots in major provincial towns, whereas others operate strictly on a local basis. Some specialize in certain classes of goods only; others carry a general range of merchandise.

General wholesalers

In the grocery and hardware trades, where retailers tend to buy a multiplicity of items in small quantities, the general wholesaler, offering many product lines, is able to maintain a quick delivery service, based on adequate stocks, to small independent traders. Recent years have seen an increase in 'cash and carry' methods of general wholesaling. The retailer has the advantage of making his purchases at a central warehouse – a kind of wholesale supermarket – and taking the goods away with him. He has the benefit of immediate possession of the merchandise, and can therefore limit his stockholding. The wholesaler is saved the cost of a salesforce as well as the cost of providing a delivery service. 'Cash and carry', as the term denotes, is conducted on a cash basis, thus relieving the wholesaler of the need to finance credit facilities for customers, and removing the hazard of bad debts.

Specialist wholesalers

In certain fields, the wholesaler is a specialist. He deals in a very limited range of goods and often provides his customers with a technical service that might otherwise have to be supplied by the manufacturer. Certain types of capital equipment are distributed in this manner. Other specialists deal in food products, such as tea or coffee, and provide a blending service.

From the viewpoint of the small retailer, the support of a wholesale house offers many benefits. To secure the retailer's regular business, the wholesaler will often provide attractive credit facilities and help him in other ways – by providing a window-dressing service, training his staff, advising him on the selection of merchandise and even lending him finance for shop modernization schemes. Many successful small retail businesses have been built on the interested benevolence of the old-established wholesale houses.

4.3   Direct-to-retailer distribution

The function of the retailer in the modern pattern of distribution is complex. Essentially his role is that of a local supplier of merchandise offering a direct service to the public. The means by which he provides this service are extremely varied. He frequently breaks bulk. He prepares the goods for resale, provides credit and hire-purchase facilities and may offer an after-sales service. The provision of expertise and advice to customers, a service that at one time was widely performed by retailers, is now largely restricted to specialist independent shops.

In former times the boundaries between one trade and another were clearly defined. New marketing concepts have blurred these boundaries, particularly as the result of 'related selling', where additional sales are created by the offer of related items of merchandise.

The last half-century has seen a revolution in the structure of the retail trade. The independent shop, once pre-eminent, has declined rapidly in the face of changes in the pattern of social behaviour, on the one hand, and the growth of large-scale retail enterprises, on the other. Shopping has ceased to be a social occasion. To 'go shopping' once was an important and, for many women in particular, one of the few opportunities for social intercourse. The advent of the two-car family, the increasing number of women in full-time employment, plus a general increase in leisure pursuits, has increased the appeal of buying a wide range of goods under one roof. The dominance established by the supermarket and the hypermarket during the 1970s and 1980s has led to the extinction of a large number of independent traders. Increasingly, these powerful enterprises are moving away from the town centre to greenfield sites, where adequate car-parking facilities provide an additional customer service.

The last few years have seen the development in Britain of the out-of-town shopping centre. Here are congregated a host of retailing outlets, from independents to chain and multiple stores, coffee shops and restaurants, under a single roof, where the shopper can browse in air-conditioned comfort and security. As we approach the turn of the century, this may well be the future pattern of retailing in this country. The inner-city High Street and the traditions associated with it must surely pass into history.

In the changing retail scene the role of the independent shopkeeper is likely to become essentially that of the specialist, providing an essential service to those smaller segments of a market in which the large retail organizations have little interest. Outlets catering for the needs of minority customer groups with specific interests, such as hobby and craft devotees, pet-owners, sports enthusiasts, campers and caravaners, and those whose leisure-pursuits include such subjects as photography, audio and visual recording, angling and sailing, should stand to benefit from the greater leisure and disposable income enjoyed by many of today's consumers.

The stock check system

The importance of adequate shop distribution of the product has already been mentioned. A producer who achieves a good level of sale of his brand *into* retail outlets cannot be sure of the success of his marketing plan unless he can establish also the level of sale to consumers that is being achieved by the retailer. If he is to control the distribution of his product, he must know the pattern of consumption. This means having a method of checking the quantities of his brand *bought* and *resold* by retailers over a given period.

This information is available by means of retail audit systems conducted by agencies specializing in distribution research. The basis of this research is the establishment of representative panels composed of many hundreds of retail outlets – independent shops, multiple and cooperative stores – throughout the country. It is a syndicated service, providing statistical information on the movement of all products which are of interest to subscribers by brand, size and quantity.

At agreed intervals (usually every two months) auditors of the research organization call upon each retail outlet in the panel. A check is made of the stock held in every brand whose manufacturers subscribe to the service. A note is also taken of all deliveries of these goods made during the two-month period. The following calculation is then carried out:

1   Opening stock of each brand.
2   Plus deliveries made of each brand during the period under review.
3   Less the stocks held at the end of the period.

The final figure represents the sales of each brand to the public during the relevant period. If the final stock figure is then divided by half the sales figure, the answer provides the number of months' supply of each product held by the retailer concerned.

Working to the same premise we examined in the case of market research, namely, that what happens in the control panel, because it is representative of its universe, must be true for the whole country, the research organization provides for its subscribers a set of statistics giving the following information:

1   The percentage of all the retailers in the country who stock each of the brands that have been checked.
2   The number of those retail outlets that currently hold stocks of these brands and the number that are currently out of stock.
3   Listed under each product field are shown the percentage of purchases made and stocks held of each competing brand and the sales made to consumers during the period under review.
4   Figures of the average sales of each brand per outlet are provided.
5   The number of months' supply of each brand stocked by retailers is shown.

The value of the retail audit to the producer depends very much upon the use he makes of the information. He can assess the underlying factors indicated by the statistics. The great value of the audit is its continuity. At regular two-monthly intervals he gets a picture of the situation of his own brands and those of his competitors. In particular, the figures will indicate:

(*a*)   Where distribution density is low.
(*b*)   The effect of competitors' promotion schemes and other merchandising activities on the movement of his own brands.
(*c*)   The effect his own promotional activities are having on competitive brands.

A poor distribution result in any particular region will show up immediately from the audit figures. Sometimes a producer may be surprised by the degree of penetration achieved by competitive brands in areas where his own distribution is low. Obviously he will look first at the sales effort being devoted to those areas, but this may not be the whole story. We have seen the importance of advertising in promoting consumer interest in a brand. This in turn affects the propensity of retailers to stock the product. The cause of the weakness may therefore be insufficient advertising.

On the other hand, there may be resistance on the part of retailers because they are not happy about the presentation of the product. The point-of-sale material provided for their use may be unsuitable for these particular outlets.

Ambiguities of this kind should be investigated. The main value of the retail audit is that it pinpoints marketing weaknesses in a company's strategy.

From the retailer side, too, there has been a growing tendency for the use of statistics to assess the movement of branded products. For example, branch managers of the larger multiple concerns are given information on the gross margin earned by each product per square metre of shop space allocated to it, together with details of its shelf movement and shop stocks. Using these figures as a guide, firms can plan the placing of orders more effectively.

4.4 Mail-order distribution

Producers who decide to bypass 'the trade' and sell directly to the consumer by mail order are adopting a distribution method requiring very specialized techniques.

Mail-order trading is essentially a twentieth-century phenomenon that depends for its success upon the existence of a fully reliable postal service. In company with many trading innovations it began in the United States, and it is in that country that most of its techniques were evolved. Its development in Britain and elsewhere has been somewhat slower, partly because of the size of the market and also because the proportion of people living in or near large urban areas, well supplied with shops and stores, is greater than in America. Nonetheless, mail order plays a significant part in retail distribution.

It offers several attractions:

1 The manufacturer retains complete control over the distribution of the product.
2 The entire nation is his market, yet he does not incur the expense of a nation-wide salesforce.
3 The location of his premises can be outside urban areas, where overhead costs will be lower (there are, however, two provisos: he must be close to good postal facilities, and he must also have access to an adequate supply of labour).

4   By using the postal services for carriage of his merchandise, he is saved the cost of providing his own transport facilities.

   The difficulties of mail order trading are:

1   The total lack of face-to-face selling at any stage of the distribution process.
2   The need for products having a unique selling proposition.
3   The need for specialized marketing skills.

The scope for mail-order distribution

Mail-order businesses range in size from giant organizations such as Britain's Great Universal Stores to one-man enterprises, many of them run from private homes. It has been said that anything that will sell can be sold by mail order. If this is an exaggeration, it is certainly true that the scope of mail-order trading is extremely wide and varied. Product lines range from concrete garages to chocolate for the connoisseur, wines, tools, kitchen equipment and a vast assortment of clothing. In recent years financial services such as unit trusts have joined the more traditional mail-order lines of correspondence courses, books and recorded music.

The market for mail order

Before venturing into mail order as a distribution channel, a company should assess the market closely. The first step will be to find out who are the people who buy through the post.

   In a country such as Britain, where the vast majority of the population has easy access to conventional retail outlets, the practice of buying goods by post may seem at first sight unnecessary and inconvenient. One might assume that the consumer would prefer to see and handle the merchandise before agreeing to part with money. The successful record of mail-order trading in this country and other countries with similar urban populations is undoubted proof that such an assumption is a fallacy. Many millions of pounds are spent annually by vast numbers of people, drawn from all sectors of the community, on goods they have not examined personally until they are delivered to their door.

   Let us examine this phenomenon, to establish the motives which cause people to take the trouble to buy through the post:

1   *Adventure*. There are many people who derive enjoyment from the action of reading an advertisement, writing a letter, enclosing postal order or cheque, posting it and waiting, with pleasurable anticipation, for the arrival of the wished-for parcel. The motiva-

tion may be likened to the sensation experienced by a child expecting a birthday gift or a present from Santa Claus.

2 *Prestige*. There are people who suffer from a feeling of inadequacy when they enter a shop or store to make a purchase. They are but one of many hundreds of shoppers. When they order by mail, they have the satisfaction of receiving goods addressed to them by name. They believe they have acquired prestige because a large business organization has conducted a transaction with them *personally*.

3 *Convenience*. For many people, shopping can be a hazardous, if not harrowing, experience. Those who are infirm due to age or ill-health find the problems of travel, even over short distances, too exhausting to be undertaken with pleasure. There are other groups of customers who dread the necessity to visit retail shops. Some have a fear of large cities or large stores. There are people who are nervous of having to confront shop assistants and ask to be shown items of merchandise. Such individuals are often extremely self-conscious or timid; they are afraid they may appear foolish, and dislike the prospect of having to buy goods they do not like as the alternative to walking out of a shop without making a purchase. There are others, still, who have extreme difficulty in making up their minds, especially when faced by an unsympathetic salesperson waiting with impatience for them to reach a decision. For all such people, the offer to 'decide in the comfort of your own home' is a powerful attraction.

4 *Exclusivity*. There are, however, many well-adjusted people who buy via mail order simply because the article they want is apparently only available to them through the post. Certainly there are many product lines brought to the attention of consumers by means of mail-order advertising in the popular press and in hobbyist magazines that it would take a great deal of time to find in conventional retail outlets.

5 *Economy*. Perhaps the most powerful motive behind the majority of mail-order purchases is the popular belief that goods bought through the post offer better value for money. A large proportion of mail-order advertising stresses the factors of low price and superior product quality. It is this aspect, coupled with the belief that they are cutting out the 'middleman' and buying straight from the manufacturer, that attracts many mail-order clients.

The choice of product for mail order

When we come to consider the type of product most suitable for mail-order distribution, it is obvious that the range is extremely wide. Every really successful mail-order proposition, however, should endeavour to offer the customer one or more of the following:

exclusivity, ease of ordering, economy, value for money, low cost of distribution.

Exclusivity
An item that is not readily available from a local shop obviously will sell more readily through the post than one which customers can buy during normal shopping trips. If one's mail order proposition is likely to be paralleled by several others that are offered in the same newspaper, one can expect to enjoy only a percentage of the available demand. Many products of similar, or, indeed, identical nature are advertised side by side in mail order sections of the national press. Wherever possible, however, the firms concerned endeavour to offer a slightly different proposition, in terms of price or credit facilities or money-back guarantees.

Ease of ordering
Lethargy on the party of potential customers is the main factor which the mail-order trader has to combat. The majority of people are prone to put things off, to postpone the actual placing of the order, however interested they may be in the proposition put to them. Much research has been conducted by mail-order practitioners to overcome this problem by providing means whereby *with the minimum of personal effort* the customer can place an order.

Economy
The proposition offered by the mail-order trader should convey to the customer an element of economy. As we have seen, many of those who purchase goods through the post are motivated by the idea that they are saving money because they are dealing direct with the manufacturer. They believe that the price they will pay will be less than they would have to pay for the same article purchased from a shop, because the retailer's profit has been excluded. In many cases this is true, although the producer who distributes by mail order still incurs advertising and other costs which he must pass on in the price he charges the consumer.

Value for money
There can be no doubt whatever that every product which is sold through the post must represent value for money. Ethical considerations apart, it is a sheer waste of advertising investment to supply inferior merchandise. All the successful mail-order houses have been built upon a reputation for fair-dealing, and any firm which, knowingly or not, misleads the public cannot last long in this highly competitive field. It is because people who repeatedly make postal purchases have confidence in the suppliers, based on past experience, that mail-order trading has been so successful. Undoubtedly mistakes

will occur, orders will be incorrectly executed, goods will get lost in transit. All reputable mail-order firms – and these are the great majority – will immediately put things right to satisfy the client, because they know how vital it is to their continuing prosperity that they should do so.

Low cost of distribution
From the producer's point of view, there is one other factor that applies to the type of product suitable for mail-order distribution. Its mailing or transportation cost, generally speaking, should not be much above 10 per cent of its selling price. Every mail-order transaction is an individual sale. Whether the product in question is a magazine that can be posted conveniently or sections of a greenhouse that have to be carried on a truck, if the cost of physical distribution bites too sharply into the profit margin, the sale could be made at a loss. The figure of 10 per cent has been found, through long experience, to be a useful yardstick when assessing product suitability.

Techniques for mail-order trading

There are three basic techniques used in the mail-order business:

1 Direct from advertisement.
2 Enquiry follow-up.
3 Direct mail.

Most firms engaged in mail-order trading use one or other of these methods or variations upon them. Many employ a combination of all three.

Direct from advertisement
Using the first method, the producer places an advertisement in a suitable newspaper or magazine, describing in considerable detail the product he is offering, together with an illustration. All the essential information the customer needs is provided, with details of price and how to order. Some advertisers include in the advertisement a small order form which the purchaser may cut out and enclose with the remittance. The order form is important, because provision is made for the customer's name and address, and the form is usually coded to enable the producer to classify the response his announcement has drawn from several different journals.

   The main advantage of the direct-from-advertisement method is that the manufacturer obtains an immediate response to his announcement. It also avoids the cost of sales literature which is necessary in the other two methods. The chief disadvantage lies in the greater advertising costs incurred. The advertisement has to do the whole selling job, so that a larger space has to be taken in the newspaper or journal concerned.

Selling direct from the advertisement imposes certain conditions on the choice of merchandise to be offered. It is likely to be most successful for products that are easily recognizable to the public and do not require lengthy description. Products should have a fairly unique selling proposition, and a reasonably long profit margin is desirable to cover the comparatively high advertising expenditure. The product should also be relatively easy to mail or ship, and be unlikely to incur damage in transit.

Enquiry follow-up
In this method the newspaper advertisement is restricted to a broad outline of the proposition, with an invitation to the reader to write to the producer for further details. In response the supplier sends a range of literature describing the product in detail, together with a carefully constructed selling message.

Generally the enquiry follow-up consists of:

(*a*)   A sales letter.
(*b*)   An illustrated leaflet.
(*c*)   An order form.
(*d*)   A reply envelope, usually pre-paid.

In addition, some manufacturers provide a premium coupon, offering a discount to the customer providing an order is placed within a specified time.

(*a*)   *The sales letter*. This is the most important part of the manu-
        facturer's response. It will stress the benefits to be derived from
        the product, its price, the terms under which it is offered,
        together with a guarantee of satisfaction. The letter should
        expound the 'sales story' and punch home all those consider-
        ations which should induce the recipient to order the product.
(*b*)   *The illustrated leaflet*. The purpose of the leaflet is to inform. It
        should describe the product fully and anticipate and answer
        questions that the potential customer is likely to raise about its
        appearance, specification and utility.
(*c*)   *The order form*. This simplifies the customer's task in ordering
        the product, avoids the omission of name and address (a not
        infrequent occurrence) and says how much money to send and
        how to send it (by cheque, postal order or cash by registered
        letter).
(*d*)   *The pre-paid reply envelope*. Once again, this will help the
        customer to order and prevent the delay or possible postpone-

ment that can occur if a suitable envelope or postage stamp is not immediately available.

There are two main advantages in the use of the enquiry follow-up method. The first is that the manufacturer, on receipt of the enquirer's name and address, can follow-up again and again. If his first letter does not produce a favourable result, he can repeat his message at intervals until he either secures an order or decides that the enquirer has no further interest in the product. The considerable response mail-order firms achieve from their second or third follow-ups is an indication that customers do not always make the effort to order upon receipt of only one mailing of promotional material. It seems that the successive approaches create a cumulative effect.

The other advantage of this method is that one is not restricted to a few words only to describe the product and put over the sales message. There are many products which simply cannot be described adequately within the limitations of a newspaper advertisement. It is for this reason that the enquiry follow-up method is frequently used for the sale of correspondence courses and for technical products demanding considerable explanation before their value can be fully ascertained.

Direct mail
The use of direct mail as a means of selling goods by mail order has increased steadily. The essential difference between this method and that of enquiry follow-up is that with direct mail the names of prospective customers are obtained by means other than press advertising. Use is made of the mailing lists of the direct-mail houses – firms that specialize in the supply of names and addresses of people who are likely to be interested in the purchase of various services or types of merchandise. Apart from these sources, manufacturers using the direct-mail approach cull names from telephone directories and professional lists, or lease mailing lists from other mail-order firms marketing non-competing products.

The advantage of direct mail over rival methods is again one of economy. Instead of spending money on advertising, which is directed to all the readers of a journal, many of whom will have no interest in one's particular product, direct mail directs the sales message to a mailing list of people with known specific interests. One may assume, for example, that a direct-mail campaign for gardening equipment, using a mailing list of the names of people known to have recently purchased rose bushes through the post, will be received with far greater interest among those approached than would an advertisement for the same gardening equipment projected towards the very varied readership of a Sunday newspaper.

4.5   The physical movement of goods

The marketing principle that insists goods should be at the right place at the right time to satisfy the needs of the consumer often confronts the producer with a dilemma. Among the benefits consumers seek from the goods they buy, one of the most significant is price economy. Yet in order to bring goods to the right place at the right time (and secure an acceptable profit margin), the producer must maintain an economic level of costs. A major factor mitigating against such economy, however, is the ever-increasing cost incurred in the physical movement of goods.

Despite regular improvement in the road system and also in the efficiency of road haulage vehicles, transportation costs continue to escalate. It is for this reason that physical distribution management (PDM) has become an important function within marketing-orientated companies supplying goods to nationwide markets.

In very basic terms PDM seeks to find a point of balance between the cost of getting the goods to the right place at the right time and the benefit, expressed in terms of increased demand, that this facility provides for the customer.

Marketing affects this process, because every additional benefit introduced into the marketing mix represents increased cost. Changes to the place element of the mix will affect the formulation of the mix and may necessitate change in the price element.

An equally important reason for marketing's effect on the planning of physical distribution is that operational economy is only half the picture. To take a crude example, should a company decide to close its regional depots and make long-haul deliveries from a central warehouse, a considerable saving may be achieved in its distribution costs. But if this results also in falling regional demand due to customer dissatisfaction, because the quality of delivery service has declined, the firm's longer-term marketing objectives may not have been served. Alternatively, requests by sales for improvements to delivery services in peripheral areas of a company's geographical market may appear justified in view of the additional demand for the firm's products such facilities might attract. But the additional costs that distribution may incur in the provision of the benefit may be disproportionately high relative to the margin of profit the extra business will create.

4.6   The distribution mix

A conceptual approach to the problem focuses on the main variables with which physical distribution management has to contend. These may be categorized as follows:

1   Order-processing.
2   Material-handling.
3   Stock-control.
4   Warehousing.
5   Transportation.

Any one of these categories has an effect on the others. To take but one example, in a situation where the order-processing section of a company is not operating efficiently, there will be frequent occasions when 'panic' measures will have to be taken to placate customers whose delivery instructions have not been complied with. Material-handling will be forced to interrupt its scheduled procedure in order to find the specific goods in the warehouse, which in turn will become disorganized while other stock is disturbed in the process. The stock-control section is also brought in, because the stock of goods that may have been allocated for imminent despatch to other customers will have been unexpectedly depleted. Finally, transport is called upon to change the scheduled deployment of vehicles to make special unforeseen journeys.

The interdependence of the above five elements, and the contribution made by each of them to the quality of the physical distribution operation, provide the basis for the concept of the distribution mix. Like those of the marketing mix, each distribution element may be varied to achieve a mix formulation intended to match the benefits of a company's distribution service to the perceived needs of its customers.

In order to achieve this objective there is an obvious need for close liaison between the distribution and marketing functions within the organization. Distribution will need to be informed of the projected level of demand for each of the company's products, and the geographical spread of that demand. Seasonal and other likely fluctuations will need to be anticipated. Whenever an organization decides to introduce a new product to its market, or to enter new markets with new or existing products, distribution management will require adequate time in which to plan for the changing situation. Additions to warehousing and transportation facilities will require the reformulation of the distribution mix to ensure the continuity of the quality of service rendered to the company and its customers.

Discussion questions

1   Discuss the channels of distribution that are open to producers of consumer products and select a preferred channel for the distribu-

tion of: (a) a fine-art ceramic decorated plate in limited edition; (b) a boxed set of artists' oil paints; (c) a child's crayoning book.

2 Describe how the retail stock-check system operates.

3 Select a product you consider suitable for mail-order distribution, justify your choice of this channel and describe how you would prepare a marketing plan.

4 State the major elements that constitute the physical distribution mix, create three scenarios depicting differing demand situations to which a supplier organization must respond and devise appropriate strategies of response.

5
The marketing of services

The past twenty-five years have seen a remarkable growth in service industries in the advanced countries of the world. Many such countries, Britain included, have ceased to be manufacturing-based, and are now service-based economies. This means that the output value of their service sectors and the numbers of people employed in them has outstripped those of manufacturing and agriculture.

The main reason for this phenomenon has been the greatly increased affluence of consumers in developed nations. Generally speaking, their percentage of disposable income is very much larger than that of previous generations. This has enabled a majority to demand services many of which were previously within the grasp of only a privileged minority. In addition, many now seek the provision of services that, a generation ago, they would have provided for themselves.

An equally important factor in the upsurge of service activity results from the increased complexity of modern life. The technological revolution that has brought many benefits to the consumer has created the need for expertise in the maintenance and repair of equipment such as household appliances, audio-visual apparatus and computers. It has similarly increased the demand for accountants, marriage counsellors, legal firms and employment agencies to guide and assist consumers in their personal lives.

The pressures and complexities attending business managers in the modern world have created a similar need for specialist assistance in commerce and industry, giving rise to consultant services in computer technology, advertising, marketing and research.

If we look at just a selection of the service activities on offer today, the enormous diversity of the services sector becomes apparent:

Accident claim assessors	Advertising agencies
Accountants	Air conditioning consultants
Adoption agencies	Airline services
Adult education agencies	Animal welfare societies

Antique and art restoration
Antique and art valuers
Architects
Art dealers
Auctioneers
Audio-visual services
Banks
Beauty consultants
Bookmakers
Building consultants
Building societies
Bus and coach services
Business centres
Business enterprise agencies
Business transfer agents
Careers advisory services
Catering consultants
Catteries
Central heating services
Chimney sweeps
Chiropodists
Cinemas
Cleaning and maintenance
    services
Colleges
Computer services
Conference and exhibitions
Convalescent homes
Conveyancing
Copying and duplicating
Copywriting
Courier services
Credit investigation services
Curtain and carpet cleaners
Dancing schools
Debt-collection agencies
Design consultants
Detective agencies
Direct-mail agencies
Discos and dance halls
Dog-breeding kennels
Domestic cleaning services
Double glazing installers
Dress hire agencies
Driving schools
Dry cleaners and launderers

Dry rot and woodworm
    consultants
Employment agencies
Energy conversion consultants
Estate agents
Export agents
Facsimile bureaux
Factoring agencies
Farm management services
Finance companies
Fireproofing consultants
Floor cleaning services
Flying schools
Forestry consultants
Forwarding agents
Garage services
Garden services
Golf clubs
Hairdressers
Health clubs
Hospitals
Hotels
Industrial consultants
Insurance agents
Laboratories
Language schools
Leasing and contract hire
Legal services
Leisure centres
Libraries
Livery stables
Management consultants
Marinas
Marketing consultants
Marriage bureaux
Medical practitioners
Model agencies
Nursery schools
Nursing homes
Patent agents
Pawnbrokers
Pet services
Photographic agencies
Piano-tuners
Plant hire contractors
Printers

Removers and storers
Road haulage services
Roofing services
Safari and wild life parks
Saunas and solaria
Secretarial services
Ski centres
Sports promoters

Ticket agencies
Tourist agencies
Training services
Veterinary services
Waste-disposal services
Wedding services
Window cleaners
Zoos

5.1   Services and product marketing compared

The provision of a service is totally different to the production of a product. Products are physical objects. They have size, shape, texture, colour. They can be examined for suitability for the purposes for which they are intended. By means of mass-production processes, they can be made uniformly, and uniformity of production means uniformity of quality.

Products may be patented to provide protection for the manufacturer against direct imitation by rivals. They can be made in quantity in advance of immediate requirements and stored until they are needed. Supply can be balanced against fluctuation in demand.

On the other hand, services have no physical existence. They are intangible. This intangibility makes them incapable of precise description. Services cannot be mass-produced, lack the assurance of uniformity, and, in consequence, their quality is likely to be variable. Services cannot be patented. The provider therefore has no legal protection against competitors' imitations.

Services exist only at the moment of their provision. They are perishable. They cannot be stored until needed, which means that the provider has no simple means of balancing supply and demand.

These are some of the essential problems that service marketing has to overcome. There are others.

Providers of a service are inseparable from the service they provide. A producer of a product can set up a machine to manufacture the product and walk way to do other things while the machine maintains the production process in his absence. Furthermore, this inseparability is not merely a physical linking. The quality of the service provided is specific to the skills of the individual provider. This means that multiplication of service provision is difficult: which presents problems for business expansion.

Provision and consumption of a service are instantaneous. This means that, in a commercial situation, a service is sold to the consumer before it is provided. Sampling is possible but frequently impractical, so that a customer has no means of judging a service until he has bought it.

It can be seen therefore that services have a number of special characteristics that do not apply to manufactured products, and present major difficulties for marketing. However, measures can be taken to overcome these problems.

Intangibility

In the marketing of a manufactured product it is common practice to emphasize the distinctive features of the product to attract the customer's attention. The intangible features of a service, however, seldom make much impression upon potential users, because we are up against a conceptual problem. It is all in the mind, and different people visualize things differently. Those with experience of service marketing prefer to stress the benefits to be derived from the service, because these are easier for consumers to visualize and apply to their specific needs.

It is possible to reduce the effect of intangibility in customers' perception of a service by using physical surrogates to depict its benefits. An illustration, showing a beach of sun-drenched golden sand stretching away to the blue of the ocean, with bikini-clad holidaymakers sipping cool drinks in the shade of swaying palm trees, may be a cliché of the tourist industry brochure. It does, however, provide an example of the use of physical representation in the promotion of tourism, by encapsulating a major benefit of the service being offered.

Another method increasingly being used to overcome the intangibility problem in the marketing of services is to create an individual identity for a specific offering by means of branding. As in the case of product branding, the brand image, when applied to a service, provides a 'personality' immediately recognizable to consumers as the result of national advertising. Where the specific service is being provided from multiple outlets – the nationwide spread of roadside restaurant chains in Britain is an example – the consumer, on seeing the sign, has immediate recollection either from personal experience, from advertisements or from recommendation, of the nature of the benefits on offer.

Inseparability

The fact that the quality of the service provided is so dependent upon the skills of the provider does pose difficulties in the extension of a service company's field of operations. A product manufacturer may, if he chooses, set up a string of factories in different locations, install identical machinery in each, and produce goods uniformly to specification. The quality of a service, however, is liable to differ when provided by different providers, because of the human factor involved.

Human idiosyncrasy constantly bedevils one of the principal objectives of marketing, which is to provide the consumer with the benefit of a consistent level of quality. It is an objective much easier to achieve in product marketing, because of the almost total use of mechanization in the production process. Unfortunately service industries are hugely labour-intensive in their operations.

The obvious way in which to reduce the effect that human idiosyncrasy has upon the quality of service offerings is to apply, wherever practicable, increased mechanization in the provision of the service. The problem is that in many sectors of the service industry it simply is not practical to mechanize. A glance at our selected list of services will prove the point.

Nonetheless, the continued growth and profitability of the service industry may ultimately depend upon increased use of technology. One international organization, McDonald's has introduced a high level of mechanization to its fast-food restaurant operation, pioneering where others will be bound to follow. A less dramatic but equally significant example of mechanized service is the installation of automatic cash dispensers on the exterior walls of their premises by High Street banks.

The use of technology may aid some sectors of the service industry in reducing the effects of the human factor on the quality of their operations, but it will not assist all. There are a large number of service situations where the presence of a human provider remains essential. In many branches of health care, in financial services and in consultancy, for example, opportunities to introduce mechanization are rare because of the advisory nature of the service being performed.

There are other sectors of the service industry where displacement of human providers by automation destroys at least one of the major benefits currently on offer. A good example here is the quality restaurant, where discreet, highly professional personal attention to diners is integral to the nature of the service being provided. In situations such as these, where retention of the human provider is essential, a high standard of staff selection, training and motivation is necessary if an organization wishes to multiply the number of its outlets and maintain a uniform quality of service to its customers.

Perishability

A service exists only at the moment in time that it is provided. Unlike a product, it cannot be produced in multiples, stored and brought out to meet a surge in demand. So we have yet another inherent difficulty in service marketing: that of dealing with fluctuation in supply and demand. Like the other problems we have discussed, it can be eased but not eradicated.

On the supply side service industries traditionally have recognized the need for flexibility in staffing to cope with fluctuating demand levels. Their problem, however, is not merely that of catering for periods of high demand, important though this may be from the point of view of customer satisfaction. Periodic low demand creates the problem of insufficient use of valuable and often expensive resources. Staff may be stood down in low seasons but many overhead costs, such as rent, business rate tax and the financing of loans, still have to be met.

A major objective of any business must be to achieve a reasonably balanced level of trade. Methods applied in some service industries consist of various price inducements offered to customers to encourage them to use the offered services at off-peak times. Leisure service organizations – hotels, coach-tour operators and airlines, for example – offer reduced low-season rates to drum up extra business in off-peak periods. Theatres and cinemas offer special rates for party bookings to attract matinee audiences.

The use of price variation to smooth demand levels is of course impractical in many service sectors. The traditional appointments system used by doctors, hairdressers or garages provides an alternative method of regulating the flow of demand.

5.2   The marketing concept in service industries

We have seen that the special characteristics pertaining to services have significant implications for marketing. Current experience of the marketing concept is based on a history of some sixty years. For most of that time it has been essentially product-related. Its application to services therefore is relatively new and should be recognized as still largely experimental. In the absence of any extensive evidence upon which to draw, it is sensible to approach the subject with a degree of caution.

Of one thing, however, we may be sure. The needs of the consumer, central to product marketing, are equally central to the marketing of services. This basic concept applies to both sectors. Where divergence is likely to occur is in procedure, which may have to be modified to deal with the intangible nature of services.

In general terms it is fair to say that service organizations often are less marketing-orientated than companies in the manufacturing sector. Among many professional firms there is a distaste for the entire notion of marketing, on the mistaken grounds that marketing is synonymous to selling. The idea of setting out to sell their services is considered in some quarters to be not only unprofessional but indeed unethical. Another factor mitigating against the marketing concept is that the quality of management personnel in some service industries is inferior to that in manufacturing industry, and the business ethos frequently is lacking.

We are, however, currently in a transitional period. The growth of the service sector in recent years has attracted increased competition. There has also been a change in the public attitude to many service industries: the removal of ethical barriers to the advertising of a range of health care and legal services in Britain provides an example. Inflation and competitive pressures have placed constraints upon the resources of many organizations such as universities and higher education colleges; these and similar factors are forcing managements to reconsider long-established and often out-dated practices and to look instead to the marketing concept to alleviate their difficulties. There is evidence of increasing market-orientated activity in specific areas, notably industrial cleaning, car hire, hotels and catering. So it would be wrong to suggest that the marketing concept has made no significant impact on service industries. Nor should we assume that marketing procedures widely adopted in the products field can be applied generally to the service sector, with its divergency of processes and practices.

As a starting point, however, we can derive a great deal of knowledge and experience from product marketing that may legitimately be applied also to services. The first step is to obtain recognition and acceptance by service organizations of the marketing concept: that the satisfaction of the customer's needs is paramount, the ultimate objective to which all available resources must be channelled.

5.3   Researching service markets

The next step will be to devise an appropriate marketing strategy, using methods similar to those already discussed in the context of product marketing. This will call for close scrutiny of the company itself, from which assumptions can be made of its major strengths and weaknesses, followed by research of the target market it is proposed to enter. We shall look specifically for a segment of that market most appropriate for the kind of service we have to offer and the kind of business organization and resources we have to provide it.

This means that the customers who comprise that segment must be identified in order that their needs may be clearly understood and the particular benefits they are seeking can be met. We shall have to be very careful here, because what customers may consider to be essential benefits can vary enormously from one type of service to another.

Research for service marketing differs little from research for product marketing. In each case its prime purpose is to discover customer needs, decide the scale of such needs and whether currently they are being satisfied. Market research, as we have seen, is an essential marketing tool. In the absence of reliable information, the scientific approach to the formulation of commercial plans cannot succeed.

It has to be acknowledged, however, that within the services sector traditionalist attitudes of mind remain strongly entrenched. Market research is often seen as a commercial device, generally acceptable in relation to manufactured goods but having vulgar implications if applied to the sensitive areas of some personal services.

Another difficulty arises from the size of many service organizations. They tend to be small operations, and the complexity and expense of market-research studies is frequently seen as unrealistic. On the other hand, many large and often monopolistic service firms are faced with little or no competition; here the objection may be that market research is considered to be simply unnecessary. Indeed, among service companies of all kinds, the prevailing view is that their direct contact with their customers rules out the need for market research.

The lack of patent protection for services does create a reluctance for management to invest in research and development for services on a scale comparable to that of the manufactured product sector. There is a preference on the part of many service companies to take the easier option of imitating the existing service offerings of competitors rather than to attempt totally new concepts. Very often, however, the underlying reason why market research is resisted in service firms is that they are managed by individuals lacking in commercial training. They cannot see the advantages that the adoption of marketing principles can bring to their businesses.

Even where a company is enthusiastic to adopt these principles, the difficulties of conducting market research in the services sector can be a deterrent. Much of the essential information for desk research is fragmented and difficult to source. There are problems, too, that are posed by the nature of services, particularly their intangibility and the difficulty of meaningful classification.

Such problems are accentuated when researching a market for new services. Because it is difficult to convey to potential consumers the concept of a service of which they have, as yet, no experience, problems can arise when they are asked to express an opinion. In product market research respondents can be shown at least a visual representation of a proposed product, but with an intangible service offering, it can be described only in very general terms, and these may not be fully comprehensible to interviewees. For this reason, the degree of positive or negative reaction one might expect to result from new product testing is likely to be considerably smaller in respect to new service testing.

The objections frequently raised within service organizations to the use of any extensive field research may be overcome by the use of what is termed *concept testing*. This approach begins with an analysis of consumer needs, on the one hand, and ideas for satisfying them, on the other. Examination of competitive activity may suggest whether such needs are currently being fully met. The next stage is to consider how such ideas can be formulated into a service offering, taking account of the resources available to the provider organization in terms of available skills and finance. Limited trials, using a selected panel of likely potential users, can then be undertaken to obtain reactions. If these are favourable, one can again look at the market to find the most promising segment. It should be possible to make assumptions of potential demand and the potential price level the targeted market segment will bear. It is obviously vital that in all pre-launch customer evaluations of a new service the selected customers fully understand the concept, and that their buying and usage intentions line up with the provider's preliminary assessments.

Providing these criteria have been met, the concept now can be modified or allowed to proceed to test marketing. Here services research possesses a distinct advantage over research conducted for manufactured products: because of the inseparability of producer and consumer at the point of delivery, a service can be evaluated while it is being consumed, providing the researcher with an instantaneous feedback of the consumer's reactions.

5.4 Defining the service offering

Having reached a point where we have a service offering fashioned, to the best of our capability, to satisfy an identified consumer need, our next marketing task is to promote and sustain its sale. Before we attempt to formulate a marketing mix of elements designed to attract customer interest, however, we must try to define what it is we have to offer.

We can of course define the features of our service in much the same way as we can define the features of a manufactured product. But features, as we know, are not enough. We need to offer benefits, and here we have a difficulty. When potential customers agree to buy our service, they may not in fact be buying the benefits we have offered.

The reason for this apparent contradiction is that a service is intangible and its benefits are purely concepts, images in the mind. Such is the infinite variety of human imagination, it is true to say that customers will create for themselves at least part of the service by means of benefits conceived by them, individually, of which we, the providers of the service, may be totally unaware. This is yet another essential difference between services and product marketing. Despite every effort on the part of the provider to provide benefits tailored to coincide with what he perceives to be his customers' needs, he will never gain a complete insight into any one customer's conception of those benefits. This means we cannot define a service by means of conceptional benefits alone.

To assist the means of definition, we need to consider how the service is to be *delivered* to the customer. Without a defined *delivery system* the consumer benefit concept is meaningless. The two things are inseparably linked. Once this link is forged, we possess a service offering that is capable of being conceived intelligibly in more precise terms. For example, if I say to you that I shall provide you with temporary individual transportation, you will have only the vaguest notion of what I am offering. However, if I say that I shall provide you with a self-drive car-hire service, you will immediately grasp the nature of my offer. Your concept of the underlying benefit – temporary individual transportation – will remain, but now you can visualize how the service will be performed. On the other hand, if I had said that I would provide you with a chauffeur-driven car-hire service, your concept of the underlying benefit of individual transportation of a temporary nature would still remain, but your visualization of the service would be different. While this distinction may seem obvious in terms of car hire, with which we are all likely to be familiar, it may be far less obvious when we are attempting to define a totally new service offering with which we are totally unfamiliar. Hence the importance of a clearly defined delivery system.

5.5   The service marketing mix

We know that the formulation and blending of a marketing mix is basic to the development of a marketing strategy. However, the essential elements we have previously discussed in respect to manufactured products will need to be augmented for services – because of their special characteristics of intangibility, inseparability and perishability. Furthermore, the benefits sought by the customer from the provision of a service are likely to differ from and be more complex than those associated with a product. It is the additional elements of the mix that we shall now consider.

The people element

Undoubtedly a main distinguishing feature of the provision of a service in comparison with the production of a product is the significance of people in any assessment of the quality of the offering. People play a predominant role in the provision process, and thereby are largely responsible for its level of quality. People also fulfil another role, as *other customers* of a service, whose physical presence also can have an important bearing on the perceived quality standard of a particular service offering.

If we look first at people in their capacity as providers, it is clear they must constitute one of the main ingredients, or elements, of the services marketing mix. This people element comprises not merely their functional performance in the service provision but also the behavioural attitude they display to customers. A personal attitude cannot be specified in the way that a required shade of colour can be specified for a curtain fabric. Standards of behaviour on the part of staff can, of course, be set, but the degree to which they are adhered to will be dependent upon human idiosyncrasy, for which it is impossible to legislate. What we can specify, however, are training programmes designed to encourage a code of professionalism for staff attitudes in their performance of the service. Professional attitudes and behaviour *can* be created among individuals of diverse personality and temperament.

One of the clearest examples can be seen in the theatrical profession. On stage trained professional performers are capable of maintaining and projecting attitudes and behavioural patterns often totally in contrast to their off-stage personalities. Similarly, among trained military personnel, we can observe the difference between the 'on-parade' and the 'off-parade' demeanour. In each case those concerned are playing a role in the execution of their professional duties.

There is nothing new in the idea that those engaged in the performance of a service to the customer should be trained to conform to specific patterns of behaviour. The apprenticeships served by recruits entering many retail trades in the earlier years of this century taught them not only the mechanics of their tasks but also how they should conduct themselves in the presence of a customer. They acquired skills that often were poorly rewarded in a service industry where wage levels and working conditions are generally acknowledged to have been deplorable. Nevertheless, the quality of retail service of those days was vastly superior to what it is today.

There is another aspect to the performance of people in the provision of a service that we should consider. The staff of service establishments frequently are required to play a dual role: that of operators within the system (similar to that of production direct labour in a factory) and that of sales personnel. In this latter capacity it is very often necessary for them also to undertake the additional role of adjudicator between the interests of the customer, on the one hand, and those of the company, on the other.

To safeguard the quality of the people element of the marketing mix, it is therefore necessary for marketing to concern itself with service staff selection, training and motivation. This additional task can be eased wherever practicable by dividing a company's staff into those whose functions bring them into visual contact with customers and those working 'behind the scenes'.

For personnel with customer-contact duties, job specifications should reflect the marketing concept in the responsibilities placed upon individual providers. A customer's perception of the quality of a service offering is conditioned by many aspects, not least the physical appearance of the personnel providing the service. Thus people quality and the consistency of that quality apply not only to behaviour but also to dress. Many service organizations therefore require their customer-contact staff to wear appropriate uniform styles of apparel, ranging from standardized overalls in a car tyre replacement establishment to dark suits and sober ties in banks and similar institutions.

Human idiosyncrasy will always make the quality of the people element of the marketing mix difficult to control. As we have seen, there are already certain sectors within the service industry where an increased use of mechanization has been introduced partially to ameliorate the problem. Changes in service delivery, designed to reduce the importance of personal contact with customers, however, should always be treated with caution. Customer acceptance of such changes should not be taken for granted. The perceived quality of the service and the concept of benefits may also change, and this could be to the detriment of the service organization.

The other constituent of the people element in service marketing is of course that of the other customers present when the service is being performed. In a wide range of service activities, such as hotels and catering, airlines, tour operations, the perceived quality of the offering frequently is conditioned by the behaviour of other customers. For example, the refreshment on offer in a particular bar may be to an individual's liking, and the proprietor and his staff may be friendly and attentive; but if he dislikes the crowd that frequents the place, he will not be seen in there again.

On the other hand, many of the perceived benefits of a service are largely dependent on the presence of other customers. A restaurant totally devoid of other diners is soulless. A major part of the enjoyment of a holiday for some people is the opportunity it affords them to sit and watch other people enjoying themselves.

Careful market segmentation is one method by which marketing can exercise some control over the 'other customers' element. The initial assessment of the potential clientele for a service should include its likely behaviour pattern and the specific needs such patterns signify. For example, the selection of suitable background music to be played during the provision of a service to create 'atmosphere' will be largely dependent upon the age of likely customers. Another method of course is the selection and training of suitable management personnel. A competent manager or manager-ess can often harmonize the reactions of a disparate clientele, thus adding to the general quality of the service provision.

The place element

We have already noted that there are certain essential elements constituting the marketing mix for manufactured products that need to be modified for service marketing. The *channel* through which the service offering is distributed and the *location* where it is actually provided will now be considered.

Owing to the special characteristics of services, particularly those of inseparability and perishability, the choice of distribution channel is limited. In many instances the inseparability of the service from its provider removes all choice, and direct sale is the only suitable method. This creates problems, because expansion of the business may be difficult to achieve, the geographical catchment area from which customers can be drawn is likely to be limited, and, because service provision is essentially perishable, the workload carried by providers at peak periods may be heavy. Such conditions apply particularly to many small service firms that are heavily reliant on a handful of highly skilled and experienced providers, such as solicitors or business consultants.

There are, however, situations where a service organization may choose deliberately to limit the number of customers it serves and operate by direct sale because it suits its purpose to do so. It is able to keep tight control over the business, has the advantage of direct feedback regarding the acceptability of its offerings, and, by ensuring a high standard of personal service, is in a strong position to defend itself against competition. Examples can be seen in small independent restaurants, where the personality of the proprietor and his personal attention to a regular clientele provides, among many others, the benefit of exclusivity; and advertising agencies that specialize in the handling of a very limited number of prestige-type accounts.

For organizations whose service offerings are capable of a high degree of standardization, expansion can be achieved by the use of intermediaries, such as agents, dealers or retailers. Examples are found in such industries as employment, tourism, travel, insurance, industrial cleaning and many others.

At first glance it might appear that the ability to provide a service through such intermediaries conflicts with the notion of the insepar-ability of the service from its provider. It must be recognized, however, that many such intermediaries are essentially sales agencies, acting on behalf of the service provider as an extension to his own sales department. Thus an insurance agent is a salesman of insurance; he may provide a consultancy service of advice and guidance to assist the client but the service of insurance provision is performed by the insurance company. In a travel agency the staff are salespeople; the service they perform is the supply of reservations (a seat on an aircraft, a hotel room). It is the airline that provides the transportation service and the hotel at the traveller's destination that provides the hotel accommodation.

There are, however, means by which a service organization can expand its field of operations virtually indefinitely by the delegation to others of the provision of the service. Dealership arrangements are a long-established method of delegation, where an organization trains the personnel of a service intermediary to perform the service and licenses its sale.

The most revolutionary use of intermediaries in service distribution has been the development of *franchising*. A franchise may be defined as an agreement whereby one party (the franchisor) grants to another (the franchisee) the right to exploit a commercial idea, using its trade name, its process and its established goodwill, conditional upon the franchisee operating the business in strict accordance with explicit regulations laid down by the franchisor. In consideration for this right, the franchisee pays to the franchisor a regular management service fee or royalty. Within the terms of such an agreement, it is normal practice for the franchisor to provide training in the provision of the service and give support in the general business operation. He will agree a geographical area within which the franchisee is permitted to operate. For his part, the franchisee must invest substantial capital and be the legal owner of the business.

Traditionally, large commercial organizations have the advantage of professional senior management, large purchasing power and the availability of considerable resources for product or service development and promotion. Their weakness, especially when operating through multi-unit distribution points, is reliance upon branch managers who are often poorly motivated. Small firms, however, are often in a different situation. Proprietor–managers tend to be highly motivated people, yet they often lack basic management training and skills, and their buying power and resources are often extremely limited. Franchising has been a success because it utilizes the joint strength of the partner businesses and avoids their weaknesses.

Franchise operations now cover a very wide spectrum of service industries, from fast-food outlets to pest-control operations, from drain-cleaning to tax and accounting services. The franchisor is assisted in the expansion of his field of operations by each newly opened distribution point being largely financed by the franchisee. The advantage to the franchisee is that he can run his business with the knowledge that the service concept he offers has been thoroughly tested and is supported by wide promotion. The customer can place considerable reliance on the quality consistency of the service he buys due to branding.

As a result of acquisition and merger, many diverse service firms have found themselves linked as subsidiaries of large parent commercial groups, which has accelerated another important innovation in service marketing – *integration* of the sale of service offerings. This has made it possible for the customer to book a wide range of services – a seat on an aircraft, a room in a hotel, a table in a restaurant, a self-drive car, tickets for the theatre – through a single service-selling agency.

Another form of service provision that has grown speedily in recent years is the *rental or leasing of capital goods and equipment*. The attraction to rent rather than buy is considerable. Items become available for use without tying up capital that may be required for other purposes. Technical equipment that may become out-dated in a few years can be obtained on short-term leases and be replaced when improved models are available. Leasing or rental schemes facilitate business expansion plans that otherwise could be frustrated by limited capital resources. The lessee is often freed from the problems of maintenance and repair of rented items, which is the responsibility of the lessor under many agreements.

The principal gain to the lessor is that it is possible to achieve a higher margin of profit from rent rather than sale of the item, despite the additional repair and maintenance costs. In certain industrial situations the lessor may benefit from the repeating sale to the lessee of products used with the rented equipment. The renting of tea- and coffee-making machines to offices and factories is a case in point. The gain to the lessor achieved by the renting of the machine is often minimal, after maintenance costs and depreciation have been taken into account, but profit comes from the sale of the drink-making ingredients supplied on a repeating basis.

Service business locations

The location of a business is a major consideration for any enterprise, and its suitability is as important for the provision of a service as it is for the distribution of a manufactured product. There are locations traditional for the provision of particular services. Banks, building societies, auctioneers and estate agents tend to huddle in city centres, because this is where their customers expect to find them. But a number of banks and other financial-service providers are now setting up branches also in out-of-town shopping centres, following their customers away from the inconvenience of the High Street, with its restricted car parking and declining facilities. There are services such as fast-print firms and employment agencies that operate in the shadow of giant commercial office blocks, because it is here that their customer demand is concentrated. For the same reason, theatre booking agencies, hairdressers and beauty shops often occupy ground-floor locations beneath major hotels, in airport environs or close to main railway terminals.

There are, however, services that are performed not at a specific location but at the consumer's home, such as lawn care and central-heating installation, or at the customer's factory, such as plant maintenance and industrial cleaning. For operations of this kind the physical location of the provider's premises may not be particularly important. The emphasis here should be on the provision of a good channel of communication for customers; this is vital for emergency-type service provision, such as plumbing or electrical repairs.

The yardstick for any decisions on service business location must be customer convenience. Where a particular location is considered to be inconvenient – lacking adequate parking facilities, inaccessible by means of public transport or simply too difficult to find – potential customers will either seek a competitive provider, delay buying the service until a later date or simply go home and provide it for themselves.

The element of tangible association

The perception customers have of the quality of our essentially intangible service offering will be influenced strongly by the tangibles associated with its provision. This concept is exemplified by the common reaction of a customer upon entering a restaurant. A combination of thick-pile carpeting, subdued lighting, white damask tablecloths and gleaming cutlery will immediately suggest an up-market establishment offering a menu of distinctive dishes at relatively high prices. Conversely, an eating house where the floor is plastic-tiled, the tables are melamine-covered and the decor is bright and colourful, will create a different impression. Each establishment will satisfy the needs of a different segment of the catering market. Each will indicate very clearly to the potential diner the likely quality of the service on offer and the likely price he will be asked to pay for it.

The use of tangibles to promote intangible services is not restricted to inanimate objects. Much financial-service advertising, for example, focuses on the relation between the consumer and the human provider of the service. Scenarios depict friendly bank managers or caring insurance assessors sitting down with customers in their homes or places of work to offer advice and assistance to resolve their financial problems.

By the use of tangibles to represent the service, we can achieve two objectives. First, the association of physical objects, or service personnel, with the service makes it simpler for the potential customer to comprehend the nature and quality of the service offering. Second, the repetition of this association, by means of advertising and other forms of promotion, identifies the specific offering and dissociates it from those of competitors.

It is of course essential that the tangibles used to represent the service appear relevant to the benefits the segmented market is seeking. Organizations using tangible surrogates should have an accurate understanding of their potential customers and the factors that will influence their buying decisions. The use of tangible clues to the quality of a service should not imply promises that cannot be kept in practice. Apart from the fact that in many countries, Britain included, misrepresentation of the nature of goods and services by advertisers can have serious legal consequences, the raising of un-realizable expectations can create a damaging effect on the image of the offering and that of the service operation offering it.

Tangibles associated with a service are of two types. First, there are objects that are themselves of minimal value yet form an aspect of the provision process and pass into the customer's possession. These include hotel bills and appointment reminder cards issued by dentists and opticians. In the same category are chequebook and credit-card wallets presented by banks, shoeshine wipes in hotel bedrooms and lollipop sweets handed to child patrons in popular restaurants. Second come tangibles that are essential to the service provision: the exterior appearance of the premises in which the service is provided, its internal layout, and its fittings and furnishings. Other examples include the type and condition of equipment used in the service provision, such as the grills and griddles of open-plan steakhouses or the machines brought to customers' homes for the provision of a carpet-cleaning service.

Tangibles of this nature, visible to customers, affect their perception of the quality of the service offering. So, too, does the 'atmosphere' of the place where the service is provided. The indefinable feeling we often have about a place results from messages we receive from our senses, of which sight is only one. Smell can be evocative, too. It can entice. It can also revolt. Sound can create a mood of exhilaration. It can be soothing, but sometimes it is irritating.

In formulating the service marketing mix therefore, the use of the element of tangible association plays an essential part:

1 By helping the customer to grasp more easily the nature and quality of the service and the benefits it offers.
2 By differentiating the specific offering from those of competitors.
3 By creating an appropriate 'atmosphere' in which the service is provided, and thereby increasing the customer's sense of satisfaction.

5.6   Operating systems for service marketing

In the final analysis it is the efficiency with which the service operation is conducted that has the greatest effect on gaining the customer's approval. Words such as 'speedy', 'fast' and 'trouble-free' seem to abound in service advertising, yet the unfortunate truth is that, in the experience of a large proportion of consumers, the smooth-running operation is more the exception than the rule. Efficiency can be achieved only as the result of careful planning and control at every stage of the provision process.

In the design of appropriate operating systems a number of factors should be considered. We know that services exist only at the moment of their provision and that, in consequence, the providers are inseparable from the service provided. It might be concluded therefore that customers are inseparable from the service they consume. But this is not always true. There are instances where the physical presence of the customer is essential to allow the service provision to occur, e.g. the meal in the restaurant or the shampoo and set in the hairdressing salon. But there are many other types of service normally carried out in the customer's absence, such as car maintenance and repairs or dry cleaning.

Where the physical presence of the customer is essential, we need to take account of the degree of his or her participation in the operation. It can have a significant effect on the quality of the service and the time-scale of its provision. Customers can dislocate a carefully balanced operating system by demanding attention to unforeseen special needs, by registering complaints that require immediate attention, or merely by arriving to consume the service in greater numbers than have been anticipated.

The other major factor to be considered is whether the service to be provided should be standard or bespoke. Obviously a standardized offering simplifies the operation management, in the same way as the production of standard physical objects assists manufacturing management, by permitting a high degree of streamlining in the sequence of processes. Standardized services generally allow the acceptance of high levels of demand, as may be seen in the popular segment of the catering market. Providing such levels remain relatively consistent, there may be scope to introduce the mechanization of some processes in standardized operations, thereby reducing the highly variable human element of the marketing mix.

The scheduling of bespoke service operations, such as financial services, consultancy or high-class catering, is, however, more difficult. Here the range of offerings may be numerous, requiring individual tailoring to accord with customers' needs. Opportunities for mechanization may be very limited, with consequent much greater reliance on the human element. Demand levels, too, are likely to be less predictable, creating problems in calculating optimum capacity requirements.

It can be seen that most of the operational difficulties in service provision stem from the special characteristics of inseparability and perishability that distinguish service marketing from the marketing of products. The service can be provided only when the providers are present to provide it. It cannot be stored to meet surges in demand.

These problems, as we know, are not capable of solution, but their effect can be diminished. As with all marketing activities, the first step is to investigate the current situation, identify the problem areas and discover the underlying cause of apparent difficulties. Each stage of the provision process needs to be examined to find out if it really is essential to the operation or whether it can be removed, reorganized or combined with another process stage for improved efficiency. There are indeed some service operations where the arrangement of the various processes appear to owe more to historic accident than logical planning. Faulty arrangement can be the cause of bottlenecks, as can an imbalance in the capacity levels of the various processes.

Solutions to many operational difficulties may be found by increasing the mechanization of processes, by introducing programmes to train staff in multi-function skills, or by the employment of part-time staff and the introduction of shift-working. Some service organizations ease their operational problems by sub-contracting certain processes to outside providers.

It is the function of marketing not only to create demand but to control it. One way of harmonizing demand with supply is to increase the customer's participation in the provision process. There is nothing new in this – it is another way of describing self-service. It has happened in restaurants, it has happened on petrol filling station forecourts, and it is certain to happen increasingly in many service industries in the years to come. There are of course other options. One is the appointment system, used by professional services to control the arrival of customers: up-market restaurants, for example, 'hold' customers in bar-lounges to balance demand with dining-room and kitchen capacity levels. Another option for many service industries, such as travel, tourism and hotels, is differential pricing, which is considered the most effective method of controlling demand.

One must recognize, however, the essentially conservative bias of the majority of people. They dislike and often resent change. This applies equally to those who are the customers of a service and to those who form the workforce employed in its provision. In an environment where so much that once was familiar already has changed so rapidly, people have had to accept change as inevitable, yet some prejudices remain deeply ingrained. Marketing always takes a risk whenever it attempts innovation either in the way people are asked to work or in the way they are asked to spend their money.

Both employee resistance and customer resistance to new ways of doing things should always be anticipated.

This is work for personnel and consumer research. People usually are less hidebound in their attitude the more they can appreciate the need for change. Staff rescheduling, the introduction of automation or increased customer self-service may offer benefits to employees or customers or both. These innovations need to be actively promoted, internally and externally, to ease the process of change and to ensure the retention of goodwill.

Discussion questions

1 Itemize the principal differences between services and products and discuss the problems these pose for marketing.
2 Define specific strategies for controlling demand levels in three different types of service provision.
3 How would you define the service sector of the economy?
4 State the reason for the considerable growth of the service sector in recent years.
5 What are the additional elements that need to be included in the marketing mix for services?

6
Marketing and advertising

When we think of advertising, it is natural for our thoughts to turn immediately to the promotion of consumer goods, because it is in this form that it appears to dominate our daily lives. Obviously the advertising of branded consumer goods must figure largely in any study of advertising in relation to the marketing process, but one should not overlook its importance for all forms of commercial enterprise. Because it appears less overt in the promotion of industrial products, it is not less effective, although the techniques employed in advertising to industrial users differ considerably from consumer advertising. For the sake of simplicity, however, we shall discuss the two spheres separately.

6.1 Consumer advertising

Marketing management may not require an in-depth knowledge of advertising theory and practice, but it should have an understanding of its basic structure. How to engage the services of advertising practitioners, what to expect from them, and, above all, how to calculate with reasonable accuracy the amount of investment a company should undertake in the advertising of its products or services, are questions vital to the formulation of the promotion element of the marketing mix.

Advertising alone does not sell either goods or services. At best, it can only stimulate interest. This interest will have to be converted into a buying decision by means of other marketing tools: personal selling, distribution channels and packaging appeal.

The brand image

We have seen that few consumer products, whatever their intrinsic qualities, can hope to hold their own in a highly competitive market without the support of a superimposed and individual personality –

known in marketing parlance as the 'brand image'. This is because competitors are watching one's product constantly. Any improvements one makes will be copied rapidly. If it becomes impossible to advance the sale of the product by means of quality or utility, there is of course the alternative of reducing one's price, which also may be matched quickly by the competition. A round of price reductions unrelated either to reduced production and distribution costs, or to increased sales and output, can be suicidal.

The brand-image method of solving this dilemma sets out to create certain attitudes towards the product in the minds of consumers. These can be summarized as follows:

1 Awareness of the existence of the brand.
2 Recognition of the brand in retail outlets.
3 Persuasion to try the brand by making a purchase.
4 Retention of loyalty to the brand by making repeated purchases in future.

Perhaps the most important factor in consumer advertising is the creation of brand loyalty. It provides the manufacturer with the means of protecting the demand which he has established for his product from the attack of his competitors. Brand preference is a delicate flower, likely to wilt easily in the fierce heat of competitive pressure unless it is irrigated regularly by means of a constant reminder of its virtues. This is the essential function of brand advertising: to create and maintain a favourable image of the product in the mind of the consumer. The ultimate effectiveness of one's advertising campaign can be judged only when the shopper, hesitating before a supermarket display of several competing brands, decides to buy *your* product because it is the one that has achieved the most lasting impression on his/her mind.

The creation of a successful brand image is not the result merely of intuition or inspiration on the part of advertising experts. Consumer research, aided by the discoveries of experimental psychology, has established certain behaviour patterns to which the majority of men and women conform. These patterns, when studied and systematized by advertising specialists, provide a ready guide to the response one might reasonably expect from a given advertising theme or 'platform'.

Why some products fail

If modern advertising techniques are so well advanced and the hold over the consumer, by means of the creation and maintenance of a dominant brand-image theme, is so compelling, why, one may well ask, do so many products fail?

One of the answers may lie in the profusion of these fruits of psychological study. Increasingly one finds that products of more or less comparable quality are struggling to hold their market share, each using much the same methods of popular persuasion. Because these methods eventually become overworked, their effectiveness becomes diminished or destroyed. Constant innovation in one's choice of advertising themes is therefore essential.

In spite of all the research that has gone into trying to discover why some products fail while others succeed, it is still possible only to generalize about the reasons for product failure. Experience shows that it is most likely to occur where one or more of the following conditions apply:

1 *Excessive established competition.* The market is already highly competitive and is already catered for by a large number of products offering basically very little difference in quality, utility or appeal, such as toiletries, alcoholic drinks, cigarettes and confectionery.
2 *Capital-intensive production.* There is a high degree of capitalization and repeat sales of a high volume are essential to achieve a profitable return. In such circumstances success is dependent on rapid sales growth and the achievement of a major share of the market in a very limited period of time.

One could argue that failure brought about by either of the above factors cannot be attributed to failure on the part of advertising. It is the result of mistaken marketing judgement, because the selling attributes of the product – its unique selling proposition – are inadequate. Advertising can only do its job when other factors – product suitability, good personal selling and effective distribution – have played their part. One should bear in mind always the overriding premise for successful marketing: the matching of the product to the consumer's need, together with the correct identification of the market segment one intends to penetrate. Only then can advertising be expected to do its work of promotion and persuasion.

Deciding the appropriation

Before it can be decided how much advertising should be undertaken, it is necessary to know how much one should spend. The usual answer to this question is another question: 'How much can we afford?' Unfortunately there are no established guidelines for arriving at an optimum advertising appropriation.

The budgeting of advertising expenditure has been the subject of many theories but few definite conclusions. The problem of course is that the effectiveness of advertising is almost impossible to measure.

For this reason company managements and their accountants often are distrustful. They recognize the necessity for a certain amount of advertising but can never prove how much is enough.

One of the most favoured arguments justifies the amount spent on advertising if the *marginal revenue* which the company earns because of the advertising is greater than the cost of that advertising, plus the *marginal cost* of satisfying the additional demand. It ceases to be justified if the *marginal cost* of providing the additional goods or services, plus the advertising cost, exceeds the marginal revenue.

Many very successful business organizations establish a relation between advertising expenditure and sales volume on a percentage basis. The theory is that a final satisfactory profit figure will be achieved if the investment in advertising is held at a fixed percentage of sales turnover. An immediate objection, however, is that promotion begets sales, not the other way round! Apart from this, one must consider the situation of the multi-product company. Where there are several products competing in different markets and each perhaps at a different stage in its life cycle, one cannot relate optimum advertising expenditure strictly to the volume of sales.

If, in spite of these difficulties, one opts for the 'percentage of sales' approach to the calculation of an advertising appropriation, it is still necessary to decide *which* sales one takes into consideration – this year's or last year's? There are firms that take the total value of their sales for last year and decide to spend, say, 3 per cent of that figure as this year's advertising budget. The notion is that, having achieved a certain level of sales last year, one stands a good chance of at least doing as well this year, and that 3 per cent of the sales turnover is an affordable sum for advertising. The trouble with this historical approach of course is that one cannot be sure that this year will compare with last year. Market conditions may change, the level of the sales of the product may go up or down. Either way, the work that advertising has to do may be different from what it had to do last year.

The alternative is to budget the *anticipated* sales for this year and agree a percentage of that figure for advertising expenditure. But further problems arise. When we speak of 'sales', are we talking in terms of value or volume? We may sell more goods at a lower price or less goods at a higher price. More pertinently, how many actual *sales* of the product are we asking advertising to induce?

One of the more popular methods of arriving at an optimum advertising appropriation, particularly in highly competitive consumer-goods fields, is to follow the competition. One establishes how much competitors are spending on their advertising programmes and relates one's own expenditure to theirs. But is the other person's appropriation right? Does the competitor spend enough or too much? How much of the expenditure is ill-advised and wasteful?

Above all, do we want others always to lead while we merely follow?

The pundits of this approach argue that if the relation between one's own advertising expenditure and that of the competition is maintained, then one's market share also will be maintained in relation to theirs. This can be dangerous ground. Marketing success is not dependent on advertising alone. One must not discount the part played by selling techniques, pricing policies or the effectiveness of distribution methods.

Theoretically, the best way of budgeting for advertising is probably that which is called 'The Job to be Done' method. One calculates how much must be spent to achieve certain objectives in the current market situation, taking into account:

1   The degree of consumer acceptance achieved by the product.
2   The activities of competitors.
3   The scope for further market penetration that exists.

The next step is to cost the product. If one then assumes a ruling price and deducts cost from price, what is left represents that which is available for profit and product promotion. Finally, one must decide what is to be the net profit required from the product and deduct this figure. The remainder is what is available for advertising.

If one relates the cost of what needs to be spent on advertising to achieve one's objectives to the sum of money available, it could be found that there is insufficient to pay the bill. Should this occur, there are only four alternatives to choose from: increase the price of the product, cut some other costs, trim one's proposed advertising programme, or decide to 'invest' some of one's net profit in the advertising budget.

The merit of this system is that it provides an effective means of controlling advertising expenditure. One either keeps the advertising appropriation within the bounds of what is affordable or one must find means of cutting back, either in other costs or in one's net profit objective.

The social acceptability of advertising

Advertising is rather more than a substitute for face-to-face selling. While it is true that nothing can equal the effectiveness of personal contact between seller and buyer, advertising, because it is impersonal, can attempt things that a salesperson cannot. Its chief asset is that it can repeat the sales message over and over again. It can follow the consumer around, and, virtually, wherever he is and whatever he is doing, he cannot for long escape its propaganda. Thank to micro-circuitry and transistor electronics, commercial radio and television are repeating the advertiser's message on the beaches, in the parks, in cars, in public houses, as well as in most homes in the land. Apart from broadcasting, the consumer is subjected to persuasion every time he opens a newspaper or magazine, or when he travels in trains or on buses. At numerous sporting events eye-catching signs repeat the message.

One may well question the morality of all this commercial propaganda. There are those who hold strong views on the subject and consider that, because one simply cannot escape from the influence of advertising, it has become an infringement of our liberties. The case for the anti-advertising lobby is expressed often enough, and, certainly, in many countries there is a growing concern about the long-term effects of too much commercialization upon the outlook and way of life of society.

For those with a product or service to take to market, advertising is an essential part of their work and for those who may be seeking justification for adding to the general hue and cry, the following factors are worth consideration. Good advertising should be socially acceptable because:

1   Demand is stimulated quickly, enabling production and distribution costs to be reduced.
2   Correctly applied, it can even out peaks and troughs of consumer demand and achieve a consistent level of production, thus creating security for both the investor and the worker.
3   A high and consistent level of demand enables transport costs to be reduced through better routing methods.
4   The consumer is protected, because the value of a good company name which advertising has created is a guarantee of quality and fair-dealing.
5   The revenue from advertising supports the free press and provides competition in the mass media by financing commercial television and radio.

Let us now consider some of the objectives of an advertising campaign.

We have seen the importance of creating and maintaining a persuasive brand image for consumer goods. Readers, in their role of consumers, will have been receptive to consumer advertising sufficiently long to recognize it for what it is. The purpose behind the promotion may not be so apparent.

Pre-selling to the trade

When a new product is to be launched upon the market, advertising has several jobs to do. First, the product has to be pre-sold to the retailer. He has to be convinced that by allocating valuable shelf space to the new brand and tying up capital in stocking it, he is making a good investment. Obviously advertising that is directed towards the retailer must tie in with the efforts of the salesforce. In this instance advertising supports the work of the salespeople, expands the message they are trying to put over, and then goes on repeating it as frequently as the advertising budget will allow.

The best assurance a retailer can have that he should carry the product will be the knowledge that a considerable consumer demand for the brand will be created. Therefore, when advertising his product to the retailer in the trade press or by means of hand-out literature supplied by the salesforce, the manufacturer will provide also full details of his forthcoming advertising programme directed to the general public, such as the number of television commercials scheduled to appear at peak viewing times or half-page announcements in the popular press.

Buyers for retail outlets are themselves consumers, and advertising directed to the trade should combine both retailer and consumer motivation. This applies not only to 'convenience goods' such as grocery, pharmaceutical, toiletry and confectionery products, but also to those items of merchandise that require an element of personal selling, including furnishings, clothing, electrical goods and appliances of all kinds. Shopkeepers must be assured that should they agree to stock the line, they will attract good consumer demand promoted by adequate advertising. They will also need to know what are the special selling features of the goods – durability, ease of maintenance, aesthetic appeal, fashion-worthiness, reliability, safety or whatever – in order that they may recommend them to their customers.

A major apprehension of retailers is that of 'missing the boat' with a new line. If they are convinced that other shops and stores have accepted it and will stock it, they may well feel obliged to stock it themselves, because failure to do so might lose them a valuable share of future business. Furthermore, there are some retail buyers who adopt a 'me-too' policy, and prefer to follow a trend rather than create one. When engaged in 'selling-in' a new product to the retail trade, one should bear this in mind: the advertising should emphasize the degree of trade acceptability that the new brand has already achieved.

The objectives of consumer advertising

If we turn now to the question of advertising directed towards the consumer, it will be found that the main function of consumer goods promotion is to influence customers' predisposition to buy the product *before* they enter the shop. The public has become accustomed by its experience of modern advertising methods to the pre-selling process, so much so that a new product – especially in foodstuffs, toiletries and other heavily branded items – that has *not* been extensively advertised is often greeted with suspicion. The housewife expects to be informed about a new product before she encounters it in the supermarket.

This is the case especially with products that have what is known as a weak unique selling proposition (USP). These are products that, regardless of their intrinsic quality, can claim no superiority of uniqueness against that of brand rivals. A product in this category will usually require a greater amount of advertising than one that does possess the attribute of uniqueness. Indeed, if one is proposing to market a product whose USP is weak, it becomes necessary to decide the minimum level of advertising that is essential. If this level cannot be maintained, it may be unwise to put the product on the market at all.

In deciding the objectives of consumer advertising of branded goods, the first question we should consider is the coverage necessary to ensure adequate market penetration. This immediately poses a second question: To whom are we selling? The advertiser needs to know who buys his product, why they buy it and for what purposes they use it. He should also try to understand what it is about his particular brand that apparently makes it different, in the eyes of his customers, from those of his competitors. Having established who the customers are – that is, having defined the market segment at which the product is aimed – he must decide how to reach them. Advertising media that are likely to exert the most influence upon those particular consumers have to be selected.

The assessment of objectives does not stop here. One must decide how much weight should be put behind the message to achieve sufficient impact on this consumer group. Decisions in this matter will be influenced by the extent of competitive advertising. In a market where one's competitors are shouting their sales messages loudly and repeatedly it is a sheer waste of the advertising budget to attempt an occasional whisper. One simply will not be heard.

The nature of the product also will influence the assessment of advertising objectives. Very often the consumer's view of a product differs from that of its manufacturer. Here again consumer research plays a vital part, because one needs to know just what it is the consumer imagines he or she is buying.

Equally vital is consistency. Once an advertising theme has been established for a particular brand, the message one is trying to put over must be seen by the consumer as consistent. If the advertising method is varied too widely, potential customers receive a distorted impression of what is being said. The result can be bewilderment and loss of impact. It should also be remembered that customers do not make conscious buying decisions unless they appear logical. An advertising message which does not seem logical – which 'simply doesn't make sense' – will have no constructive influence.

To summarize, an assessment of advertising objectives will therefore include the following:

1 The market segment at which the advertising is to be directed.
2 The extent of advertising necessary to cover that market segment adequately.
3 The weight of advertising needed to put over the message effectively.

Effective brand promotion does not stop of course with the advertising campaign. The message must be supported by the merchandising of the product, packaging design and the use of point-of-sale material.

6.2 The use of an advertising agency

Having established, very broadly, the objectives of our advertising campaign, we must now consider how these may be best achieved. Such questions as when, where and how shall we advertise lead us at once to the next stage of the discussion. Should a company use the services of an advertising agency or rely solely on an advertising department within the firm?

The services of an agency are not cheap. Apart from the question of cost, however, there are other considerations. To what extent can an agency really understand the marketing philosophy of its client? How much reliance should be placed on the advice, guidance and responsibility of personnel not under one's own direct control?

Most firms do use advertising agencies, especially for national campaigns directed towards consumer markets. Advertising is a highly specialized field, and the major agencies provide services based on wide experience and backed by facilities seldom available within the advertising departments of even the largest manufacturing organizations. The cost of using an agency is usually cheaper than if one attempted to do the job oneself. The agency will recoup a high proportion of its costs from the media owners by means of commission on all advertising time or space booked on behalf of the client.

Apart from the questions of cost-saving and the comprehensiveness of its services, the advertising agency possesses a most important attribute: that of objectivity. Because of this the agency can often appreciate its client's position and assess its advertising needs more clearly than its client company's own management, who are 'too close to the trees'. Often the problem of understanding the consumer's view of the product is facilitated by this objectivity on the part of an agency not obsessed with the history of the brand's conception and development or with the day-to-day problems of production and distribution.

What does an agency do? Very much more than is generally realized. A good agency does not merely create advertisements, it becomes an extension of the manufacturer's marketing organization. It provides advice on market research to assist the preparation of the marketing plan. It can add to the company's marketing knowledge experience gained with other clients operating in other markets. Above all, it can guide the company in the selection of the most appropriate media through which to promote the product in its targeted market.

The creative services of an advertising agency include not only the preparation of television and press advertisements but also posters, direct-mail shots, leaflets, booklets, catalogues and price lists. The agency will organize competitions and gift-offer schemes. It will provide point-of-sale material such as showcards, stands, dispensers, mobile displays and electric signs. Indeed, so comprehensive has become the brand-image philosophy, that today many firms place in the hands of their advertising agents responsibility for the design of everything that carries their 'house style', including letterheads, product packaging, wrappers, cartons and even the 'livery' of their delivery vehicles.

Selecting the agency

How does one set about selecting a suitable agency? In Britain the Institute of Practitioners in Advertising will provide a list of agencies, but most agencies obtain new clients by means of recommendation. Where a suitable introduction does not present itself, a company can choose an agency by assessing its results. If one sees a series of advertisements that appeal, and makes contact with the agency concerned, there will be, initially at least, harmony with the creative personnel. Care should be taken, however, to ensure that the agency selected has some knowledge and experience of the market in which one's product is to be sold. Most agencies specialize, and the approach they have developed successfully for one type of market, or for one class of products, may not necessarily be suitable for others. Communication with the agency's personnel is facilitated when they have some related experience of the client's market and class of product. They are able to grasp the essentials of the subject better, and a good rapport can be created quickly.

Another important consideration is the size of the agency in relation to the scope of the advertising campaign one has in mind. A small outfit may have insufficient resources at its command to handle a large and intensive compaign adequately, whereas a fairly modest advertising appropriation may not evoke sufficient interest for one of the leading agencies, the majority of whose clients may be spending vastly greater sums.

Finding the right agency is therefore never an easy task. Even when a decision has been reached, it is an obvious precaution to limit the initial contract to a trial period only. This will enable the two organizations to discover whether they can work together – whether their talents will combine effectively.

The time to bring in the agency is *before* marketing plans have been finalized. So often companies define their objectives and set in train all their various marketing forces before the agency is consulted. This is to lose the informed advice of the agency's specialists, based upon accumulated experience in other products and other markets. By the time they are brought on the scene, the agency personnel may find that their client has already committed itself to a particular line of approach, and they will have to try and create an advertising 'platform' within unnecessarily narrow parameters.

The agency's response to your initial overtures will probably be an invitation to what is known as a 'presentation'. Owing to the high degree of competition that exists among rival agencies for the advertising accounts of client companies, particularly in the consumer-product field, 'presentations' have a tendency to become somewhat grandiose occasions. Some agencies will go to ridiculous lengths to win important accounts. On occasion, a lot of money is expended entertaining client personnel, and creating a highly theatrical performance of the agency's past achievements and present qualifications – aimed not merely to impress but sometimes to overawe the visiting directors and marketing personnel of would-be client firms.

Those whose critical faculties have not been too impaired by such a display of showmanship will appreciate the value of a good rapport between the staff of the two organizations. On the agency side an 'account executive' will be appointed to liaise with the marketing personnel of the client company. This individual will attend to all matters of detail and introduce to the discussions the various creative and other specialist staff of the agency, as and when required.

Briefing the agency

The agency personnel should be given as much information as possible about the company, its products and its marketing objectives. In the early days of association it is important that the agency people get the 'feel' of their new client and form an accurate appreciation of its outlook regarding its products and markets. Copywriters and designers need to understand the kind of 'image' they are being asked to establish.

To get the best results from the agency, the company should present a lucid exposition of its aims and requirements. A statement should be prepared on the following lines.

The product
1   The production processes employed in the manufacture of the product and any specific technical requirements.
2   The history of the product's inception, screening and initial testing.
3   Its current life-cycle stage.
4   Its pack sizes.
5   The packaging, transportation and physical distribution arrangements.
6   The product's shelf life.
7   The after-sales service provided.

The market
1   Who uses the product, how they use it, when they use it and why they use it.
2   The company's distribution policy: via wholesaler, direct to retailer, or direct to consumer via mail order or other agencies.
3   The market share currently held by the product.
4   The proposed market share.
5   The company's pricing policy for the product, including distributors' discounts.
6   The scope of the company's sales effort allocated to the product.

Previous advertising policy
1   The amount of the previous advertising appropriation.
2   The amount spent by competitors on advertising.
3   The percentage of previous advertising budgets spent on conventional advertisements (press, radio, TV, etc.).
4   The percentage of previous advertising budgets spent on special promotions (premium offers, competitions, sales aids and other merchandising activities).

Proposed advertising policy
1   The amount of the current advertising appropriation.
2   The desired 'image' for the company.
3   The desired 'image' for the product.

The advertising platform

Detailed information of this kind will enable the agency to create what is known as an advertising 'platform' or general theme. This is the vital part of the whole exercise, because this theme, once agreed upon, will be the basis on which the entire advertising campaign will be built. Such a theme will have to be unique in the particular product field concerned. It must also find appeal with all the various attitudes and living habits of the consumers who make up the targeted market segment. Its purpose will be to convey to the consumer an agreeable impression of the product and encourage its purchase.

Table 6.1 shows some of the more obvious examples of advertising 'platforms':

Table 6.1 Advertising 'platforms'

Type of product	Possible theme or 'platform'
Inter-city rail travel	Fast journey times coupled with relaxation.
Cars	The experience of 'power' linked with safety.
Pre-cooked meals	Appetizing nourishment combined with a saving in time and labour.

Having established a proposed 'platform', the agency will consider the aims of the advertising campaign and how these will relate to the general objectives laid down by the company. The first aim of all product advertising must obviously be to tell prospective users that the product exists. As we have seen earlier, however, in a market already crowded by other makes, each possessing similar character-istics, the existence of yet another brand, largely indistinguishable from the others, will make little or no impression upon potential users. It is here that the artificially created identity of the product, those special features designed to attract and maintain recognition – distinctive shape, distinctive pack design, and, above all, distinctive brand name – will give it a personality which, because it is unique, will set it apart from its rivals. Once recognition has been achieved, the other basic aim of the advertising campaign, which is acceptance of the advertising 'platform' or selling theme, can be pursued.

The agency will now present its proposals to the company for approval. These will include the 'platform' and suggested media for the propagation of this theme with a view to achieving the greatest impact on the market.

The selection of media

The selection of suitable media will of course play a decisive part in the success of the campaign. Media research is a major function of the advertising agency. The company management that has put its trust in an agency will be wise to accept its guidance regarding this highly complex subject. It will, however, be in a better position to understand the advice it receives if it has some knowledge of the factors behind media selection and we shall now consider what these are.

What are we selling?

The first question to be asked is what exactly do we think we are selling? To say that we are selling a breakfast cereal, shoe polish or a toothbrush, to pick random examples, is not enough. We make the mistake of approaching the subject from one direction only. Marketing must be consumer-orientated. We must rephrase the question and ask: What do users think they are buying? We can go one better and probe the housewife's likely motivation that results in her decision to purchase. If she is seeking merely a breakfast cereal, then she will buy any cereal, regardless of brand. But the sales figures for the various makes of breakfast cereal show that she does not in fact buy *any* brand. The majority of housewives show an allegiance to a particular brand by their repeated purchases. One would not perhaps have thought that there was a marked degree of difference in quality or price between one nationally known make of breakfast cereal and another. Therefore it is logical to assume that the housewife, in choosing a specific brand, makes a distinction on grounds other than quality and price. Is she influenced in her choice because the brand she selects carries with it a premium offer of some kind? If this is so, then perhaps it is the premium offer, rather than the cereal itself, that she is really buying.

Let us consider the toothbrush. Brand loyalty in the toothbrush market may not be as prevalent as it is with breakfast foods. People have occasion to buy a new toothbrush less frequently than a packet of cereals. The manufacturers of toothbrushes tell us that, according to their market research, not everybody uses a toothbrush. Of those that do, a large proportion continue to make do with brushes that have become worn and have ceased to do an adequate job of dental care. It is also an established fact that many people buy a new toothbrush immediately before going on holiday, from which it is inferred that they would feel ashamed of the condition of their toothbrushes if these were to be seen by hotel chambermaids! Thus we can perhaps say that consumers' motives for buying new toothbrushes are:

1 Concern for the care of their teeth.
2 Concern for the opinion of others about the way in which they care for their teeth.

If this is true, we are selling not just a toothbrush but also health and social acceptability.

Similarly, with our other example, shoe polish, we can point to the well-known fact that shoe leather needs a regular application of oils if it is to remain supple and in good condition. When a pair of shoes is seldom cleaned and polished, the leather is liable to crack and become porous. Regular shoe-cleaning therefore is a form of thrift. But clean shoes have another merit: that of imparting a good appearance to the wearer. Thus we find that we are not merely selling shoe polish: we are selling economy and, once again, we are selling social acceptability.

Advertising specialists will endeavour to establish these underlying motives for consumer purchases and to reflect them in their preparation of the advertising 'platform' for the product.

To whom are we selling?

When we come to consider who our customers are, a similar depth of penetration is required. Once more we must get down beneath the obvious to discover who it is, in the consumer market for our particular product, who really makes the buying decision. Let us refer again to the example of the breakfast cereal. Who, in the main, eats cereals at breakfast time? Research shows that, generally speaking, it is families with children who buy the most cereals. The majority of parents care about their children's well-being, and conscientious mothers try to ensure that their offspring leave each morning for school with something nourishing inside them. But mothers with a family to get off to school in the morning do not have an abundance of time in which to prepare complicated meals, and one of the merits of the breakfast cereal is that it does not require cooking. It is easy and quick to prepare. Furthermore, it is easy and quick to eat, and therefore likely to be popular with children. From this we may deduce that the mothers of young children are likely to be the people to whom we are selling when our product is a breakfast cereal.

There is, however, something more to be borne in mind. We must remember the old saying that it is one thing to take a horse to water but another to make it drink. Mother may put before little Johnnie a dish of cereal, but she cannot necessarily get him to eat it. If Johnnie prefers Brand X and Mother has bought Brand Y, then Mother may have a problem on her hands. So far as she is concerned, the nutritive value of X and Y may be indistinguishable and both are quick and easy to prepare. But it is not to Mother alone that we are selling but to Johnnie as well. This is why the majority of advertising for breakfast cereals is orientated towards both the mother and the child.

When shall we advertise?

To answer this question, we must examine our findings to the previous questions of 'what' and 'to whom' we are selling. The in-depth understanding we have obtained under these headings will be our guide to *when* to do the selling. If we refer again to the example of breakfast cereal, it does not demand a great deal of imagination to realize that the best time to advertise such a product is when we can reach the greatest number of children and mothers. In radio and television terms this will be after school hours and up to perhaps eight or nine o'clock in the evening.

On the other hand, if we look at our shoe-polish example, we may decide that it is men rather than women who, in the main, use this product. Many younger men wear shoes made of synthetic materials, however. Perhaps it is to the older men that we should direct our advertising? In terms of television, we might decide to run several 'spots', choosing a peak viewing period when a regular sports programme is being broadcast. But how sure are we that men do in fact influence the choice of shoe polish? Even if they do use it more than women, are they likely to insist upon one brand in favour of another? Or do they leave it to the women in their lives to purchase it along with all the other items of shopping at the supermarket?

How you answer that question – backed, one hopes, with some elementary market research – will decide the *time* at which you choose to advertise.

Types of advertising media

When it comes to selecting media for advertising, one has the choice of one or more of the following:

Press advertising
1 *Newspapers*. The amount of money spent on newspaper advertising still remains very much in excess of that spent on television commercials in Britain. Apart from the national daily and Sunday newspapers, there are regional dailies and Sunday papers that possess very considerable pulling power. In addition, there is a very considerable readership of local weekly newspapers throughout the country. Of these, a significant number are what are colloquially known as 'freebies', delivered free of charge to all households in local areas.
2 *Periodicals*. General interest magazines, read by all the family, have largely disappeared from the bookstalls in Britain. Their place has been taken by a wide range of journals targeted at specialist segments of the market, such as motoring, gardening, yachting, sports of all kinds, do-it-yourself and hobby interests that include photography, audio-visual recording, antique collecting, together with a whole spectrum of other leisure pursuits. Magazines for women are also widely read by men because their editorial content covers not only fashion and beauty but also home subjects, such as furnishings and interior design.

Television and radio advertising
1 *The Independent Broadcasting Authority* controls commercial radio and television in Britain by issuing licenses to regionally based companies.
2 *Satellite broadcasting.* A comparative newcomer in Britain and likely to have a very considerable influence upon the shape of British broadcasting and the scope for consumer advertising during the next decade.

Poster advertising
One of the oldest and still a very effective means of advertising consumer goods and services.

Direct-mail advertising
The use of the postal services for the distribution of advertising matter by means of letters and circulars has increased enormously in recent years, with encouragement from the General Post Office which has introduced special schemes to attract advertisers' business.

Handbill advertising
One of the simplest methods of dissemination of the advertiser's message is to print handbills and have them put through letterboxes.

Cinema advertising
Despite the decline in cinema audiences, cinema advertising still attracts a not insignificant volume of advertising expenditure, targeted towards the younger age groups.

Miscellaneous advertising media
Telephone and other directories, postal franking machines, labels, special gifts and novelties.

From this welter of advertising opportunity it is no simple task to select media most likely to be suitable, in terms of the relation of cost to pulling power, for a particular product or service. It is here that advertising research comes to our aid.

Advertising research

Advertising research is a highly specialized function. There are research organizations solely engaged in a study of all the various advertising media to measure their relative effectiveness. Most advertising agencies rely upon the services of research consultants to advise them on the choice of suitable media and guide them in the preparation of advertising copy to achieve the best results from any specific medium.

Readership research

Newspapers and periodicals publish their circulation figures, but it is not the total number of readers of any particular journal that interests the potential advertiser so much as how that readership is made up. He wants to know the breakdown according to age, to social class, where the majority of these readers are to be found – in the country or in large cities – whether the readership is predominantly men or women, how many of the women are housewives or are working, the average number of children per reader and the children's ages. He wants to know the kind of occupations of the majority of readers – artisans, office and factory workers, executives – and their likely income bracket. In addition, he is anxious to discover what their special interests may be: how many of them are likely to be keen gardeners, for example, how many do their own home decorating, how many own their own car.

It is information of this kind, presented in the form of statistical tables, which the advertising researcher makes available to agencies or directly to intending advertisers.

Television audience research

One of the problems of assessing the size of one's audience when advertising on television is that there are no 'circulation figures' to provide conclusive evidence of the actual numbers of people who watch television programmes at specific times. The BARB organization does provide advertisers with the number of television sets which it is estimated are tuned in to the programmes of the British Broadcasting Corporation and the commercial television companies. This assessment of the number of homes in which one's advertisement will be screened gives a fair indication of the total audience being reached. What cannot be assessed by this means is the actual number of people who are consciously absorbing the advertising message. In many homes the TV set is switched on for several hours per day, but whether or not anyone is actually viewing – whether or not anyone is actually in the room – throughout this period of time is problematical.

Copy-testing

Although readership and TV audience research can go a long way towards establishing the identity and numbers of consumers reached by advertising, one is still confronted with the question of the effectiveness of the advertising message one is trying to put across. Here again researchers have devised various methods to aid the advertiser.

In one of these a small sample of readers of the particular newspaper or magazine in which a specific advertisement appears is invited to answer certain questions and undertake some simple tests. The researcher asks them which advertisements they have seen and whether they can describe them. Subsequently, the reader is shown the particular advertisement in which the researcher is interested and is asked whether he, or she, has read it all, or in part. From the responses obtained, it is possible to assess the effectiveness both of the various positions of advertisements in a paper in relation to one another and also the pulling power of different types of advertisement layout and copy.

Copy-testing is also influenced by semantics, which is a branch of linguistic research concerned with studying changes in the meaning of words. Philological studies of this kind have established the words in the language which are most frequently used, and are therefore most likely to be understood by the majority of people.

6.3   Point-of-sale advertising

However effective your newspaper or TV advertising may be in persuading consumers of their need for the type of product you are offering, and however well you may have convinced them that it is your particular brand they will prefer to use, the battle has not been decided until customers enter a shop and buy it.

Decisiveness is not a prevalent human virtue. Memories, too, have a way of being capricious. It is necessary therefore to bridge the gap between the work done by press and TV advertising and the point at which the customer makes the ultimate decision to purchase: at the shop counter. As she, say, goes to make that decision, there is the danger that the time lapse that has occurred since she was last exposed to the advertiser's message may have brought about a diminution in the effectiveness of that message, or it may indeed have been completely forgotten. Consumers often are the victims of tremendous pressures in their workaday lives, as well as the pressures of competitive advertising. It thus becomes very necessary to repeat and re-emphasize one's sales message, right there, at the point in time and place at which the final purchasing decision is reached.

There are of course a large number of everyday purchases which we make on impulse. A man finds that he has run out of tobacco and enters the first tobacconist's shop he comes to and buys a packet. In the supermarket, the housewife spies a display of biscuits and remembers she must buy some. The child sees the ice-cream vendor in the street and demands an ice-lolly. All these are impulse purchases and seldom carry with them any conscious reference to a specific advertisement seen or heard hours, days or weeks previously. It is essential therefore to remind the shopper of one's pre-selling message. In fact the omission of adequate point-of-sale advertising can result in a waste of much of the appropriation that has been spent on TV commercials and press announcements, because their effectiveness has been allowed to dissolve before the purchasing decision has been reached.

The suitability of display material

We have seen that the purpose of point-of-sale display is to remind the shopper of all the interest and persuasion that has been created previously by advertisements in other media, and to exploit it at the moment of decision to purchase. We must remember also the importance of consistency and repetition, which means that point-of-sale material must put across the same selling message in the same style. Consistency is vital because, in a crowded store, the customer is unlikely to have the time or the inclination consciously to read what we have to say. Thus the layout of the advertisement display, the colours and print type employed, and, above all, the phrases and slogans used in the final message, must be the same as those used in the general advertising campaign. If the product we are selling is contained in a package, then the colour of the package and the print type should again be consistent to achieve that final visual recognition of the brand which we have been building up, at a high appropriation cost, for days or weeks beforehand.

One should not attempt to say too much in point-of-sale advertisements. The story should be condensed to its basic essentials. This is your last 'punch' before the customer's final decision wins or loses you a sale. For this reason you may be tempted to spend a great deal of money on large or complex point-of-sale equipment, such as illuminated signs or mobiles. Before doing so, you must consider the attitude of the retailer.

The retailer looks for the support of his suppliers to help him to sell his merchandise. The provision of suitable point-of-sale material will often influence the distributor to run a particular line or to give a specific brand a greater share of his limited display space. But the emphasis is on suitability, and the manufacturer must take account of the circumstances which are likely to exist in the majority of retail outlets where his brand is to be displayed. For example, some of the large national multiple stores have clearly defined regulations concerning the size and type of manufacturers' display material they consider to be acceptable. A counter display unit which may be eminently suitable for the counter of a personal-service retail shop could be useless in a supermarket that has no counters. A piece of display equipment that takes up a comparatively large area of floor space may be impracticable for the small shopkeeper, and offer a danger hazard for shoppers accompanied by young children.

Any equipment requiring erection on site needs careful design. There is often reluctance on the part of both salespersons and retailers' assistants to spend time erecting display material if they feel their energies are better employed in their conventional selling activities. For this reason such equipment needs to be easily portable, and capable, wherever possible, of being stowed in the boot of the salesperson's car.

When insufficient heed is paid to these considerations, the result can be a high rate of wastage of time, money and effort. All too frequently, companies spend an inordinate proportion of their advertising appropriation on point-of-sale equipment that is never fully used. It will be advisable therefore to give some consideration to the practical conditions in which display material has to do its work.

Display 'positions'

The first consideration is the position in which such material will appear in the retailer's premises. The most desirable positions, from the point of view of achieving the greatest impact, differ in service shops compared with self-service stores and supermarkets. In service shops the most favoured positions, in descending order of merit, are:

1 The window.
2 The counter top.
3 The floor area immediately adjacent to the counter.
4 The shelves or fixtures behind the counter.
5 Adjacent to the till.

In some trades, such as groceries, toiletries and pharmaceuticals, there has been a tendency for the window to lose its first-rank position for point-of-sale material and the counter and its immediate vicinity has acquired greater importance. In the case of those kinds of merchandise for which the shopper tends to 'shop around', such as clothing, furnishings, electrical goods and durables of all kinds, the window display is still a major source of attraction for the potential shopper and an obvious point-of-sale 'pitch' for the product manu-facturer. In self-service shops and supermarkets, however, where usually there are no window displays, it has been found that the check-out points are the most effective positions for display material.

One must consider also the question of visibility. It will be obvious that every manufacturer of branded consumer goods is trying to secure a maximum share of the available display area in retail shops, and there is just not enough space for all the posters, showcards, display stands and dispensers which the retailer has offered to him. The only way to overcome this problem of display saturation is to try to be original and to find means of telling what is likely to be the same old story in a new, interesting and arresting manner – providing, of course, that it remains consistent with one's general advertising platform.

This brings us back to the question of layout and copywriting for point-of-sale material. We have emphasized that it should be complementary to and consistent with the main advertising campaign. However, because such material is handed over to the retailer for his own use within his premises, some manufacturers fear that at least a proportion of it will be wasted. They prefer to reduce its cost by designing the material themselves and using their own printer. In doing so, they run the risk that their point-of-sale material may not be in sufficient harmony with their main campaign, and the emphasis on consistency will be lost. It is advisable therefore to arrange for both design and production of point-of-sale material to be handled by the agency responsible for the entire advertising campaign.

Wastage of point-of-sale material is always a problem. It can be reduced considerably, however, if the views of the company's sales-force and of retailers themselves are canvassed in advance. Sales-persons calling on shops and stores have a good insight into what may be wrong with existing material. Frequently they can provide management with good advice about improving the value of such material. It is a subject worth discussion at sales meetings.

Some manufacturers actively seek the assistance of the retailer. They select a limited number of retailers, present them with a supply of showcards, a display stand or an illuminated sign, and ask them to report any noticeable increase in the sale of their brand.

6.4   Industrial advertising

Companies supplying capital equipment, components or raw materials to industrial users have a rather different need of advertising from that of the producers of consumer goods. In the first place, the advertising appropriation of the industrial product manufacturer is usually smaller. Secondly, industrial markets tend to be more seg-mented than those for consumer goods and, generally speaking, somewhat easier to identify. On the other hand, advertising research into industrial markets has lagged behind that of the consumer field and evaluation of the available advertising media can be more difficult.

Media suitable for the promotion of industrial products include the following:

1   Industrial and trade press advertising.
2   Public relations.
3   Sales literature.
4   Direct mail.
5   Trade exhibitions.
6   Demonstration films and videos.

A major difference between the relevance of press advertising between consumer and industrial products lies in the question of branding. We have seen that in consumer-product marketing the establishment of a satisfactory brand image is often essential to achieve loyalty from consumers and to protect one's market share from attack by competitors. With industrial marketing, the situation is often quite different. Here one is selling on the basis of quality, service and price, usually in that order. Industrial buyers have no option but to purchase such components and materials that their production departments require. Thus advertising does not create the demand for industrial products. It provides, instead, a backdrop for the other promotional tools of the marketing effort: salesforce, direct mail, public relations and trade exhibitions.

One of the functions of industrial advertising is to provoke enquiries for the company's goods or services from potential clients which the salesforce can convert into repeat business. This is something that can be achieved by means other than press advertising. Indeed one may well ask whether there is any particular wisdom in spending a modest publicity appropriation on advertising at all. Sometimes a better job can be done by spending the money in other ways – by means of high-quality literature, the use of regular direct-mail shots to likely users of the product, or simply by an improvement in public relations.

If it is decided to advertise, one of the problems is the multiplicity of trade and technical journals. Indiscriminate use of such media can obviously be extremely expensive. Quantuplication analysis – the method of discovering the overlap of readership between more than two journals – is often insufficient help in the task of industrial media research. While it may be true that an advertisement in any one of the trade journals ensures that it is aimed at a readership likely to be directly engaged in the trade or industry served, many such publications contain such a welter of advertising matter that there can be little assurance that one's message will have much impact.

Some industrial products manufacturers therefore eschew the trade press and use the columns of the 'quality' national newspapers and journals, on the grounds that these are read by the widest selection of people who occupy decision-making positions in their respective organizations. Advertising rates in the national press tend to be considerably higher than in trade journals, but the advertising content in relation to editorial is often much smaller.

Industrial-product advertising usually divides into 'hard sell' and prestige advertisements. The 'hard-sell' type often features a specific product or group of products, and aims to engender the interest of potential users by means of detailed information with regard to quality or performance, accompanied by an invitation to the reader to write to the company for fuller details. This approach is backed, in trade journals, by the frequent inclusion of a reader-reply-card system. Anyone requiring additional information has only to detach from the journal a pre-paid reply postcard, insert his or her name and address and the code number of the advertisement. The journal has a system by which the enquiry is passed on to the advertiser concerned.

A prestige advertisement, on the other hand, has a much less specific purpose. Its aim is to create a favourable impression of the company and its products, and by repetition to instil that impression into the minds of existing and potential customers. To some extent industrial prestige advertising bears a close relationship to the brand-image advertising of the consumer-goods field.

The question of which type of advertising to use is always difficult to answer. The 'hard-sell' promotion has the merit of being more easily measurable in terms of the number of enquiries which it evokes. 'Prestige' advertisements seldom produce any direct response, but have a better long-term effect. When the same message is propagated month in and month out, the company concerned has the opportunity of building an image of consistency and, by infer-ence, of reliability, which can be of major assistance to its salesforce.

Planning an industrial advertising campaign

The first step towards the planning of an industrial advertising campaign is to set out a programme of activity. As we saw in the case of consumer-product advertising, an organized approach to the spending of the appropriation is essential if unnecessary wastage is to be avoided.

An industrial advertising programme should be organized on the following lines.

Establish the marketing plan
Once again it is vital that a company should have a clear notion of its objectives and the role advertising has to play in helping to achieve them. We have already stressed that advertising alone does not sell. Its functions are to generate interest in the product or service which is offered, and to create as favourable an impression as possible of the company concerned. In practical terms it is likely that what an organization is seeking by the use of advertising is greater penetration

of its existing market, and the opportunity to broaden that market by bringing its product to the notice of users with whom the salesforce is not yet in touch.

A company may decide to use the services of an advertising agency specializing in industrial advertising. Before doing so, it should establish exactly what it is that it is selling and to whom it is selling.

What are we selling?

In the industrial field, product quality and service often tend to be of equal importance as selling features. A product of superlative quality, in comparison to those of competitors, will have little appeal to customers if they find that the service which backs it is completely inadequate. Reliability in his supplier is often a more important asset in the eyes of the industrial buyer than quality supremacy. The product usually has to be only good enough to do the job for which it has been designed; but the service which the manufacturer provides must be more than adequate if it is to succeed in a highly competitive market.

What, then, are we selling? The product or the company's reputation for service and reliability? Perhaps the two are indistinguishable from the viewpoint of market acceptability.

Let us look again at the product. Is it much the same, in terms of quality and utility, as its competitors? Or does it possess some specific edge? If so, then this surely is the factor we should hammer home to the trade. This will be our unique selling proposition, and its exploitation by means of a 'hard-sell' campaign seems indicated. On the other hand, if there is little to distinguish our particular product from that of others being offered to the market, we must conclude that its unique selling proposition is weak. An attempt to 'hard-sell' in these circumstances may not prove very effective, unless our potential for outstanding service, by means of ex-stock supplies from regional warehouses, or an expert advisory service, is superior to that of our competitors. Unless we have some specific advantage to offer – a unique selling proposition – it may be advisable to restrict our advertising to a series of 'prestige' advertisements with the object of keeping our product and our company name to the fore as a backdrop for our other marketing tools.

To whom are we selling?

What we are really asking under this heading is who are the decision-makers among our potential customers? Some of the answers will come from the sales department, because it will know to whom it is already selling the product or service: managing directors, purchasing managers, stylists and designers, works managers. Another source of information will be market research, which should be able to designate the decision-makers within user organizations for specific goods or services.

The marketing plan should also tell us how much of the market we wish to penetrate. This will be dependent upon the increase to existing sales we are seeking, and in turn will be related to our available resources and capacity. Again market research should be able to indicate the size of the total market for our product and where it is to be found.

Briefing the agency
With a clear idea of what it wants, the company should now be in a position to brief the agency personnel. It should furnish them with the fullest information on how the product is made, what are its special features (unique selling proposition), as well as the situation appertaining to competitive products and the degree of market penetration the product has so far achieved.

Armed with this information, the agency should be able to respond, in due course, with a rough plan of campaign on these lines:

1   The proposed theme or 'platform'.
2   Suggested artwork and copy for advertisements.
3   Recommendations for media.
4   A proposed budget for the campaign.

6.5   Direct-mail advertising

Reference has already been made to the use of direct-mail advertising as an alternative or adjunct to press advertising for industrial products. There is a history of considerable success for this method of promotion, which permits far greater control than most other media. One of its greatest merits is the comparative ease with which its effectiveness can be measured.

Direct mail is simply the sending of advertising matter to known recipients through the post. The size of the operation may be either modest or extensive, according to the magnitude of the task to be done, and the available budget. Its effectiveness, in comparison with other forms of promotion, is dependent upon several factors, the most important of which are the following.

The possession of an adequate and accurate list of names and addresses
There are several ways of building a list of names and addresses of people and firms to which direct-mail advertising may be sent:

1   *Existing customers.* Every business organization possesses a list of

its current customers and the names of the individuals who occupy the decision-making positions.

2 *Known potential customers.* The sales department should be able to supply a list of those users of the kind of product one is offering.

3 *Trade and local directories.* These list the names and addresses of firms that are active in specific trades and industries, but care should be taken because, inevitably, directory entries quickly become out of date.

4 *Use of list brokerage services.* There are a number of firms that specialize in the supply of mailing lists either for hire or outright purchase.

The mailing list is the foundation of any successful direct-mail campaign. The list must not only be adequate, it must also be accurate. A great deal of money can be wasted if one is continuously posting matter to proposed recipients whose companies are either defunct or have moved away, or who themselves have left their company's service. The Post Office in Britain can assist you if you seal the envelopes and mark them with the request: 'If undelivered please return to sender'. In the event of their failure to deliver, the postal authorities will return the envelope and contents marked 'Gone away'. There is no extra charge for this service, which enables you to remove such unwanted names from your mailing list.

A more difficult problem occurs when your letter is delivered to the company concerned but fails to reach the individual to whom it is addressed because he or she has left the company or moved to another department. Business people have a 'nose' for circulars, and an envelope addressed to an ex-colleague long since departed will probably end up unopened in somebody's wastepaper basket. The best way of avoiding this difficulty is to send to each company on the mailing list, at periodic intervals, a pre-paid reply card asking them to assist you in keeping your mailing list up to date by crossing through the names of individuals no longer interested in your product and adding the names of people within their organization who may be interested in receiving your future announcements. Not every firm will bother to send back the card. But even a negative response has its use because it tells you that the company concerned is probably not going to be interested in anything you send it in future, and it may be advisable to remove its name from your list.

It is to the field salespeople, however, that one should look for the regular supply of information which will keep the mailing list up to date. The company's sales representatives should be instructed that it is part of their routine work to notify head office of any changes that occur among the personnel of client firms. It is a good idea to provide them with a suitable form for the purpose such as that shown.

MAILING LIST UP-DATING FORM

From: To: Date:

Name of company:
Address:
Name(s) of contact(s):   Position held:

Sales area coding:
Trade classification coding:

Provision of suitable facilities for the preparation and despatch of regular mailings

To be successful, direct mail needs to be properly organized and efficiently executed. Although it is often cheaper to operate than press advertising, it can place a heavier burden on the company concerned because, unlike a conventional advertising campaign, it is not so easy to 'farm out' the bulk of the work to outside agencies.

Your advertising agent can of course sub-contract to a direct-mail specialist. As a general rule, however, advertising agencies do not display a great deal of interest in the use of direct-mail publicity. They place the bulk of their clients' promotion programmes with conventional media owners, from whom they receive a commission on the space or time booked. It is because they are not greatly interested in direct-mail publicity that one finds they often do not possess the expertise that this particular advertising medium requires.

Where this is a problem, a company can exclude direct mail from the advertising agency's sphere of responsibility and contract with a direct-mail house, of which there are many, supplying a very comprehensive service, including:

1   Provision of mailing lists.
2   Preparation, design and printing of sales letters and literature.
3   Addressing and despatch of letters.
4   Evaluation of the response obtained.

Nevertheless, even when all this detailed work is handled by outside specialists, one has still to create the ideas and assemble the factual information upon which a mailing campaign is based. To be effective, like any other form of advertising, direct mail must be repetitive. A 'one-off' effort, without adequate follow-up within a reasonable period of time, is likely to be a waste of money. Regular mailings are essential because their effect is cumulative.

The main uses of direct-mail firms to industrial firms are:

1 To inform customers and potential customers of new products or product modifications.
2 To remind customers and potential customers of one's standard products.

The preparation of suitable direct-mail material for the promotion of a new product is usually not difficult. The very fact that the product *is* new to your range gives it a 'news' value. The technical specification and the selling message incorporating the special features of the new product and the benefits they provide should be enough to ensure an interest on the part of recipients of your letters or bulletins.

What is not so easy is to maintain a series of mailing shots about products which are already well-established in the market. To do so requires a combination of good product and market knowledge, combined with imagination and a flair for copywriting. This is where the company's own advertising department should come into its own. It should be the responsibility of the advertising manager to organize the gathering of material for direct-mail publicity. He and his staff should make it their business to find out as much as possible about the applications to which the product is put, with a view to establishing interesting case histories. To do so they will need the active support and interest of the salesforce.

One of the hazards of the use of direct mail lies in the fact that one is making a *direct* approach to the client on a personal basis. There is always an element of risk in that the recipient may regard what you have to say as an impertinence. A press advertisement suggesting to its readers that their firms have a need for a particular item of office equipment to improve their efficiency is entirely impersonal and cannot cause offence. A similar suggestion, contained in what purports to be a personally addressed letter, to the managing director of a client firm may provoke an entirely different response. It may be regarded as an implied criticism of his company's efficiency. People can be touchy about what is said in letters addressed to them personally.

The brash approach is therefore likely to be inappropriate for direct-mail advertising addressed to business executives. This does not mean that one must resort to a staid, dry-as-dust style. One can write a dignified letter that can still impart a compelling message. The point to remember is that direct mail, as opposed to press copywriting, is addressed not to a faceless multitude of casual readers, but to individual men and women occupying decision-making positions in their organizations, and with rather more than average intelligence, who will expect to receive correspondence couched in fluent yet courteous terms.

6.6   Trade exhibitions

Most industries are catered for by trade fairs usually held on an annual basis. Whether or not to take part in trade exhibitions is a question many organizations have to face.

For some very large firms, there is little option but to exhibit, at least at major shows organized for the specific industries they serve. Their standing may be such that their non-appearance could provoke widespread criticism. In much the same way as small retailers welcome the presence in the High Street of the large stores because they attract shoppers to the vicinity, so smaller exhibitors at trade fairs expect influential companies to take part to maintain the prestige of an exhibition and ensure the attendance of a large number of visiting buyers. Smaller firms may not be under the same pressure, but often feel obliged to exhibit simply because their competitors do so and they fear loss of face if they stay away.

This negative attitude results in part from the proliferation in the number of trade fairs within recent years. Exhibition-organizing has become big business. Unfortunately, exhibitions can be very expensive for companies taking part, in terms of site fees and stand construction costs, plus the incidentals of stand-staffing and entertainment of visitors. There is also a high lost-opportunity cost to be considered when members of one's salesforce are withdrawn from their territories to staff the exhibition stand, and the areas for which they are responsible are left unattended for a week or more during their absence.

It is these considerations that a company must weigh against the advantages of exhibition attendance.

One of the most important of these advantages is that of having a sales 'pitch' in the industry's major marketplace, to which will come a large proportion of the buyers and users of the product or service one is offering. Of no less importance is the opportunity an exhibition provides for customers and potential customers to get a broader view of the company and its activities. It is not always appreciated how limited is the view that customers have of their suppliers. Apart from the visits of salespersons and, on occasion, that of the sales manager, they see little of the firm that supplies them other than its delivery vehicles. When a customer steps on to the exhibition stand, however, he has the chance of seeing a complete range of the company's products, as well as meeting members of the management team and technical staff whom he would be unlikely to encounter in other circumstances. Equally, the company's senior staff has the opportunity to meet the representatives of client firms, who cease, henceforth, merely to be names that appear in sales reports and take on flesh and blood personalities.

A decision to exhibit will ensure being in the right place at the right time, with a chance to gain from the interest and activity which the fair organizers seek to generate. By staying away, one denies oneself that opportunity. Indeed it can be an indirect way of aiding one's competitors, because the interest of potential buyers will be concentrated solely on competitive products. Furthermore, regular customers often expect to see their suppliers at major trade exhibitions. They may well question the motives of a company that appears either too mean or too disinterested to take part.

Before one contracts to 'show' at a trade fair, there are certain elementary precautions it is wise to take. In the first place, some enquiry should be made of the experience and competence of the exhibition organizers. To put on a successful trade exhibition requires considerable capital investment, particularly in advertising and other forms of promotion, organizational skill and experienced and capable management. Next, one should look to the accommodation provided, both for exhibitors and visitors, the provision of lounges, bars and other catering facilities, and the adequacy of car-parking arrangements. If the exhibition is designed to attract a large number of visitors from other parts of the country and from overseas, the availability of good-class hotel accommodation in the vicinity will also have to be considered.

Once satisfied on these grounds, a company should consider the site which is available for its use in the exhibition hall. To ensure fairness in the disposal of sites, exhibition organizers often invite intending exhibitors to ballot for the more attractive positions. If one is unlucky and finds oneself saddled with a position that is unattractive, or a site whose area is considerably larger or smaller than required, it may be prudent not to exhibit at all. The size of the site one needs will depend upon the amount of money allocated to exhibition purposes, the relative importance of the particular show, and the number and nature of the products one is offering.

The construction of the stand itself will usually be undertaken by one of the many firms specializing in this kind of work. The stand contractor will, if desired, design and build the stand; arrange for the supply of water and electricity; provide carpeting, showcases and other fittings; and arrange for the hire of any furniture you may require.

In discussions with the stand designer, certain essentials should be kept in mind. The layout of the stand should be such that it invites entry by casual visitors, who may be dissuaded from doing so if entry points are obstructed by showcases or other fitments. Thus an open, uncluttered area at the front of the stand is a desirable feature, which will facilitate the reception of visitors by the stand personnel. One also needs to cater for the more confidential kind of conversation that may occur when a regular customer or an important potential client comes on to the stand for discussions and negotiations with senior company personnel. For these occasions one needs an enclosed area, furnished with two or three chairs and a small table for papers and refreshments, away from the goldfish-bowl atmosphere of the rest of the stand.

One of the problems of designing exhibition stands is to strike the right balance between aesthetic appeal and practical utility. When it is finally dressed with exhibits, showcases and furnishings, the stand should look attractive. It must be pleasing to the eye, not only to give a good impression of the company, but also because it must vie in visual appeal with the attractive-looking stands of competitors. It is a mistake, however, to overdo the aesthetic quality to the detriment of the function of the stand as a sales 'pitch'. It must be remembered that it is your products that visitors have come to see, not the fruits of the artistic genius of your publicity manager or the stand designer. This is where the ingenuity of the designer must show itself, by the use of artistry to enhance and not to detract from the commercial attractions of the exhibits.

If one wishes to avoid the expense of a tailor-made stand, stand 'shells' are available from contractors. These basic units may be hired or purchased, and are cheaper than a stand designed and constructed to one's specific requirements. Alternatively, there are stand-construction kits available, which have the advantage that they can be put together in various ways, thus permitting re-use from exhibition to exhibition, with adaptation to suit differing sizes and shapes of site.

One of the hazards of which the multi-product company should beware is that of cluttering the stand with too many exhibits. The analogy of the typical 'cheap-jack' retail shop window in comparison with that of a high-class store window display should be borne in mind. A firm that tries to cram too many exhibits on to its stand will defeat its object. Visitors will get a blurred impression of what it makes, because the sheer multiplicity of merchandise will be confusing. It is better to rely on one or two excellent examples of one's product range, prominently but tastefully displayed, and to relegate lesser items to subordinate positions, where they will not obtrude too forcefully upon the visitor's first impressions.

With an exhibition that lasts for a week or more, one has the problem of keeping exhibits in good condition, free from dust and grime. Wherever possible, items of a delicate nature, or those made of synthetic substances liable to static dust attraction, should be confined behind glass.

The staffing arrangements for exhibitions need careful planning. The normal procedure is to appoint a stand manager, preferably a senior member of the management staff who possesses good organizing ability. Another useful qualification for the stand manager is the capacity to remain calm and reasonably unruffled while all about him is in chaos! It will be his, or her, responsibility to ensure that all the services for operating the stand, including cleaning, procurement of refreshment supplies, water and electricity services, are functioning satisfactorily. The manager will liaise with the exhibition organizers to ensure that regulations governing the stand and its general maintenance are complied with. A further responsibility will be control of the company personnel who have been designated to staff the stand. For industrial exhibitions it is customary to bring salespersons in from the field and to support them with one or two technical personnel to deal with the more complex type of enquiry. Export staff are also normally in attendance to deal with export enquiries and conversation with non-English-speaking visitors.

Exhibition visitors, like shoppers in a retail store, have a tendency to come and go in droves. One moment a stand appears deserted but for what seems an over-abundance of the company's staff standing about looking bored. A moment later and visitors appears as though from nowhere and each member of the staff seems to be trying to deal with three callers at once. The stand manager should be alive to the bad impression given to a stand populated by weary-looking staff, waiting, during the doldrums, for visitors to turn up. It is easy to criticize, but only those who have done it for long periods know just how tiring exhibition work can be. The atmosphere often is heavy and sultry, and field sales personnel, unaccustomed to being indoors for days on end, tend to become jaded in such conditions.

To keep the staff interested, cheerful and enthusiastic, it is desirable to have a rota for stand attendance. Where possible, permit salespeople to alternate, with perhaps no more than two or three days on the stand in a row. Meal breaks should be taken in rotation, too, to ensure adequate staffing of the stand throughout the day. Ideally, arrangements should be made for staff to take meals away from the exhibition hall. They should not be expected to subsist on a hasty sandwich eaten on the stand. The maintenance of good staff morale will go a long way towards getting the most out of the business opportunity that exhibiting provides.

Some system will be needed to record all enquiries received on the stand and to ensure that they are adequately followed up later. An exhibition visitors book should be available, and the stand receptionist should be instructed to invite every visitor to sign it, with the addition of the name and address of the firm he/she represents. This provides a permanent record of the number of visitors received during the exhibition, and the names and addresses will make a useful addition to the company's mailing list.

When the exhibition is over, it is a good idea for the sales manager to write a letter of appreciation to each visitor, thanking him or her for calling at the stand and enclosing some general literature which will enable recall of the products or services the company offers. Where specific enquiries have been received, the sales manager should instruct the area salesperson – or, in the case of an overseas enquiry, the export manager should instruct the local agent – to follow up the contact made during the exhibition to cement good relations for the future. This is, after all, the ultimate purpose of industrial fairs: to make contact with potential clients. If the follow-up process is neglected, much of the company's investment in the exhibition will have been wasted.

6.7   Public relations

For many people, public relations is a nebulous activity. Its meaning is barely understood and its practitioners, sad to say, are sometimes regarded as charlatans. This is regrettable, because public relations has an important part to play in all forms of corporate understanding. For the modern business organization its role often is vital.

Once a firm has grown beyond the stage when it is personified by its proprietors or the members of its board, it has a need for a public-relations service. Unfortunately, public relations (PR) is often suspect, because it is equated in the eyes of some of the public with an attempt to deceive, to 'pull the wool over our eyes'. Yet this is the very opposite of its real purpose, which is to explain that which may not be fully apparent and to remove prejudice and misunderstanding based on ignorance of the facts.

Just as advertising will not repeatedly sell a product or service that fails to provide value for money, neither will PR, however skilful its methods, create permanently a good impression of an organization whose activities are opposed to the best interests of its customers, its shareholders, its employees or the public at large. While no company, any more than an individual, is likely to be wholly perfect, one must concede that all successful businesses must possess the virtue of enterprise, coupled with fair dealing, in order to remain successful. In the highly competitive world in which we live, however, it is not enough merely to be virtuous. One must be *seen* to be virtuous. PR takes account of this need to focus public attention on all the favourable aspects of a company's activities. By doing so, it endeavours to create a good climate of opinion in which the organization can pursue its legitimate aims.

The task of PR therefore is to ensure that the company is seen to have an effective and valuable influence upon the well-being of the trade or industry in which it operates. A good public image is not something that occurs accidentally. It requires conscious effort, and that effort needs to be channelled correctly to be effective.

Good PR is synonymous with good communications. This requires a knowledge of communications media, especially the press, radio and TV. It is for this reason that many PR personnel are former journalists or have had journalistic training.

What makes for good public relations? The creation of a good public image is likely to be based on the following:

1 An examination of the *existing* impression that the company makes.
2 A decision on the *desired* impression the company would like to make.
3 The establishment of *whose* opinion the company is really concerned about.
4 The preparation of a proposed programme of PR work to correct wrong impressions and to promote an improved company image.

Let us consider each of these steps in turn.

What is the existing impression the company creates?

The answer will be found by some elementary opinion research conducted among:

(*a*) the company's senior and junior management personnel,
(*b*) the office and sales staff,
(*c*) existing and potential customers' personnel.

An attempt to canvass the views of the company's employees on so emotive a subject as their opinion of the firm for which they work can produce a highly inaccurate response if carried out by a member of the firm's own management. Better results will be obtained if this is put in the hands of an outside agency experienced in this kind of work. Use of a prepared questionnaire which provides for answers of the 'yes' and 'no' type only is desirable, and a pledge of strict secrecy to respondents is essential.

When questioning the personnel of the company's customers, it is usual for a PR agency to disguise the identity of its client by making the subject of the survey a general one, aimed at discovering the opinions of user firms with regard to all suppliers of a particular product or service. This will ensure an uninhibited response.

What is the desired impression the company wishes to create?

This will depend on the company's marketing strategy. Whereas a reputation for square-dealing, efficiency and dependability is universally desired, not every company is looking for the same kind of public image. Very often firms operating in another sector of a market prefer not to have the same image. A company whose products have the renown of high craftsmanship, appealing to the 'quality' end of the market, may seek to give an impression very different from one that is operating in a more popular sector and offering a range of medium-quality, lower-priced merchandise.

Whose opinion is the company concerned about?

When we were discussing the preparation of an advertising campaign, we examined the need to identify the decision-makers to whom we wanted to appeal. Similarly, with PR, it is necessary to identify those whose opinion really matters, because not everybody's opinion will have the same value for our particular purposes. In our efforts to create a good impression of the company are we concerned especially about the views of the company's customers, its shareholders and its employees, or are we seeking the goodwill of a wider public? Firms whose trading interests are world-wide are sensitive to international opinion, and cannot afford to limit their image-building to a narrow section of a purely domestic market.

A proposed programme of work

Finally, we come to the consideration of a programme of PR activity to:

1   Correct any mistaken impressions of the company that may exist.
2   Establish the desired company image.
3   Direct this image to those whose opinion really matters to the company.

Mistaken impressions of the company that may exist – concern among employees regarding labour/management relations, concern on the part of local residents about the hazards of environmental pollution, concern on the part of existing or potential customers about the company's trading policies – call for energetic remedial action by PR. If the neighbouring community fears the danger to health threatened by factory effluent, PR must explain the facts, if necessary with the active support of the local health authorities. If labour relations within the company's plant are strained, PR should try to dispel the tension by a clear explanation of the firm's viewpoint, backed perhaps by factual releases to the local press describing the action being taken to improve working conditions.

From the point of view of marketing, it is important that PR should emphasize to the trade such aspects of company policy that will correct mistaken impressions regarding its trading arrangements. Business is built on confidence: the confidence of suppliers that the company will pay for the goods and services it buys in accordance with agreed terms; the confidence of employees that the company will ensure that their health and safety are protected while they are at work and that their wages and salaries will be paid regularly and promptly; the confidence of customers that the products the company supplies will be to specification, and that, if they have legitimate cause for complaint, the company will resolve the matter in a fair and responsible manner; above all, the confidence of shareholders that the company is well-managed and following policies that safeguard their investment.

In establishing the desired image, PR will take into account not only the products or services the firm is offering but those underlying factors we examined in our discussion about the advertising platform. For example, a manufacturer of food products is selling, in addition to a nourishing and time-saving pre-cooked meal, an assurance of hygiene and reliability in its preparation. PR will seek to stress these additional attributes by means of organized visits by groups of consumers to the company's factories, where housewives can see for themselves the stringent conditions in which the foodstuffs are handled. Similarly, the PR department of a leading manufacturer of chemical products will publicize, by means of press bulletins, lectures delivered to trade association meetings by members of the company's technical staff. Such lectures, given to an audience of qualified people within the trade or industry, provide an indication of the calibre of the technicians employed by the company to maintain the high quality of its products.

The chief methods of PR work can be summarized as:

1 Liaison with all communications media, including the editorial departments of national and local newspapers and trade journals, and also of radio and television networks.
2 The organization of press conferences for the announcement of important items of company news, such as new product launches or plant extension programmes.
3 The preparation of press releases of items of news such as new uses for existing products, the winning of important export contracts, the personalizing of directors and senior management personnel. Items likely to engender public goodwill, such as the company's charitable activities, participation in international trade missions and conferences, trade-association activity or the achievement of quality or similar meritorious awards, will also be publicized by the PR department.

6.8 Sponsorship

Another means of corporate image-building is the sponsorship of sporting and cultural activities. It is an aspect of public relations that has received much attention in recent years, and large sums of money are now channelled into this form of promotion by leading national and international organizations. Its basic objective is to raise corporate awareness by the close association of the company or brand name with popular activities or causes. This deployment of company funds to support arts festivals or sporting championships receives general public commendation and also has very considerable commercial value.

As a commercial strategy, sponsorship of a social activity depends for its success upon adequate promotion by the company of the sponsorship. The PR resources of the company must be utilized fully to gain the widest possible publicity for the sponsored activity in the media, thereby ensuring wide publicity and public awareness of the company or brand name associated with that activity.

Sponsorship will not attract product enquiries or sales leads, which is the task of advertising. What it will do is to promote a desirable popular image of the organization to assist those other elements of the marketing mix in achievement of the company's objectives.

Discussion questions

1   Discuss the purpose that the branding of a product is intended to achieve.
2   List some of the objectives of a consumer product advertising campaign.
3   What are the major considerations that affect the selection and use of an advertising agency?
4   Provide a proposed theme or 'platform' for advertising three different products or services of your choice.
5   What are the main benefits a company can expect to derive from participating in a trade exhibition and what principal considerations apply to this form of promotion?

7
Merchandising

Merchandising is a term used in marketing to denote all those sales-promotion activities that aim to generate the customer's interest in the product or service other than conventional press and television advertising, direct mail or the use of PR. The purpose of merchandising is to bring product and customer into the closest possible proximity in order that the attributes of the merchandise may become fully apparent and, in effect, sell themselves.

7.1 The principles of merchandising

The principles of merchandising are as old as trading itself. The pedlar who travelled from village to village in Norman times presented his wares by inviting his clientele to see, touch, hear or smell the goods he had to offer. The market stallholder through the centuries has practised the art of merchandising by encouraging his public to examine his merchandise, to pick up items and test them: knives for sharpness of blade, silks for fineness and delicacy, cloths for weight and firmness of weave.

In our more sophisticated age we have seen the same principles of merchandising exploited with success by such stores as Woolworth and Marks & Spencer, pathfinders of the self-selection method of retailing. Merchandising techniques have been developed as an aid to the retailing of practically every class of product. Much of the success of marketing depends on one's ability to find novel ways of getting one's goods literally into the hands of potential users.

The greatly extended use of merchandising techniques has not resulted just in response to marketing theory. There has been an important practical consideration that has coerced both manufacturer and distributor to adopt new methods of presentation – the steady rise in the cost of labour in retail distribution, coupled with increased difficulty in attracting a sufficient number of men and women to work in retail shops and stores. The quality of the labour force of the distributive trades has fallen while its cost has risen. As a result, personal selling has largely disappeared in many trades. Means other than the persuasive ability of the shop assistant have had to be found to sell goods to the public. The result has been the rapid development of merchandising as a means of reducing the shopkeeper's dependence upon the selling skill of his staff.

The modern self-service store may be said to have been born of merchandising out of labour shortage. Supermarkets can be operated almost entirely without skilled labour. Staff is needed only to replenish the display racks with merchandise drawn from the stock room; cashiers, aided by adding machines, check the goods purchased and collect the money. No personal selling of any kind is required.

7.2   Factors in merchandising

There are certain factors that have become apparent from the experience of self-service retailing that are important for all types of marketing. The first is the undoubted fact that goods sell by sight and touch. The old notion that customers should be asked not to touch the merchandise unless they intend to buy has become an anachronism.

Secondly, the positioning of goods within the retail outlet plays an important part in selling them. It is probably not surprising that items placed at eye-level sell faster than those placed either above or below the level at which the majority of customers are likely to look. What may be less apparent is the fact that a large display of one item of merchandise will promote greater sales than a large selection of different products. Furthermore, the artistically constructed pyramid that the customer dare not touch for fear of producing an avalanche produces less sales than a jumbled display that invites handling and examination.

In a personal selling shop, assistants can suggest additional items of purchase to the customer to create extra sales. The self-service store does not have this facility. In order to draw the attention of shoppers to special offers or slow-moving merchandise, it is necessary to get them to circulate. One of the ways this can be done is to scatter the display of 'demand goods' – those that are bought regularly – all over the shop, thus compelling customers to move about and visit each part of it. If one alters the position of these displays frequently, this mobility will be maintained; otherwise regular shoppers quickly learn where to find their essential items of purchase and defeat the merchandiser's attempts to make them look at every shelf and be conscious of the slower-selling goods he hopes to promote.

Another important factor in self-service retailing is that the whole shop should be treated as one for the purposes of merchandising.

This is a breakaway from the traditional departmentalism. It aids the juxtaposing of goods to create related sales – eggs and bacon or fruit and cream as menu ideas – bearing in mind that research shows that the majority of purchasing decisions are made after and not before the customer enters the shop.

These are merely the rudiments of the merchandising of consumer goods. They are important for firms in pursuit of a marketing approach to the promotion of their goods, enabling them to anticipate and grasp more readily some of the opportunities that the use of merchandising techniques may offer. More sophisticated methods are to be seen in the development of so-called 'package-deals', such as the supply of deep-freeze refrigerators together with a contract to deliver to the user a regular supply of frozen goods. The 'free-trial' offer of the mail-order trader, in which he permits his prospective customer to have the use of an appliance, a book or a set of audio tapes for seven days and return them if he is not satisfied, is a good example of a more advanced form of merchandising. It provides the consumer with unfettered experience of the product before he buys it. Car distributors encourage potential customers to have a free ride in the model of their choice before making up their minds whether or not to purchase. Similarly, many manufacturers of food products, upon introducing a new brand, invite shoppers to taste a sample before buying the package.

Most distributors of domestic appliances will arrange demonstrations in customers' homes. Some of the most imaginative examples of merchandising are in fact designed to introduce the product in the home. Part-time agents are recruited to promote a variety of merchandise by means of organized coffee parties, at which groups of housewives are invited to drink coffee at a friend's home and witness a free demonstration of the product. They are able to seek information, discuss the product's attributes and, by a process of mutual conviction, be assured of its merits and desirability.

7.3   Planning promotions

In view of the significant role merchandising will play in the marketing of its product, a company should consider the types of promotion it may be decided to use and to formulate a strategy on the following lines:

1   *Objectives*. The objectives of the company's merchandising activities for the next twelve-month period should be sent out in detail. These may include:

   (*a*)   The launching of a new product.

(*b*)   The launching of an existing product into a new market.

(*c*)   Increasing the product's market share.

2   *Methods.* The merchandising methods to be employed to achieve these aims will depend upon the nature of the product and the market. One or more of the following may be suitable:

(*a*)   Free demonstrations.

(*b*)   Special displays.

(*c*)   Price reductions.

(*d*)   Deal-ins or trade promotions.

(*e*)   Deal-outs or consumer promotions.

Under this heading also one should define the product or products, the geographical areas and the class of customers it is intended to feature in the promotions.

3   *Cost.* Merchandising activities can be expensive and erode profits quickly unless kept under tight financial control. The cost of every promotion should be budgeted in advance, and related to the increase in revenue it is designed to achieve.

4   *Training.* The salesforce will have to be briefed on all promotional arrangements, and may require some special training in order to play its part to the full. Some large firms, particularly those producing grocery and pharmaceutical products, employ specialist merchandising staff who operate alongside and in addition to the salespersons. The merits of this system are the saving of the time of the salesforce, saving in the cost and inconvenience of having to train salespeople to undertake merchandising work, and the assurance that the merchandising effort is being undertaken by persons experienced and qualified in this specialized aspect of marketing. On the other hand, there is the hazard of possible confusion that can result from divided responsibilities, and the inconvenience which may be caused to distributors who have to deal with more than one representative from the same supplier.

5   *Coordination.* Successful merchandising depends upon proper coordination of the activities of all departments in the company likely to be engaged in special promotions. The production, despatch, advertising, PR and sales departments should all be kept fully informed, and cooperate with the merchandising personnel to obtain the maximum results from the exercise.

6   *Programming.* Good organization is vital to merchandising. Arrangements have to be made well in advance not only with other departments within the company but with such outside agencies as printers; manufacturers of merchandise for premium offers; distributors of coupons, samples or sales literature; as well as with retailers. A programme of dates for each stage of the

merchandising campaign should be prepared and circulated to all concerned.

It is fairly standard practice, in the field of packaged groceries, soaps, detergents and toothpaste, for promotions – or 'deals' – to be in two parts. The first part, called the 'deal-in', usually consists of an offer by the manufacturer to the retailer of a price reduction for a specified period, conditional upon the retailer accepting an agreed minimum supply of the product. In the second part, known as the 'deal-out', a special attraction is offered to the consumer. This can take several forms. It may be the offer of some desirable item, such as a kitchen utensil, or a toy or gadget, which the housewife can purchase at a reduced price upon presentation of two wrappers or labels of the product. Alternatively, it may be entry into a competition, with the chance to win a holiday for two, a car, or a considerable cash prize; or the offer may perhaps be merely the opportunity to buy the product at a reduced price.

7.4   Trade promotions

The purpose of a trade promotion is to induce the retailer to acquire an increased stock of the product. If this can be achieved, then certain advantages must automatically accrue. The trader who holds a large stock of one's brand is compelled to make a special effort to sell it. He will take an active part in the manufacturer's 'deal-out' campaign to attract increased sales of the product to the consumer. This propensity of the retailer to push the sale of one's product is especially important where brand preference on the part of the buying public is known to be weak. The shopkeeper can bring influence to bear on the consumer's choice of product, either by giving it prominent display in the fastest-selling position in the store or, in the case of personal service shops, by instructing his staff to introduce it to customers. The pressure of a heavy stockholding can produce advantageous results for the manufacturer, particularly where the retailer has been stocked with a new product or an improvement to an existing product, and where fast build-up of consumer sales is seen as vital.

One of the side effects of a successful 'deal-in' is that, having been induced to purchase a large consignment of one's own brand, the retailer's current cashflow situation may compel him to limit the stock he holds of competitive brands. In some markets where competition is particularly fierce it can be almost as important to deny the opportunity for sales to competitors as it is to achieve sales for yourself.

There are three main methods employed by manufacturers to

encourage retailers to accept a bulk supply of their particular brand. The first is the provision of either a percentage discount or a straight cash allowance for each case of the product ordered during the period of the promotion. This discount is given for every case of the product that the retailer orders, not merely on the excess quantity he accepts over and above his normal ordering quantity. An alternative method is to increase the case content, i.e. if the normal case contains ten items of the product, during the period of the promotion cases containing, say, twelve items will be supplied at the normal price applicable to ten items. The third method, one that often appeals to the proprietors of small independent shops, is the offer of a gift in kind for the placing of an order of a given size. The manufacturer buys a quantity of gifts at a discount, and the cost to him of a promotion of this nature often will work out considerably cheaper than the provision of a cash allowance.

Apart from the tactical advantage to be gained from filling up the retailer's shelves with one's product and thus denying sales to competitors, the 'deal-in' offers the manufacturer a further benefit. It provides a means of rapidly transferring his own stocks and freeing his capital for other forms of investment or to create additional liquidity should the need arise.

7.5   Consumer promotions

The 'deal-in' will, of course, achieve greater long-term benefits if it is accompanied by a 'deal-out' or consumer promotion, designed to help the shopkeeper to sell quickly these additional stocks that he has acquired on good terms. There are five frequently employed techniques for consumer promotions:

1   The use of coupons.
2   The use of self-liquidating offers.
3   The supply of bargain packs.
4   The provision of samples.
5   The offer of 'give-aways'.

Coupon promotions

In this type of promotion, the product manufacturer supplies to the consumer, by hand or by post, a coupon that offers a price reduction of a stated amount against the purchase of the product, provided it is made within a specified time. The consumer 'redeems' the coupon by presenting it to the shopkeeper at the time the purchase is made. The retailer obtains from the manufacturer repayment of the value of the coupon, together with a small handling charge.

Coupon-promotion schemes provide an incentive to the consumer to buy one's products. They are also an additional incentive to the retailer to stock it in order that he may enjoy the business to be obtained by consumers wishing to redeem their coupons.

It is not surprising that the higher the coupon value, the higher the redemption rate will be. There are, however, certain problems. Where a brand is already established in the market, many people who will be redeeming coupons would have bought the product in any case. Each sale to a regular user therefore will be made at a lower price than would have occurred if the promotion had not taken place. Another difficulty is that known as *malredemption*, when the shop-keeper accepts the coupon in part payment for goods other than the product for which it was intended. There is no easy answer to this problem, and producers who embark on a coupon scheme have to accept it as part of the cost of the promotion.

Self-liquidating offers

A self-liquidating offer is one in which the product manufacturer, having purchased in quantity a particular article for promotional purposes, advertises it to the consumer at virtually cost price plus a number of labels from his product. The benefit to the consumer is that he/she is able to buy the article concerned at a very low price because of the manufacturer's bulk purchase. The manufacturer and the retailer benefit from the extra sales of the product that result from the consumer's additional purchases to obtain the necessary labels. The offer is termed self-liquidating, because the consumer's purchase of the article reimburses the manufacturer for his original outlay.

Bargain packs

This method consists merely of an offer of the product, usually in a special pack or wrapper, at a reduced price for a limited period of time. The consumer is invited, for example, to 'save 10p' by 'buying while the offer lasts'. The manufacturer hopes to win for his brand new customers who will be tempted, by the opportunity to save money, to try the product. Retailers, anxious to attract additional sales during the period of the offer, are likely to give the product extra prominence and to undertake special displays. The problem that arises, once again, is that advantage will be taken of the offer by many regular customers who would have bought the product anyway.

Sampling

The offer of a free sample has undoubted appeal for many people, and some product manufacturers run promotion schemes by giving away either a full pack or a sample of their product in the expectation that, once tried and found acceptable by the housewife, it is likely to be purchased regularly in the future. This is not, however, a method that recommends itself to a brand leader or a producer whose product already holds an appreciable market share, because too great a loss of revenue can result from the use of free samples by users who would normally have bought the product. For a manufacturer new to the market, however, there is advantage in the sampling method. Not only does the new brand obtain wide distribution and testing by consumers, but during the period of the promotion a drop in the sales of competitive brands is likely to occur.

'Give-aways'

The provision of 'give-aways', such as plastic flowers, small toys or novelties, with each item of the product that is sold is yet another method of motivating the consumer to buy one's brand in preference to that of competitors.

There are considerable advantages to be gained from the use of promotions. It has been established that an increase in sales of up to 1,000 per cent can be achieved during the period of a well-considered and well-run campaign. There are, however, disadvantages. After all the extra effort and outlay – on special printing, the provision of additional display material, the distribution of coupons and samples – has been costed, it has often been found that there has been no lasting increase in sales. Consumers who have been attracted to buy the product during the promotion period rapidly revert once the campaign is over to their former buying habits. Indeed the very profusion of coupon schemes, self-liquidating offers and bargain packs provided by competing manufacturers has the effect of weakening the brand loyalty that the producers' advertising seeks to promote.

Discussion questions

1   Describe the meaning and scope of merchandising.
2   Describe some of the ways in which marketing uses merchandising techniques.
3   Discuss the principal considerations that apply in the planning of:
    (a) a trade promotion; (b) a consumer promotion.

8
Marketing and sales

Market segmentation enables us to differentiate between the needs of various customer groups that collectively comprise the total market for any given product or service. By means of the marketing mix, we can formulate a standard package of benefits designed to match the perceived needs of any one segment. What we should not lose sight of, however, is that even the smallest segment realistically must consist of many thousands of people. A standardized package cannot hope to have equal appeal to every single individual.

For the vast majority of branded goods this is not a problem. Individual preference is largely catered for by the wide variety of such products on the market. Because they are generally low-priced, consumers can shop around until they decide upon the offering that approximates most closely to their particular requirements.

There are, however, other situations where customer needs can only be satisfied by personal contact between seller and buyer:

1   Where the customer needs personal advice in the selection of the product.
2   Where the customer needs special benefits not provided by the standard offering.
3   Where the price the seller wishes to charge and the price the buyer is prepared to pay are not in accord, and negotiation is required.

In all such situations, advertising and promotion alone will not effect a sale. Where satisfaction of the *individual* needs of the customer is paramount, personal selling is essential.

When the seller meets the buyer face to face, he can assess by observation and by conversation the specific needs of that buyer. He can present the standard features of his product in the form of specific benefits for that buyer. When he meets a second buyer, he will assess that this buyer's needs, although very similar, are not precisely the same. Now he will present the standard features of his product in the form of specific benefits to suit these somewhat different needs of the second buyer. This is what personal selling is all about.

8.1   The role of the sales department

In many organizations the role of marketing manager and of sales manager are still combined. Where this occurs, one usually finds that the manager is trying to do two jobs: to control the company's marketing activities from the office and trying to control the sales-force in the field. Neither one task can be tackled efficiently without neglecting the other. This is bad organization, because direction of a salesforce is a full-time job. The effective performance of any group operation is dependent upon the effectiveness of its leader, and this is particularly true in the management of sales.

Ask most young salespeople to state their ambition, and you are likely to be told they want to become sales manager. A laudable aim no doubt, but the fact is that a good salesperson does not necessarily make a good manager. A characteristic of many successful sales-people is an individual outlook, an ability and desire to work on their own initiative, with the minimum of assistance or interference from colleagues and superiors. Good salespersons are not necessarily good organizers. They may be able to organize themselves, but often lack the desire or ability to organize others.

In view of these factors, one cannot be sure to find a good sales manager merely by promoting from among one's best salespeople. Fortunately, however, a good sales manager does not necessarily have to be a good salesperson. Indeed those who, above all else, want to sell may find it difficult to settle down to the task of management. They may find the detailed work of organizing others irksome, and may tend to revert to being super-salespersons, thus not only neglect-ing their new duties of management but also duplicating and interfer-ing with the activities of the salespeople under their control.

The sales manager, ideally, should be a person with a philosophical nature protected by a reasonably thick skin. Certainly sales manage-ment is no task for either the sensitive neurotic or the unfeeling slavedriver. A good sales team will only work at its best if it is led by a person judged by subordinates as fair-minded. An effective sales team takes time to create. Once created, it needs astute control to ensure that morale is maintained at a high level. As we shall see later, both morale and motivation are essential features of the personal selling element of the marketing mix.

The functions of the sales manager

The function of a sales manager is not, primarily, to sell. It is to organize the activities of the salesforce to ensure maximum effectiveness in promoting and maintaining the flow of orders from customers. The aim should be the highest appropriate sales volume at the lowest operational cost. The manager should interpret to the salesforce the objectives of the company in the market in which it operates, and the specific role that sales has to play in their achievement.

In the field of grocery or pharmaceutical products, for example, this will include the maintenance of good relations with wholesale or retail customers to ensure they not only maintain adequate stocks of the firm's products but are making sufficient efforts to resell them. The sales personnel should also be ready to assist by offering advice on the display of the products and by obtaining for distributors point-of-sale materials to associate with promotional advertising in the press or on television, with the view of bringing the consumer to the point of decision to make a purchase.

A sales team responsible for selling consumer goods in wholesale or retail outlets usually requires persons of varying calibre. Selling to large multiples means negotiating with highly experienced buyers, located in central purchasing offices, to set up satisfactory 'deals'. It is obvious that only those possessing considerable experience and ability will succeed at this level of commercial transaction. Once such 'deals' have been struck, however, another category of salesperson is needed to represent the company to the individual supermarket or shop managers. The task now will be to ensure that these retail branch outlets are properly serviced with adequate stocks and display material, and to sort out any major or minor problems that from time to time are bound to arise.

Some multiple firms not only place their contracts from a central buying point but also call forth supplies centrally, giving instructions to the supplier to deliver direct to the branch shops. There are others, however, who operate differently. Having placed their contract for the supply of a particular brand, they leave to the individual branch manager the placing of call-off instructions against the contract. Here the salesperson calling on the retail outlet has a full-scale selling job to do. The retailer's selling space is limited and he has room to stock only a certain quantity of any one commodity. It becomes the responsibility of the salesperson to ensure *his* product maintains as good a share as possible of this limited space, because this will make sure that his brand will be readily available to meet consumer demand and will also limit the space left for competitive brands. In the packaged foodstuffs market, for example, this battle for precious retail display space is very real.

Before deciding upon a detailed sales policy, a company should examine its current sales situation. Are the resources at the disposal of the sales department adequate for the tasks they have to perform? It may find that they are adequate in total but are not being correctly deployed. This is a not uncommon failing, and many firms discover they have fallen into the classic error of devoting, perhaps, 80 per cent of their selling effort to chase business that is producing only 20 per cent of sales revenue.

An enquiry into salesforce performance should consider, first, the number of sales personnel the company employs and how they are organized on a territorial basis. Calling patterns should be examined to establish the number of calls that sales representatives make on average in a week, and the frequency with which calls are made on different types of outlets: retail shops and supermarkets, wholesalers, the central buying departments of multiple stores. How many of the total number of such outlets in the country are in fact being visited regularly by the company's sales personnel?

Secondly, to establish a guide to the effectiveness of current selling techniques, one should examine the ratio of orders received to the number of calls made. What is the average size of order obtained by each individual member of the sales team? How does this compare with the average achieved by the total team?

Thirdly, attention should be given to the existing level of distribution the company has achieved for its products throughout the trade. How does this compare with competitive brands?

Finally, what are the current methods for training and supervising the sales team? Are there training schemes for new entrants or refresher courses for established salespeople? What methods exist for communication between the sales department and sales representatives in the field? The current system for reporting sales calls may need review, together with the methods used to keep the salesforce informed of special promotions, new advertising campaigns and any changes to product formulation or package design.

Salespeople's journey cycles

In order to establish the optimum number of salespeople needed to sell the company's products into a given segment of any market it will be necessary to examine the current journey cycles of the existing sales team. A journey cycle is the period of time it takes a salesman to call once upon all the customers allocated to him. Thus an eight-week cycle means it takes that length of time to make one visit to each of his customers. Put another way, if the nature of the product to be sold and the geographical scatter of customers results in an average of six customer visits per day, a salesman working a five-day week will take five weeks to service 150 accounts.

It will be apparent, however, that, out of a total of 150 retailers, some will require more frequent attention than others. In deciding the frequency of calls necessary for individual outlets there are various factors to be considered. One is the amount of stock particular retailers are prepared to hold. A trader who is prepared to hold only a few weeks' stock of any one brand will require more frequent visits from his supplier, in order to place orders to replenish this stock, than one willing to order sufficient supplies to cover his requirements for a considerable period. Another factor is the frequency of visits undertaken by one's competitors upon major retail outlets. We have already referred to the battle that exists between product manufacturers in fast-selling grocery fields for a maximum share of the retailer's precious shelf space for their products. It is only by frequent calls that the salesperson can maintain a strong personal relationship with the shopkeeper and thus ensure a fully adequate display for his company's brand.

On the other hand, one must consider the costs of sales calls, plus the cost of the execution of the orders received, including the movement of the goods from the warehouse, transportation, the issue of delivery notes and invoices, and the subsequent collection of payment, and set this against the value of the business secured. Small or medium-sized outlets may need regular sales contact, but this can be provided by telephone sales personnel based at head office to ask for repeat orders and to check that everything is satisfactory. This can be supported by visits from the area salesperson at intervals of perhaps every six to eight weeks.

8.2   Appointment and control of the salesforce

The recruitment, training and control of the salesforce is an important part of sales management. In small or medium-sized companies it is a task that all too frequently is given less attention than it deserves. Finding people who want to enter selling is not difficult. A high proportion of young people, failing any other specific bent, opt for a sales career in the belief that the job carries with it a considerable personal freedom, favourable employment conditions and an enviable social status. While these attributes undoubtedly apply to selling, there is another side to the coin. Field sales personnel work in all weathers, often for long hours at a stretch, away from the comforts and security of home. They may at times be treated in cavalier fashion by customers, and should they fail to maintain a satisfactory level of sales, their lives may be made miserable by the badgering of a sales manager under pressure to produce improved results.

It is little wonder therefore that there can be a considerable turnover of salespeople, and the composition of a sales team is seldom static. Apart from the fledgling who becomes disillusioned and quits selling for more tranquil fields, one has the problem of keeping the more successful personnel, who may fail to see the prospects of advancement they want and who decide to move on, possibly to a competitor, where the grass appears to grow a little greener.

Staff turnover in the salesforce is something to be avoided as much as possible. It takes even an experienced salesperson a considerable time – anything from six months to two years – before he or she is fully established and has become sufficiently well-known and accepted by customers to obtain the best results. Where company policy, or the nature of the product or service to be sold, results in the recruitment of inexperienced personnel, a period of several weeks or even months may elapse before new entrants have been sufficiently trained to take over a territory.

As trade and industry continue to expand, competition between employers to recruit people with suitable selling potential increases. The proportion of sales management time that must be devoted to recruitment also increases, and with it the costs incurred by the sales department.

Recruitment and selection

The means adopted to recruit salespeople will depend upon the degree of experience one is seeking, the nature of the market to be approached, and the type of product to be sold. The calibre of salesmanship the job demands will have a bearing on the source from which applicants will be drawn. Generally speaking, one looks for a different type of individual to sell materials and components to industrial users than one seeks to sell branded consumer goods into wholesale or retail outlets. The task of selling, for example, a piece of capital equipment to the managing director of a large engineering firm differs from that of negotiating the sale of a new brand of biscuits to the chief buyer of a national grocery chain. The basic principles of salesmanship will apply to both situations. There will, however, be modifications in the method of approach. The expertise required of the industrial salesperson will be neither greater nor less than that required of the biscuit salesperson, but there will be differences in emphasis and in the background training of one to the other.

There are also differences in the level of negotiating ability required in any specific trade or industry. The person who will negotiate the biscuit contract with the major retail food chain will exhibit skills which clearly would not find adequate expression at the branch shop level of selling, where the collection of stock orders and the handling of routine queries was the principal function.

It is important therefore to decide in precise terms what it is that the salesperson has to do. A job analysis should be prepared, listing the functions to be performed, the responsibilities the person will carry, the limitations within which he or she will have to work, and the results the individual will be expected to achieve. Such an analysis will clarify management thinking on the 'job to be done'. It will also create a picture of the kind of person required to do it.

There are five main sources from which the salesforce may be recruited:

1 *By recommendation.* Customers often provide a source for the recruitment of experienced sales personnel. Aware that a salesperson, representing another organization, and of whom they have formed a good opinion, is dissatisfied with his or her current situation, they will often 'pass the word on'. When an applicant is recruited in such circumstances, much of the initial screening for suitability will already have been done. The problem of course is that it is purely coincidental for a suitable recommended candidate to turn up just at the time one is about to recruit new staff. If the individual is highly suitable, however, it may be sensible to try and find room for him/her within the existing sales team in anticipation of future expansion.

2 *By direction application.* A similar situation exists when an individual seeking sales employment makes a direct approach to a company entirely on his own initiative and not in response to any advertisement. Here again, if he is of a calibre suitable to sell the company's products, it may be a wise move to engage him against the day when further sales personnel are required. The initiative that prompts someone to make a direct approach to a firm not currently seeking staff has its own virtue. If that person is already experienced in the particular trade or industry in which the company operates, he has made a specific choice. He has a preconception of the company and its products, which obviously appeal to him, and if taken on, he could well make a significant contribution.

3 *By internal promotion.* There is much to commend the practice of recruiting sales personnel from within the organization. Apart from the consideration that 'the devil you know is better than one you don't', the principle of internal promotion is a morale-booster for inside staff. But the particular virtue of internal promotion to the salesforce is that it enables a company to 'grow its own' recruits, rather than have to go outside the firm each time a new salesperson is needed. A person selected from within the company will know broadly how it operates, and will bring to the new task a knowledge of its products and many of its customers. Above all, such an individual will be unsullied by bad training or bad experience gained elsewhere.

4 *By means of recruitment agencies.* Such agencies have proliferated in recent years to meet the increasing problems of staff recruitment. The cost of using the services of an agency usually differs little from that of a display announcement in a national newspaper or leading trade journal, plus the cost of management time spent in the screening of unsuitable applicants from advertisements.

The agency will ensure that the qualifications and experience of applicants notified to the company at least accord with the specification that has been given. Where a company seeks to recruit people with no previous sales experience, however, the use of an agency is of little value. In the absence of any selling 'track record', the assessment of the individual must depend to a large extent upon the personal opinion of the interviewer, and sales managers will usually prefer to form their own judgement of an applicant's suitability.

5 *From advertisements.* In spite of the usefulness of the above methods, it is in response to company advertisements in the press that the majority of salespersons are recruited. It can be an expensive method, and time-consuming for management personnel. Where an organization is highly successful in its operations and the need for the recruitment of additional members for the salesforce is a reflection of that success, management may decide that time spent in this task is well worthwhile. However, if repetitive recruitment is the result of salespersons leaving the company because they have failed in their jobs, or have become disillusioned with the firm and have decided to go elsewhere, the sales manager may only have himself to blame. He will need to improve his selection methods.

What makes a good salesperson?

Various test methods have been applied to answer this question. Unfortunately it has been impossible to measure a person's selling aptitude accurately. One of the methods that has been tried is to establish an analysis of the interests of successful salespeople and to use this in the selection of applicants possessing a similar pattern of interests. It has been found, however, that skills and interests are not the same thing. There are millions who follow football with avid interest, for example, but comparatively few of them actually play football and fewer still are skilled players.

An alternative method has been to put to the candidate a number of questions about his or her motives and opinions, with a view to comparing these with the objectives and views of people with good sales records. The problem, however, is that intelligent people are quick to anticipate the general drift of the questions and provide answers they think will succeed in getting them the job!

The major difficulty in arriving at any satisfactory method of human assessment is that no two people are exactly alike and can only be loosely classified by means of very generalized characteristics. In spite of the many abortive studies undertaken in this field, there has been growing realization that two aspects of human character play a predominant part in the establishment of selling ability. These are known as ego-drive and empathy. Ego-drive means the over-riding need for success: there is a dominant urge to succeed that transcends all other considerations. A person with strong ego-drive will stop at nothing to achieve set objectives. Unfortunately ego-drive alone does not make for success in selling. Those with ego-drive and nothing more will be over-persistent and oblivious to the feelings of others.

A good salesperson is one whose ego-drive is matched by an equally strong degree of empathy: the ability to adjust to the re-actions of others. The salesperson with good empathy will be creative in his sales approach and will be capable of modifying that approach to suit changing circumstances.

Efforts have been made to permutate empathy and ego-drive. There is a degree of both ego-drive and empathy in most people, and the theory is that, where both elements are strong in an individual, he or she will have good selling abilities and be capable of 'closing' sales. Tests have shown, however, that comparatively few people possess these qualities in equal proportion. Thus a person with strong empathy and reduced drive is likely to possess excellent personal qualities but, because of his lack of drive, he will often fail to 'close' business. Equally, someone with a high degree of ego-drive and weak empathy will tend not only to ride roughshod over both colleagues and customers, he will also fail to win business because of his lack of understanding of the reactions of his clients. An individual with a low degree of both ego-drive and empathy will undoubtedly make a poor showing in selling. His personal qualities and understanding of other people will be limited and he will possess little of the driving force needed to achieve sales.

8.3   Training and salesforce improvement

Sales training should be continuous, not confined solely to the induction training of recruits. Experienced members of the sales team will benefit from refresher courses that add to their product knowl-edge and assist them to improve their sales performance.

In drawing up a training programme, you should consider certain basic objectives. Sales personnel need to be told how to achieve the optimum level of sales in their territories. The sales approach should be explained fully, with a structured method for the presentation of the range of products to individual customers, together with guidance on the planning of journeys and call frequencies to make the most economic use of their time. The standards of performance required of salespeople should be set by the sales manager during the period of induction training. Their maintenance will be achieved only by fre-quent visits on the part of the manager to the various territories,

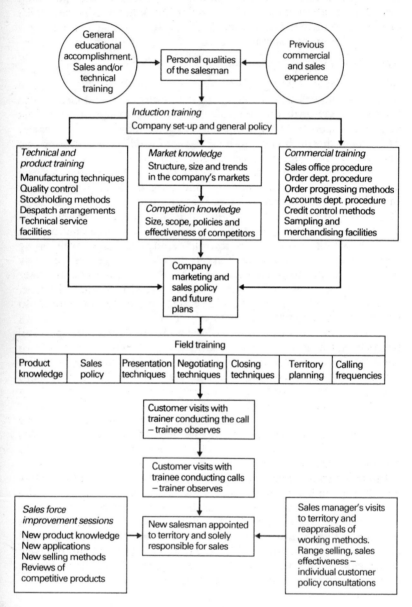

Figure 8.1　*Training and salesforce improvement*

when a number of joint calls should be made with the individual salesman or saleswoman, to assess the continuing effectiveness of his or her performance. See Figure 8.1.

Appointing a training instructor

In a company that employs a large number of salespeople it may be necessary for the sales manager to delegate certain aspects of sales training. Some firms put their new recruits in the care of their best salespersons, with the intention that they should learn by example. This can create problems, because the best salespersons may not be performing their duties in the manner prescribed by the manager. The top-calibre salesman, say, may long since have discarded the orthodox approach, with no disadvantage to his sales performance. In all fields one finds that rules and regulations, devised to safeguard the unwary, only cramp the style of those whose knowledge and experience is such that they have outgrown them. Unorthodox methods employed by top salespeople, however, may well prove disastrous for a tyro. At the very best, the recruit may be confused by the contradiction between what he has been told by the sales manager and what he sees practised by one of the firm's top salesmen. Furthermore, it is one thing to be a successful practitioner, another to be an equally successful instructor.

If the recruit is to be instructed in accordance with the principles and practices set by the company management, it will be advisable to consider the appointment of a training officer. Sometimes this can be achieved by withdrawing from the field a senior salesperson and putting him or her through a course of instruction on how to train recruits. Managers who are reluctant to use one of their better salespersons for this purpose should remember that the loss of one good person from the field can be more than offset by the advantages to be derived from reinforcement of the sales team of properly trained newcomers.

Induction training may need to be spread over a few weeks or a few months, depending upon the complexity of the product range and the firm's markets. The whole of this time need not be spent under instruction. It is important that the recruit should be given adequate opportunity to put into practice that which has been taught. It will also allow the instructor to adjust the training scheme to suit the pace of an individual's progress. Weaknesses can be corrected before moving on to more complex aspects of the work.

'Inside' training

Newcomers to a company need to be given an insight into how the firm thinks and how it operates. 'Inside' training should therefore begin with the company's history and its future aims. Recruits should then be taken through all aspects of the work of the firm's various departments, with a particular emphasis on those whose activities will impinge upon their own future work in the field. The systems by which customers' orders are processed need detailed explanation to ensure the newcomers fully grasp how the sales and order sections operate. Similarly, they should be shown how the company's credit control system works, how goods are invoiced and statements prepared. The methods adopted to encourage prompt payment, such as the provision of discounts, should be discussed.

The next stage of training should enable recruits to discover how the products they will be required to sell are actually produced and packaged. Particular attention needs to be given to quality standards, and novices should be initiated into what constitutes a reject and why. They should be given every opportunity to discover the special features of the company's products and what distinguishes them in terms of quality, utility and value from those of competitors. From production they should move to the despatch department to find out the methods of coding and documentation, and the means by which goods are shipped to customers.

Having gained some understanding of the nature of the merchandise they will be selling, trainees should now receive instruction on the structure of the market and types of outlet in which the company's products are sold, as well as the nature and strength of the competition. A further and most important part of this section of the training programme will deal with the methods by which the salespersons will communicate with head office, such as sales reports, order forms and similar documentation.

'Outside' training

Before deciding how the salesforce should be trained, one must consider the duties it has to perform. These will vary from company to company and market to market. The main line of demarcation, however, lies between the selling of consumer goods to wholesale or retail distributors and the selling of materials or components to industrial users.

Let us consider, first, the role of the consumer-goods salesperson selling into grocery, pharmaceutical and related fields. In markets where branded goods are dominant, consumer demand is achieved mainly by national advertising. At first glance the need for any personal selling may seem questionable on the grounds that if enough shoppers ask for the product, retailers are bound to stock it. There is, however, more to selling than encouraging the consumer to want to buy. Having established a demand by means of national advertising and other promotions, the manufacturer must ensure that it can be satisfied. We have seen that marketing has been defined as getting the right goods to the right place at the right time and making a profit out of the operation. Unless the right goods are in the right place at the right time the consumer will be unable to buy them.

The salesforce of the branded-goods manufacturer plays a vital part in the logistics of the marketing operation. It is to ensure that a sufficient number of retailers have sufficient stocks to satisfy the popular demand that advertising has created. Furthermore, it is not enough for the retailer merely to stock the product. He must actively try to resell it. To do so, he must be persuaded to devote sufficient shelf space and display area to enable his customers to see and, if necessary, to examine the product. He must exhibit sufficient display material to reinforce the work done by the TV commercials, and thus, finally, persuade the housewife to make the decision to buy.

In order to achieve these ends the cooperation of the retailer is essential. This, then, is the salesman's function: to maintain good relations between his company and its retail distributors, to ensure that the retailer maintains adequate stocks, to ensure he is making sufficient efforts to resell them, and to ensure that adequate display material is provided and that the retailer uses it to the best advantage.

In addition to these primary functions, salesmen selling branded merchandise to distributors need to know how to handle complaints, how to obtain credit information and how to assist the company's accounts department in the collection of overdue payments. They will also need to know how to plan their journeys and how to report back to management information gathered about customers, the situation in the market and the activities of competitors.

When planning a field training programme, it is important to provide the recruit with as comprehensive an experience as possible. Accounts to which he is taken should represent a cross-section, including not merely the outlets where the customer is well-disposed but also to those regarded as 'difficult' or those that have so far failed to develop into regular purchasers of the company's products. Furthermore, a tendency to select specific accounts only on a territory, for the purpose of training calls, is to depart from one of the major tenets of correct training procedure. It will create an un-economical journey route. New salespeople should be taught from the outset the importance of systematic routing to ensure the fullest and most economical use of available time.

During the first few days of field training the calls made upon customers will be conducted by the trained salesperson. The trainee will attend only as an observer. The number of interviews achieved in a day will be fewer than would be the case for a trained salesperson operating alone. Time must be allocated for pre-interview and post-interview analysis and discussion. Each interview should be planned in advance, with the trained salesperson explaining the objectives and the methods he/she proposes to employ to achieve them. The various selling tools should be discussed, so that the trainee can become acquainted with their relative value and appropriate use. Among these tools will be the sales record book, index card or computer printout which details previous interviews and orders obtained. This case history of the account will provide pointers to the class of merchandise in which the retailer is interested, the quantities of the product he normally buys and the pattern of his ordering frequency. A study of this record will enable the salesperson, unfamiliar with the territory, to spot those of his customers who are due to reorder and the quantities of the various pack sizes they normally take. From the details of previous interviews, he/she will be able to note which of the company's various products have been presented, or represented recently, and what the retailer's response has been.

A further selling tool will be the range of samples of the product. Salespersons' samples should be carefully prepared and presented. Where the company offers a wide range of merchandise, it is important that samples should be easily portable, with quantity and size markings clearly indicated. Sample cases need careful design to enable the salesperson to find any particular item quickly and surely. Nothing is more distracting and likely to weaken the salesperson's approach than to have to fumble through a mass of items to find a specific sample.

Other sales aids include copies of the company's literature, which act as a back-up to the salesperson's spoken words and sample range, and provide the retailer with a ready means of reference to the company and its products.

The various stages of the call upon a retail grocery or pharmaceutical account can usually be summarized as follows:

1   The reception of the salesperson by the buyer and an initial discussion of any matters outstanding. These may include comment or complaint with regard to a previous delivery, an examination of damaged packages or the investigation of an account query.
2   The carrying-out of a check of the trader's stock. In many retail trades, especially grocery, it has become the accepted practice for a supplier's salesperson to examine the shelves and stock room to ensure the adequacy of the stock of his products that is being carried, and to note the quantities of each item which should be reordered to bring the stocks back to an optimum level.
3   The presentation of new lines, the representation of existing items in the product range not currently being stocked by the retailer in question, the discussion of new special offers and other types of promotional activity.
4   The achievement of a satisfactory close by obtaining an order.

Where the need for restocking of established lines has become apparent from the stock check, it may only be necessary to obtain the retailer's assent to the order. In the case of a new product line, the salesperson may need to persuade the retailer to speculate with a trial quantity 'to see how it goes'.

The ability of the salesperson to close his/her sales is the crux of salesmanship. All other activities are subordinate to the obtaining of orders. It will be apparent therefore that it is this aspect of field training that must be given the greatest attention. As we have seen earlier, this is an ability that it is almost impossible to assess in advance, which is why there are so many people employed as salespersons whose success tends to be haphazard and often purely fortuitous. The sales manager need not be too alarmed, however, if, during the period of training, the fledgling salesperson appears weak in the closing of sales. Ultimately every successful salesperson finds a method of approach to this vital aspect of sales work. We have seen that we cannot exactly assess the qualities needed to make a success-ful salesperson. For this reason, it is not possible to teach a trainee exactly how to secure an order. The most the trainer can do is to demonstrate methods which have proved successful when employed by others, and to steer the beginner away from approaches likely to fail. In the vast majority of cases good salespersons start to learn how to sell *after* their training period is over, when they are on their own and are faced with the personal challenge of achieving a sale without outside help or interference.

The question of interference is relevant when the trainee makes his first call (let us say he is male) and it becomes his turn to take the initiative, with the trainer stepping into the background. If he is to do his job properly, the trainer must accept a self-effacing role at this stage. He should avoid any interference with the conduct of the interview. If he sees the chance of a sale slipping through the trainee's fingers, he should let it slip. To intervene and take over the discussion will be to destroy the beginner's confidence. It will also damage the confidence of the retailer, who may be unaware of the shortcomings of the newcomer until the more experienced person highlights them by the intervention.

Of course if the trainer foresees the likelihood of vital damage being done to the company's reputation, he must interrupt. It is, however, very important for the beginner to be given the opportunity to make mistakes which can subsequently be pointed out to him and be corrected. It is certainly far better for him to commit errors during his period of training, when his words and actions are under sur-veillance, than later, when he is on his own and has no one to guide him.

After a period of joint calls, the trainee should be allowed to operate on his own for a few days so that he can put into practice that which the trainer has taught him. He will encounter situations not completely covered in the routine course of instruction, and these will be the basis of further discussion with his trainer when formal training is resumed. By reducing gradually the periods of accompaniment and increasing those when the salesman operates on his own, his confidence will be allowed to grow. The process should be continued until such time as the trainer considers that the fledgling has reached a degree of competence where he has more to gain from practical experience than from exhortation and example.

Industrial sales training

The training of industrial sales personnel differs from that of those in the consumer-goods field. Apart from the obvious need for product knowledge, the industrial salesperson is more likely to undertake the protracted negotiation for new business than his counterpart in the branded consumer-goods market, where purchasing decisions are frequently made only at headquarters level and where the negotiations are conducted by senior sales management personnel. Industrial buyers are concerned not with the resaleability of the goods they purchase but with their technical acceptability, as raw materials or components in their company's manufacturing process. They are equally concerned about the reliability of the service offered by their suppliers, because materials to feed a mass-production plant must be delivered at the right place at the right time if a highly complex manufacturing operation is not to be brought to a standstill. Furthermore, it is the duty of the industrial buyer to seek to reduce the cost of his purchases, and he will look for competitiveness in the prices he is offered. Because the motivation of the industrial buyer differs from that of the buyer of a retail distributor, the salesperson's approach almost must differ. This difference is, however, only one of degree. The principles of selling remain constant.

Generally speaking, industrial selling requires some measure of understanding of the technology associated with the product and the manufacturing processes employed by customers. Industrial markets can be very complex and fragmented, calling for considerable flexibility in selling techniques. The degree of sophistication required of salespersons in the industrial sector tends to be often greater than in the consumer-goods field, and training programmes generally reflect this difference. The highly structured sales presentation frequently employed in consumer markets is inappropriate for the sale of many industrial products.

Successful personal selling in the industrial sector depends essentially upon the possession of good communication skills. Industrial salespersons must above all be articulate. They should also possess knowledge of the company, its size, structure and standing within the industry it serves. They will need a detailed knowledge of the products they have to offer, and how these products are used by customers. The sole interest of the industrial buyer is what the products will do *for him*. Will they improve the quality of his own final product? Will they enable him to increase his output? Will they overcome technical difficulties he encounters currently with competitive products? In order to respond to these questions intelligently, the industrial salesperson will need some understanding of the processes employed by the customers.

Industrial-sales training must therefore be essentially technology-based. The salesperson's task is to match the benefits offered by the features of his/her products to the processing needs of the customer. Unless this match can be achieved, price is immaterial. In order to achieve this match, the salesperson must not only understand the technical requirements of the customer's processes but also be sufficiently conversant with the production processes employed by his/her own company. Although most industrial product companies offer a *standard* range of products, a high proportion of their turnover is achieved by the provision of *modified* versions of these products. Since the salesperson provides the communication channel between supplier and customer, he/she needs to be capable of explaining to his/her own management the precise nature of a customer's problems in order that the company can provide a suitable response.

Another factor to be kept in mind regarding the training of industrial salespeople is the constant change that takes place in technology. For the salesforce to be suitably equipped to keep pace with such change, training must be regular. This can often be achieved by incorporating into sales conferences sessions in which technical personnel explain new products and processes. External technical training can also be achieved by arranging for salespersons to attend seminars organized by industry associations.

8.4 Territory planning and calling frequencies

One of the most important aspects of the work of the sales manager is the organization of sales territories and the planning of customer calls to ensure that the optimum value is derived from the efforts of the sales team.

Territorial organization

Let us take first the question of the individual sales territories. If one is selling on a nation-wide basis, it is necessary to ensure that

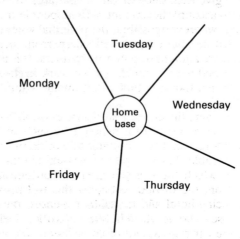

The territory divided into five
sectors, one for each day of the week

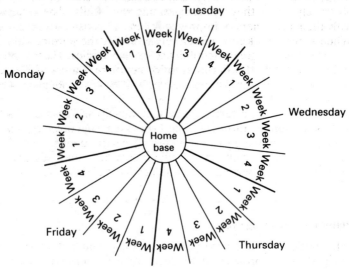

Each sector has now been divided into
four portions, representing the weeks
in a 4-week journey cycle

The salesman will visit each sector of the territory each week, working each of
the portions over a 4-week period. The arrangement facilitates the insertion of
emergency calls without major disturbance of the journey cycle

Figure 8.2   *Sales territory organization*

adequate market coverage is achieved. This must include not only one's existing customers but also all potential outlets for the product. One must aim to give each salesperson an equitable workload, which means taking into account the amount of time spent in travelling, and making sure that, wherever possible, the potential volume of sales in each territory will be about equal. All salespersons need the challenge of an adequate amount of potential business. It is a mistake for them to be burdened with so much routine work in the servicing of existing accounts that too little time is left for the acquisition of new business.

Above all, however, the geographical scatter of both existing and potential accounts on the territory should be such that the salesperson will have a reasonable possibility of working in a systematic manner. It is desirable that salespersons should live in that part of their territory in which there is the greatest concentration of customers. Apart from the obvious economy this will provide for the company in reducing hotel and travelling expenses, the salesperson needs an area close to home which he/she can work in bad weather or at times when the car may be out of commission. Figure 8.2 shows one form of sales territory organization.

Leaving aside the question of salespersons' personal convenience, which should not be underrated, salespersons can operate far more effectively when they can programme their calls. The relationship with their customers is improved when their visits are predictable. When a customer knows he can rely on seeing the salesman at regular intervals, he has greater confidence in his supplier. He will be more inclined to hold off ordering from competitive sources and await the salesperson's regular visit because he will know, in advance, when to expect it.

If the extent of a territory, geographically and in terms of existing and potential turnover, has been planned correctly, the sales manager can provide salespersons with clearly defined performance standards. These will enable their activities and success to be measured, and a periodic assessment made of their progress.

Planning the calling cycle

Sales outlets on a territory, both existing and potential, may be grouped in accordance with their relative turnover value. For example, in Group A one could list all accounts, actual and potential, with an annual turnover value for one's product of £100,000. Group B would consist of accounts worth £50,000 per annum, Group C £25,000 and Group D less than £25,000. It would then become possible to arrive at a call frequency for each group, taking account of their relative value. The result could be tabulated as follows:

Group	*Annual turnover*	*Call frequency*
A	£100,000 and over	Every 2 weeks
B	£50,000 ,, ,,	,, 3 ,,
C	£25,000 ,, ,,	,, 4 ,,
D	Less than £25,000	,, 5 ,,

Let us work in round figures for convenience and say that there are 200 outlets in the territory, made up of:

Group A accounts 20
Group B accounts 30
Group C accounts 60
Group D accounts 90

If the salesman averages eight calls per day during a five-day working week, a call frequency chart can be prepared on the following lines:

					Weeks				
	1	2	3	4	5	6	7	8	9
Group A calls	10	10	repeating						
Group B calls	10	10	10	repeating					
Group C calls	10	10	10	10	10	10	repeating		
Group D calls	10	10	10	10	10	10	10	10	10

In theory nothing could appear to be more simple. The salesman (say a man) divides his time equally between the four groups of accounts. In two weeks he has seen each of his Group A customers once. By the third week he is making a second visit to those he saw in Week 1. After the third week of his journey cycle he has also seen each of his Group B customers and thereafter he repeats the pattern. It takes him six weeks to visit all his Group C outlets and nine weeks to call upon all those smaller customers and potential customers in Group D. Thus, from start to finish, a tour of all outlets on his territory, carried out in accordance with the call frequency prescribed, will take him nine weeks.

Unfortunately, as anyone with practical sales experience will know, it never works out like this. In the first place, customers are seldom conveniently located to facilitate such systematic coverage. Secondly – and this applies particularly to industrial selling – a salesman usually has to make appointments to see his more important customers. It is extremely fortuitous if the majority will be able to see him on the days when he has planned to be in their area. Thirdly, the needs of one's leading customers must be given priority. If an important buyer has a major complaint or wishes to see the salesman urgently to discuss new business, he cannot be kept waiting for two or three weeks because the salesman is still completing his call cycle.

There are times when common sense dictates that the system must be abandoned. These times can occur quite often, and a journey cycle that, on paper, takes nine weeks can stretch to twelve, fourteen or eighteen weeks in practical terms.

This does not mean that a systematic method of calling is useless, but merely that the sales manager must accept that circumstances are bound to frustrate his best-laid plans. Allowance must be made for this in setting targets and assessing performance.

Assessing sales performance

Personal selling is one of the essential elements of the marketing mix, and, as such, the standard of its quality needs to be monitored. This is achieved by making regular periodic assessments of the performance of the individual area salespersons. This should be based on specific and measurable factors. No secret should be made of the nature of these factors, and an assessment report should be issued on a monthly or quarterly basis, with a copy sent to the salesperson to enable him/her to see that he/she is being fairly judged. It will serve to bring home to them where salespersons' weaknesses may lie and provide them with the opportunity to do something to overcome these in the future.

The following is a specimen salesperson assessment report, which can be adapted to meet specific requirements:

Name of salesperson .... Territory ....

Period on which assessment based: From ... To ....

Sales target £..........

Sales turnover achieved £..........

Number of calls on existing customers ....

Number of calls on potential customers ....

Number of orders obtained ....

Percentage of orders to calls ....

Number of days worked ....
Average number of calls per day ....

Number of new accounts opened ....

Average size of order ....

Assessment rating ....
(A = Very satisfactory, B = Satisfactory, C = Unsatisfactory)

Sales manager's comments ....
....

In addition to this statistical assessment, the sales manager should review the performance of his sales personnel periodically, with a more in-depth examination based on (1) personal attitude to the job, (2) efficiency with which the work is organized, and (3) effectiveness in customer interviews.

Personal attitude

(*a*)	Timekeeping	Does the salesman work to a schedule and is he punctual in keeping appointments?
(*b*)	Personal appearance	Is he well-groomed? Does he dress in a manner appropriate for his work? Is his car kept in a satisfactory condition?
(*c*)	Enthusiasm	Does he exhibit sufficient interest in his own and the company's progress? Is he enthusiastic about the work he is doing?
(*d*)	Human relations	Does he appear to 'get on' with other people, such as customers' receptionists and gatekeepers, as well as other members of the company's staff?
(*e*)	Loyalty	Is he loyal in his relations with his colleagues? Is he honest in his dealings with his superiors?
(*f*)	Cooperation	Does he cooperate with other members of the company: sales office staff, technical and accounts personnel?
(*g*)	Receptiveness	Is he receptive to new ideas and new selling techniques? When he has an opposing viewpoint, is he *constructive* in his criticism?
(*h*)	Self-expression	Is he capable of expressing himself clearly? Does he speak and write in a coherent, logical manner?

Knowledge

(*a*)	Market knowledge	Does he possess an adequate knowledge of the customers and potential customers on his territory? Does he know the class of merchandise and pattern of business of his individual customers?
(*b*)	Knowledge of competition	Does he have an adequate knowledge of the products of his competitors, their marketing policies and the customers on his territory to whom they are selling?
(*c*)	Product knowledge	Is his knowledge of the company's

products adequate to enable him to sell affectively? Does he understand the processes employed by his customers?

Personal organization

(a) Condition and use of records

Does he maintain his essential records in an adequate manner? Does he use his records intelligently as an aid to selling?

(b) Territory planning and calling frequencies

Does he plan his territorial coverage and utilize his time in a manner adequate to maintain an optimum frequency of calls on both existing and potential customers?

(c) Call objectives and follow-up

Does he have sufficiently clear objectives for every call he makes? Does he follow up his opportunities adequately?

Sales skills

(a) Introduction to new customers

Does he adopt a suitable approach to new customers? Are the methods he uses correctly adjusted to suit varying customer situations?

(b) Use of questions

Does he probe for information with finesse and persistence? Are his questions formulated intelligently?

(c) Establishment of requirements

How effective is he in establishing and assessing customers' needs?

(d) Persuasiveness

Are the arguments that he advances to promote sales sufficiently persuasive? Is he able to overcome customers' objections effectively?

(e) Closing

Is he sufficiently strong in the closing of his sales?

(f) Selling range

Does he concentrate on too narrow a range of the company's products?

8.5 Salesforce communications

Good communications are essential to the maintenance of salespersons' morale and to ensure the company's management is fully informed of the reaction of the market to its policies and the acceptability of the product range. An efficient reporting system is essential to the effectiveness of the personal selling effort.

Salespersons' reports

Differences in product range and markets served will affect the choice of reporting method. Let us consider, firstly, the purposes to which salespersons' reports will be put:

(*a*)   To inform the sales manager of the particular accounts where the salesperson has called, the date of the visit and the name of the person interviewed.

(*b*)   To indicate the degree of success achieved by the call by means of the value of orders booked.

(*c*)   To bring to the attention of management any deficiencies in the company's service and product quality by the detailing of complaints.

(*d*)   To inform of any changes in the customer's situation that may affect his financial standing and creditworthiness.

(*e*)   To indicate the current level of the customer's business activity.

(*f*)   To report on new developments that could result in an expansion or contraction of the level of the customer's business with the company.

(*g*)   To report the customer's reaction to the general state of the market.

(*h*)   To report the activity of competitors.

The above items are applicable generally to all products and markets. For companies engaged in the sale of materials and components to industrial users, more detailed customer information may be needed. Very often industrial products have to be tailor-made, or at least modified to meet specific requirements. In these circumstances the salesperson will need to describe fully the nature of the customer's requirements which must be met before the business can be negotiated. In markets where there is considerable price fluctuation, management needs a constant feedback regarding competitors' price activity.

For companies selling branded consumer products to intermediary distributors such as wholesalers and retail outlets, a pre-coded report form may suffice for daily or weekly reporting purposes. Where the product to be sold is of a sophisticated nature or the market is complex, a written report becomes necessary.

In setting guidelines for written reports, emphasis should be placed on the following essential factors: (1) promptness, (2) brevity, (3) accuracy, and (4) utility.

Promptness is obviously vital, because matters arising from the report may require urgent management attention. Brevity enables management to absorb the content of reports quickly and to take appropriate action without delay. Unless the information reported by the salesperson is accurate, it may be worse than useless, creating possible confusion and incorrect decision-making, which can have damaging consequences. The utility of information gleaned from customer visits may at times prove to be more far-reaching than the area salesperson might realize. Where a company has a salesforce covering the entire country, the management's picture of its national market and the trends that are occurring within it may largely result from the cumulative effect produced by the reports of its nationwide spread of salespersons.

The need for two-way communication

Salesforce communication should flow in both directions. Information from management to its field salespersons, by means of news sheets and other bulletins is important for two reasons. Firstly, it has a considerable motivating influence by keeping the person concerned up to date with what is occurring within the company and in other sales areas. Secondly, by reporting case histories and other factual information about the company's products and markets, it can be a spur that encourages an individual salesperson to greater effort. The following are some suggested topics.

Improvement to the product

Every salesperson (say a woman) is interested in possible new selling features for the product she has to sell. Not only do they give her a fresh talking point, they may enable her to counter customers' objections and gain new business. Wherever possible, one should provide a case history of the developments that have led to the improvement, because this will arouse increased customer interest and will enhance the technical prestige of the company.

New trading development

News of any changes in trading methods or new methods of approach that have proved successful in other territories are always of interest to salespersons, who will quickly seek to adopt them in negotiations with their own customers. Here again case histories are valuable. Providing care is taken not to betray confidences, a bulletin, describing how a specific sales problem in one area was overcome, can assist salespersons in other areas with similar problems.

New advertising and promotion schemes

Details of a new advertising programme or of a forthcoming special promotion scheme will act as a tonic for the consumer-goods salesperson anxious to discover the means for generating renewed interest and cooperation among retail stockists. She will be glad to learn about the preparation of special point-of-sale material that ties in with the new advertising and how her dealers will be able to use it to the best advantage.

Sales conferences

Of all the means of achieving communication within the salesforce, the sales conference is probably the most important. To be successful, an annual conference requires a lot of planning and must be properly stage-managed.

It is important that the conference should have a theme to which all the items contribute. This will provide a sense of purpose to the occasion. To illustrate what is meant by a central theme, the following may be considered:

Product themes
(*a*)   The introduction of a new product.
(*b*)   The development of new applications for existing products, illustrated by case histories.
(*c*)   The attributes and limitations of the company's products in relation to those of competitors.

Publicity themes
(*a*)   The value of current advertising and promotion schemes in support of field sales activities.
(*b*)   The adequacy of current sales literature and point-of-sale material as sales aids.

Service themes
(*a*)   The adequacy of the current service provided for customers.
(*b*)   The adequacy of current after-sales service and how this may be improved.

Sales-performance themes
(*a*)   New selling techniques.
(*b*)   Improving salesforce communications.
(*c*)   Methods for overcoming customers' objections.
(*d*)   Improved territorial coverage and journey planning.

8.6   Internal sales staff

In the achievement of company objectives by means of the marketing mix the quality of the personal selling element is a vital factor. For industrial product marketing the importance of its role cannot be overstressed. The performance of the field salespersons, however, is to a very large extent dependent upon the support they receive from the internal staff of the company's sales office. It is they who are responsible for maintaining the continuity of service upon which customers depend for their satisfaction. Activities such as telephone enquiries, customer and salesperson correspondence, the preparation and progressing of orders, and the maintenance of stock and customer records, are essential to the quality of the personal selling element.

In many types of commercial operation of course a high proportion of the selling effort comes not from field-based salespeople but from a telephone sales staff based at company headquarters. Suppliers of consumer products in particular employ 'tele-sales' teams whose function is to telephone retailers on a regular basis to take restocking orders.

Telephone selling is also used in advertising and in the printing industry, while telephone canvassing is now a widely used method for producing sales leads in the marketing of various goods and services, including window double glazing and financial services. The cost-effectiveness of telephone selling has led to its increasing adoption as a back-up to – and, in some cases, as a replacement for – routine personal selling activity.

Discussion questions

1 Describe the role of personal selling in the marketing mix and why advertising and promotion often are insufficient to achieve a sale.
2 What qualities and characteristics would you look for in the appointment of a regional sales manager for a company distributing frozen food items to the catering market?
3 In the role of sales manager, how would you propose to control the activities of a salesperson selling industrial products?
4 Describe four appropriate circumstances in which telephone selling could be used advantageously.

9
Industrial marketing

In the first chapter reference was made to the loss of direct contact between producer and consumer, and it was noted that, as the distance between them increased with the emergence of intermediary distributors, so the need for a structured approach to the identification of the consumer's requirements became increasingly apparent. The notable difference between the marketing of consumer products and those destined for industrial outlets is the vastly greater distance that many industrial product manufacturers stand from their ultimate consumers, who are the buying public.

At one time it was common practice for a manufacturer to accept raw material at one end of his production line and despatch a finished consumer product at the other. In between he conducted a variety of processes to create the various components from which the product was assembled. With rising labour and overhead costs, however, it was found that the production of such components on the necessarily limited scale dictated by an individual company's requirements had ceased to be economic. Owing to the benefits derived from the economies of scale (the more units one makes of any specific item, the lower the unit cost), it was cheaper to buy component parts in from outside firms.

As the result of this situation, there has been an increasing movement within manufacturing industry towards process specialization. Today a large number of manufacturing firms limit their production very largely to the assembly of component parts bought-in from specialist processors. This has inevitably increased the number of links in the manufacturing chain, and companies within the processing, as distinct from the final assembly, stage often are far removed from the consumers of the ultimate product.

Companies in this situation court potential danger if they rely solely upon information drawn from their immediate market for guidance on long-term levels of demand. Many large-scale national and international organizations regularly monitor markets for consumer goods in which their intermediary products are incorporated, with a view to assessing the future pattern of demand. This is not, however, necessarily common practice among producers of raw materials and manufactured components.

Owing to the technological complexity of many manufacturing processes and the heavy capital investment they need, today's management decisions may take three, five or even ten years to mature. The question that all long-term manufacturing investment must inevitably raise is whether the market one seeks to exploit will still be there. The purpose of marketing, which is to set long-term objectives and to initiate strategies by which they can be achieved, implies this need to look into the future. It is in the practice of marketing that a company should seek to ensure that this projected view is as accurate as circumstances allow.

9.1 The industrial marketing plan

As business organizations grow bigger and their operations more complex, they become more difficult to control. In a fast-changing world market conditions are increasingly uncertain. One of the major problems faced by management in industrial companies is the tendency for priorities to be dictated by events, which results in too high a proportion of thought and effort being devoted to the achievement of short-term aims.

Corporate planning of the development of all the resources of the organization in a coordinated manner is the only solution. It sets up a commitment to achieve a plan embracing the entire activities of the company. In its simplest form it entails an examination of the market the company wishes to penetrate, on the one hand, and the resources the firm has at its disposal, on the other. Taking together market opportunities and available resources, management is in a position to consider certain basic objectives. Programmes, both short- and long-term, can subsequently be put into operation to achieve a stated level of ultimate performance for the entire organization.

The basic factors to be taken into account, therefore, are (1) the market, (2) company resources, and (3) company objectives.

The market

Study of the market and the environment in which it exists should be a continuous process. All factors to do with the market need to be considered. In the marketing of industrial goods it is important to look beyond immediate user industries and consider the end-user market. The size of the population of the end-user market, its per capita income, and its future pattern of consumption, are the things which will ultimately control one's immediate industrial market.

Working back from this broader spectrum, one must assess how the possible changes in the end-user market are likely to affect the pattern of the industry, or industries, that will utilize one's industrial products. At the same time consideration should be given to the likely long-term trends in the supply situation.

The market assessment should take account of the situation of one's competitors and their probable future actions. The particular products offered by competitors should be considered, together with their market share and the likely future trend. Their marketing skill should be assessed. What are the factors that are likely to contribute to their future success or failure in the market? Are they capable of sufficient innovation, not only from the point of view of their engineering resources but in their marketing attitudes? Figure 9.1 illustrates factors influencing the marketing plan.

Company resources

An in-depth review of company resources is a function often neglected by management, yet it is essential for the preparation of a marketing plan. The firm should take a regular annual review of all its assets. Most particularly, it should make an assessment of the rate at which these are declining in value. The age of its plant, the age of its key personnel and the life-cycle stages of its principal products need to be examined.

In conducting this review of available resources, each department of the organization requires examination. An analysis of the volume and sales pattern of major products, together with sales by area, both home and export, should be undertaken.

A company's assets include the degree of goodwill it enjoys from customers and its industrial markets generally, and this should be assessed, together with the morale level that exists among the company's junior and middle-management personnel.

Company objectives

These will vary from company to company. They will establish the general strategy that the company will employ, and are likely to include objectives relating to turnover, profitability and market share.

9.2   Industrial marketing strategy

Marketing strategy consists primarily of three parts. The first is the establishment of the means by which it is intended to achieve the basic objectives that have been decided upon. Secondly, a time

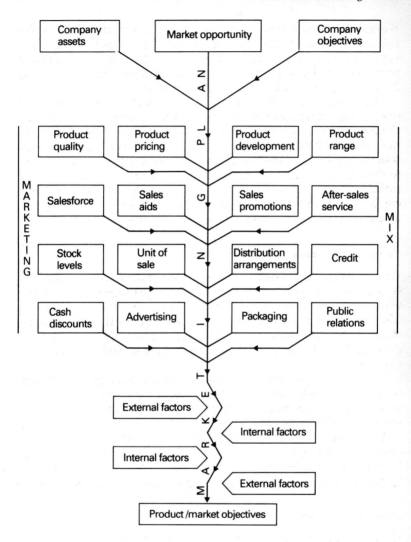

Figure 9.1   *Factors influencing the marketing plan*

programme should be decided upon for this achievement, and, thirdly, resources must be allocated to the various means by which this achievement is to be attained.

Since the underlying objective must be profitable growth, a company should plan either to expand its activities or to diversify them. This can be achieved by various methods, including:

1   Internal research and development of new products.
2   The acquisition of other companies.
3   Merger with another organization.
4   Licensing of additional products.

All such strategic plans must find their expression in the company's product/market strategy, and this will be conditioned by its markets.

None of the firm's growth objectives can be achieved unless it earns the profits that will finance its growth. Profits are dependent upon the availability of adequate resources, in terms of plant, finance, materials and manpower, to enable the organization to benefit from the opportunities the market provides. Thus it is necessary to establish the market opportunities, to utilize fully the company's assets, and to establish the correct mix of its resources.

In determining the needs of the market, one must consider both the total market and the segments of that market upon which it is intended to concentrate. A decision is needed as to how much of the total effort of the company should be applied to each targeted market segment.

Among the external factors that may affect marketing strategy is probable variation in the Gross National Product and in the consumption of the industries one is serving. Socio-economic influences generally can affect the markets of user industries, as we have noted, and will have an important bearing on general market confidence. Government regulations and the international trade scene generally are factors that also can upset the best-laid plans.

There are other external factors that may be more predictable, such as seasonal fluctuations in market demand, technological change, product substitution, and the extent and severity of competitive influence, for which some allowance should be made in the formulation of the marketing plan.

It is not only the influence of outside factors that can create a variable situation. Consideration must be given to important internal factors, the most important of which will be the availability of adequate finance, production capacity and management skills.

The elements that make up the marketing mix for industrial marketing will be essentially the same as those we have already considered in the context of consumer-product marketing, namely the four Ps: product, price, promotion and place. The formulation of the mix, however, is likely to be different in the case of industrial products, particularly those associated with high-technology market segments, where the emphasis will be essentially on product quality rather than price.

Marketing strategy and company growth

The progress of an industrial enterprise is normally assessed in terms of volume or growth of sales, profits and return on investment. By setting out one's objectives and gauging the performance that is being achieved, it is possible to assess whether the existing deployment of the company's resources will bring about a satisfactory rate of progress. If the desired performance cannot be achieved with the existing deployment, these resources may be better utilized in a wider field of company activity. When an organization reaches this situation, some form of diversification may become not only desirable but necessary.

Diversification generally means engagement in products, industries, technologies or markets which are new to the company. There are three principal methods of creating an expansion of company activity:

1   By means of specialization and the extension of markets.
2   By the acquisition of other firms.
3   By the introduction of a new product range.

Specialization
The basis of this approach is the adaptation of one's existing products to suit an increasing number of new markets. New growth is achieved by the acquisition of new markets rather than by the launching of new products.

Acquisition
The company diversifies by acquiring other firms to maintain its required return on investment. Here the company uses its existing financial and management skills to develop other businesses that lack these skills.

New products
New products can be acquired by internal development, by licensing or by purchase. When a new product range is developed internally, the situation is not dissimilar to that of *specialization*, but the firm's assets will probably be utilized in a different way or additional assets may have to be acquired for the production or marketing of the new products. Products that are added by means of investment in the company that produces them usually relate to the firm's existing product range rather than to the qualities of its management.

The starting point for new-product planning is to examine the company's special skills or the experience of its production and marketing facilities. These are known as the *differentiated assets* of the business. They may not be unique individually, but in combination they may be sufficient to give the company an 'edge' either in production or in marketing. Companies are said to have *positive* and *negative* differentiated assets, which simply means they are good at some things and not so good at others.

Once the company's differentiated assets have been established, their values should be measured against the future requirements of the markets in which the company is currently selling or to which it may wish to sell in the future. The long-term objectives of new-product planning are to make an improved use of the firm's differentiated assets, and to maximize the return of investment. There are also short-term advantages, such as the avoidance of depending upon one market only, the avoidance of staff and labour reductions due to market fluctuation or decline, and the utilization of surplus capacity. Very often an extension to one's product range enables a better service to be offered to existing customers.

When planning the introduction of new products, a company needs to answer three pertinent questions. Have the company's differentiated assets been identified? Have the strategic product objectives been established? Have screening factors for the new products been agreed? On the basis of these answers it should be possible to arrive at a specification for new products that will satisfy all the relevant criteria. This should narrow the field of search.

The screening of a new industrial product for acceptability will be along lines similar to those discussed for new consumer products. Apart from the obvious need for satisfactory performance factors, one should consider the likely stability of any new product to be introduced into industrial markets. Ideally, the newcomer should have a potential life cycle which will be complementary to existing products in the range. Its potential market should be reasonably durable and broad enough to warrant the use of the company's resources in its development and exploitation. An ideal attribute for any new product is the likelihood of stable sales even in fluctuating economic conditions.

The introduction of new products as part of a growth programme is only one aspect of the product strategy that should be pursued by the company on a continuous basis. There are three major hazards that endanger the future prosperity of all manufacturing organizations:

1 Dependence on a very limited product range which can be put in peril in the event of changing market conditions.
2 Seasonality, and a consequent violent fluctuation in demand.
3 Over-dependence on traditional consumer requirements, which are liable to change as the result of technological advance.

The product life cycle, which we examined earlier, occurs with all products. Marketing should institute regular reappraisals of the situation of the company's existing products and their future in relation to changing circumstances. The profitability of each individual product, its market share and the growth rate of its market should be considered. Has the company introduced enough new products or product modifications in the light of market trends? Are there any external influences, such as socio-economic changes or competitive activities, which can affect the stability of the current product range? What particular assets has the company and what new assets are emerging within the company that are at present under-utilized? From the answers to these questions it should be possible to establish the life-cycle stage reached by each of the firm's products. Gaps in the existing product range will be highlighted, as will the need for possible product modifications and improvements. Some products may need to be dropped from the range.

9.3 Diversification

We have seen that when the existing deployment of a company's resources is failing to achieve the desired performance, a diversification of its activities may have to be considered. As an alternative to the acquisition of new products, the acquisition of other firms can be undertaken in order to maintain the required return on investment.

There are three primary motives for diversification:

1 To replace an inadequate investment.
2 To complement an existing investment.
3 To insure against future saturation conditions.

Any one, or any combination, of these motives will justify a company's decision to redeploy part of its resources by the acquisition of other businesses.

Diversification can be conducted in a number of ways. *Narrow diversification* covers ventures into activities which are closely related to the company's existing product/market situation. Ventures into completely foreign activities are called *wide diversification*.

An *unrelated diversification* is usually limited to the financing and business management of the acquired enterprise. A *related diversification* relates to the utilization of the company's technical 'know-how', marketing expertise and production facilities in the development of the business that has been acquired. *Vertical diversification* is where the firm uses its resources to establish or acquire companies which either supply materials or provide it with market outlets.

Any diversification must lead to risk and additional costs. These can be minimized by careful planning. Every successful business plan is dependent upon (1) an evaluation of available resources, (2) identification of business opportunities, and (3) the construction of specific project plans for selection, decision and exploitation.

The cost of diversification, in the form of investigation and appraisal studies, can be kept within reasonable bounds, providing the company's objectives have been established. Diversification objectives should be considered under two headings:

1   *Qualitative:* these relate to the type of business, whether it is required purely for investment purposes or for direct operation, and the types of market in which it operates.
2   *Quantitative:* these relate to the size of the operation, the sales performance of the firm, and profits and returns on investment.

We have seen that diversification can take a number of forms. Before a company decides to embark on any one method, some consideration should be given to possible alternatives, since each of the main methods poses possible advantages and disadvantages.

Internal research and development

When a firm decides to exploit its R & D resources to develop new products, it has the advantage of being able to maintain maximum control over the project. Continuity is assured and its own staff is kept fully employed. Furthermore, all the subsequent profits earned by the project are retained.

On the other hand, the progress of the project is liable to be inhibited by any shortcomings that may exist among its own staff. If this occurs, there may be a long delay before any return on the investment can be seen. One also runs the risk that the development may not succeed and the investment will have been lost.

Using specialists

An alternative approach is to bring in specialists to lead the research and development project. This will enable the firm to maintain its control over the undertaking. Existing staff is fully utilized, and, once more, all resultant profits are retained by the company.

The trouble with this method is that the employment of specialists sometimes can have dubious effects. One's existing staff may not take kindly to the idea and morale may suffer. The research may take a long time, and one can never be sure that the specialists' abilities are all that they are said to be.

Acquiring licences

One can of course acquire licences to manufacture patented products from home or overseas producers. The big advantage is that products that are already proven with regard to production and marketing feasibility can be selected. Very often one has the added advantage of technical and marketing assistance on the part of the licenser.

The disadvantage of producing under licence is that some of the profit earned by the enterprise is lost to the company in the payment of royalties. Furthermore, the licence conditions may be such that one's own future development may be restricted. An additional danger is that of becoming too dependent upon the licenser and neglecting one's own R & D department.

Acquiring other companies

Time is the important advantage here. One immediately receives all the assets of the acquired firm, its technical know-how, its products and its profits. Very often the resources of the acquired firm can be integrated successfully with one's own. When a company is taken over, its staff gets taken over as well, and in some instances this is not the least of the benefits.

However, firms possessing useful assets and good managerial staff are usually expensive to purchase. A further problem is that one inevitably acquires some facilities and some people one does not want.

9.4   Industrial marketing research

This review of the strategy of industrial marketing will have shown the vital importance to management of an adequate, continuous and accurate supply of information in its primary task of decision-making. The nature of industrial markets is such that a true understanding of the environment in which the company operates is often difficult to achieve. As already discussed, many industrial-product manufacturers are further removed from the ultimate demand determinants for their products than their counterparts in the consumer-product field. Their reliance on market research consequently is considerable.

Industrial market research has been defined as providing information which will lead to an understanding of the markets in which the company is operating today and in which it may hope to operate tomorrow. The bulk of its work can perhaps more aptly be described as market intelligence. It is a task that can – and, wherever possible, should – be carried out within the company organization. The information it provides should be on a continuous basis. It should report on the size of the relevant markets, the nature of the products that are being supplied to those markets, and the nature of the competition. It should monitor trends in both supply and demand. It should supply regular information on prices and profitability, on technological developments, on the development of substitute products, and on changes in the structure of those industries from which demand arises.

Market intelligence should not limit its fact-finding to the current situation only. Companies have to plan today for the kind of business they expect to be in several years hence. As has been stressed previously, market information based on projections for three, five or ten or more years ahead, should be provided.

Field research in the industrial sector demands a different method than that practised in the consumer-goods field. Sampling techniques have to be modified. The 'universe' of an industrial market is not always known and therefore difficult to define. It is often necessary at the outset to decide where the market lies and what are its essential characteristics before a sampling programme can be started. A method frequently adopted by industrial market researchers is to segment the market before sampling. Instead of using a pre-determined sample, the researchers interview successive firms to establish a pattern of answers.

It is possible to use very much smaller samples for industrial research because of the smaller size of the markets. Industrial interviews may be as little as 10 per cent of the number used in consumer research; this will reduce the cost of the survey, although, generally speaking, the interviewing of senior management personnel of major industrial firms will often take longer than a series of interviews with housewives. Furthermore, a higher level of interviewing skill is generally necessary in the conduct of industrial interviews.

Among the larger organizations, market research is accepted as an essential adjunct to the marketing process. Smaller companies, however, still lag far behind in this respect; yet the need for market research cannot be denied. Its function is to reduce the risks inherent in decision-taking. Since every business executive, whatever the extent of his company's operations, must speculate continuously to take advantage of the opportunities the market situation may offer, it should be obvious that the more reliable the information available, the less of a gamble such decisions become.

There is a general criticism, however, that market research tends to be under-used by industrial companies. The reasons often advanced are that research budgets, in comparison with those of firms producing consumer goods, are very limited, that many companies believe that they can obtain a better view of their markets by means of their sales representatives' reports than by research surveys, and that those that have adequate technical knowledge and interviewing experience within the company do not have sufficient time to undertake market surveys.

These objections can be countered by pointing out that the average cost of an industrial market survey is usually much less than that of a consumer survey, and that salesmen generally are far too biased for their reports to provide a fully objective assessment of market conditions and the performance of the company within the market. Furthermore, if the firm does not have adequate personnel available for research, it can call upon the services of experienced outside consultants.

The value of using outside consultants for industrial field research work is that an agency may well be able to provide a far wider knowledge of markets than its client's own market research department, and will probably be more versed in MR techniques. It may also have greater experience in the interpretation of the results of its research to meet the needs of management.

Discussion questions

1 Describe the dangers faced by processing firms distanced by the manufacturing chain from their ultimate consumer.
2 If a company is not achieving its objectives by means of its current activities, how may it redeploy its resources expeditiously?
3 What are the basic ingredients of an industrial marketing plan?
4 A company specializes in the injection moulding of plastics components destined for the automotive industry. Describe appropriate methods of market research that will assist its management decision-making.

10
Export marketing

10.1 The advantages of exporting

The attraction of exporting is that it extends a company's scope of operations into new markets, with the opportunity for increased earnings and profits. For many manufactured products, and for services, profit margins abroad often are as attractive, if not more attractive, than those that can be achieved within the home market.

There are other advantages. An enlarged market permits longer production runs to be obtained, with a corresponding reduction of unit costs. Selling in several separate markets enables a firm to spread the risks that the peaks and troughs of a fluctuating home market may entail. A decline in demand in one country may be recovered by increased demand in another. Where an organization operates internationally, it creates for itself an enviable reputation in comparison with rivals of a more insular persuasion. The disciplines inherent in meeting the specific demands of a variety of markets in terms of quality and design, packaging and marketing techniques, tend to sharpen a company's competitive edge.

The myth that exporting is largely the prerogative only of large, highly funded organizations has been exploded in recent years by the success of many small firms that have entered the export field. Their greater flexibility and speed of decision has often given them the advantage over larger rivals.

10.2 Some exporting problems

Successful exporting is not, however, an easy option for any company, large or small. Export markets should not be considered as mere extensions of the home market – convenient dumping grounds for surplus production. Every market has its specific needs, no two markets are alike, and a well-organized and highly competitive world trade exists to satisfy them. There is, however, always room for improvement in any commercial sphere, and a firm that can offer a better product or service, an improved delivery or keener price, can establish itself in a foreign market, provided that it has sufficient and suitable resources.

The basic principles of marketing remain constant whether one is operating in the home market or abroad. However, additional considerations apply to exporting, and the question of sufficient and suitable resources often is paramount.

A new market means new needs for the organization. The first is money, because additional sales, creating the need for extra production, may increase stockholding, may require additional plant and additional labour and, very possibly, larger premises. Credit facilities extended to newly won foreign customers must be financed. All the well-known ingredients for an over-trading situation are liable to present themselves to a company that has failed to make appropriate financial provision.

The next major consideration relates to personnel. A commitment to export is a sufficiently important development that it must engage a considerable proportion of the time and energy of directors and senior managers. The effort required to launch and sustain a successful export initiative can seriously weaken the day-to-day management of a company's existing home-market operations. Entry into new markets also places additional strain on a firm's routine staff. Export documentation and correspondence are exacting, and the quality and experience of existing personnel may prove inadequate to meet requirements. While it is true that much of this specialized work can be delegated to outside agencies, it must be paid for, and will still require coordination and control within the company.

Finally, one must consider the product, or group of products, it is intended to export. It is unlikely that these can be merely shipped abroad in the form in which they are currently sold in the home market. The basic product design and composition may require modification to suit foreign needs, as may the packaging. Immediately this will create a new challenge for the firm's research and development team and for the production department. In the initial drive for exports output may suffer because of the need for special prototype production and sampling.

10.3   Special factors in exporting

There is no doubt that an organization practising a consumer-orientated policy in its home market will enter the export field better equipped than one in which production calls the tune. The attitude of mind that the modern concept of marketing seeks to evoke, namely, that the product and its presentation should satisfy the specific market need, is essential to success in exporting. Thus the starting point in the preparation for entry is consideration of some of the essentials for exporting.

Stability

Companies whose trading experience hitherto has been confined wholly to the domestic market frequently exhibit extreme naivety in their commercial approach to foreign countries. The stability of the local currency will need careful examination before commitments are undertaken. Political stability in the intended market should also be considered. The exporter should be alive to the considerable changes that can occur in a country's external trading policies following a change of government. The relative strength of the opposing political parties and their attitude towards imports should be watched. In the selection of suitable export markets care needs to be taken that a relatively large marketing investment is not put at risk in a country where a sudden change in the political regime closes the door to future importations.

Indigenous competition

The technological advance that is currently occurring in most countries of the world, and particularly in what are described as the underdeveloped countries, must tend to encourage protectionist trading policies designed to safeguard their embryo indigenous production. As a result, there are certain markets where the scope for the importer is a short-term one only, though this does not mean that the business currently available is not worth seeking. The exporter will be wise to recognize the true situation and tailor his investment in such markets to the limited degree of penetration that is likely to be available to him.

Social conditions

A consumer-orientated marketing policy, as we have seen, examines the social conditions of those to whom the product is directed. In all the various countries of the world there are marked differences in social behaviour. Religious outlook, class structure, the attitude towards women, standards of hygiene and the leisure habits of the population vary, not only from country to country but also from region to region. Climatic conditions play a decisive part in the development of social habits and mental outlook.

Dependability

Any company entering the export field must be alive to the fact that the traditional standards of commercial conduct in its domesic market do not necessarily apply to all other parts of the world. While it may be assumed that any reasonably astute exporter will establish the financial reliability of an overseas customer before trading begins, he will be advised to ensure that the buyer is in a position to pay for the goods he receives promptly. There are certain markets in which business may prove easier to get, such as some of the underdeveloped countries, but where very extended credit may be taken. Alternatively, in highly industrialized markets, such as the United States, Western Europe and the older Commonwealth countries, in spite of heavier competition, the exporter will often have the advantage of obtaining quick payment.

10.4   Export management

An export manager should possess not only a full understanding of export procedure and practice, but should also be familiar with the products or services his/her company provides and be able to settle the majority of queries regarding quality or price on the spot, without the need for frequent guidance from head office. For this reason he/she must have the full confidence of the directors of the company and be fully acquainted with the company's policy.

Ideally, an export department should be headed by an export director, delegating to an export field sales manager control of the activities of export salespersons and overseas agents. In firms where this is not feasible, an export manager will have to spend part of his time in his office managing the department, and the remainder overseas visiting the various markets in which the company is operating to establish a good personal relationship with individual customers. The amount of time the manager devotes to overseas travel must depend upon the size of the exporting effort and the number and quality of the staff available to assist him/her. It is a cliché to say that one cannot conduct a successful export campaign from behind a desk, but if the individual charged with managing the export drive is nearly always abroad, rarely to be seen or heard at company headquarters, the essential communication between the export department and the rest of the marketing organization must suffer. Furthermore, the paperwork side of exporting must be closely supervised, and an export manager who has transformed himself into an overseas representative will be in danger of abdicating a vital task.

Any serious approach to overseas trading cannot therefore stop with the appointment of an export manager, however competent that

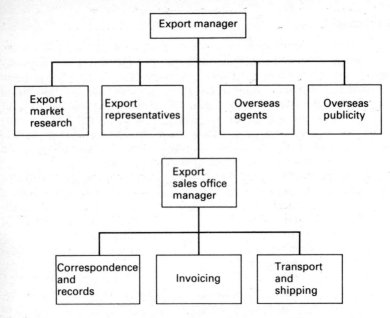

Figure 10.1   *Organizational chart for an export department*

person may be. Trained personnel are needed both in the office and at the customer end of the operations.

The organization of an export department is illustrated in Figure 10.1.

10.5   Staff selection and training

In the office

The export office should be in the care of an office manager who has a full knowledge of export procedure and documentation. He or she should be capable of handling all correspondence with overseas clients and agents during the absence of the export manager, who should be prepared to delegate all the routine work in export sales, including the receipt and progressing of customers' orders, liaison with the production department, arranging shipping, customs documentation and insurance. The export manager, blessed with the assistance of a reliable supervisor, is free to devote a major part of his time to other vital aspects of his work, such as research into new overseas markets, the scrutiny and appointment of agents, and the framing of export strategy in accordance with company objectives.

In the field

In selecting salesmen and saleswomen for work in export markets one should look for individuals with higher qualifications than is usually necessary when filling vacancies in home-market territories, because overseas salespersons must often assume greater responsibilities than their counterpart at home. They may well be responsible for far greater volumes of business, are likely to be under much less supervision than the home-based salespersons, and many of their duties, such as control of local agents, liaison with local distributors or the supervision of local depots, are of a managerial nature.

It is desirable that they should have some technical qualifications, because, unlike home-based salespersons, they are unlikely to have a source of technical assistance close at hand. An essential qualification, one that is only recently being given sufficient weight in many overseas appointments, is linguistic ability.

In arranging a training programme for export salesmen or saleswomen, stress should be placed on the need to understand the habits, tastes and general way of life of the people who live in the countries into which the company is extending, or hopes to extend, its activities. Secondly, overseas sales personnel should receive training in the pattern of the markets in which they will operate. They need to know the distribution of population, the concentration of industry and the extent and calibre of competitive activity within those markets. Instruction in the business practices of the countries concerned, together with some understanding of the political and economic conditions, are also desirable. Finally, all export sales recruits will need a good grounding in the company's products – how they are produced, their selling features and how these compare with those of competitors in the overseas markets – the company's costing policy, and how the products are packed, shipped and distributed.

10.6 The export marketing plan

The next stage in the preparation for exporting is the preliminary export marketing plan. This should seek to achieve three essential objectives: to find the most suitable market in which to begin operations, i.e. where the company's products or services may expect to obtain the best response; to design and produce goods or services that will most closely match the needs of that market; and to decide the most suitable method of presenting the company to that market.

None of these objectives is likely to be achieved until one has looked closely at one's own existing organization, because conditions and situations in the market that might be right for one company can be entirely wrong for another. It is a question, once again, of the firm's strengths and weaknesses: its financial position and its ability to raise additional funding; the quality and experience of its management; the nature of its production equipment and processes; its geographical location within the home country; and its proximity to indigenous transport facilities such as road and rail, airports and seaports, and to its potential export markets. This last can be an important factor, not only with regard to the shipment of goods but also in terms of personal contact with proposed markets abroad. The capability of the company to carry out product modification and to manufacture in accordance with export-market specifications – which may be different from those of the home market – should also be considered.

If the findings of this internal research are studied realistically, it should be possible to discard several export-market options immediately, on the grounds that their particular needs cannot be met by the company at this time. By such a process of elimination a short-list of possible export markets that will warrant closer scrutiny should emerge.

10.7   Researching export markets

This can be a time-consuming but not necessarily an expensive operation, because much of the information will be available from desk research. The particular difference about researching a foreign country compared with one's own is that there are far fewer points of reference. Managers who conduct research within their own country have the advantage of familiarity with their environment and its social, commercial and political norms; with a foreign country they must often start from scratch. It is very important that all such research should provide accurate clues, because the selection of the right export market for the company and its products can be decisive.

There are five essentials one needs to know about each short-listed potential market:

1 *Demand.* Does a demand currently exist for the product or service it is proposed to offer at a price level the company can manage?
2 *Competition.* How effective is the competition? From where does it emanate? Is it indigenous, from importers, or both?
3 *Market conditions.* What is the position regarding tariffs, import controls, government buying agencies, or local taxation policies? Do any of these disadvantage an importer?
4 *Special regulations.* Are there governmental or technical specifications covering product acceptability or composition?
5 *Other factors.* Are there factors of an economic, cultural,

geographical, or political nature that could impede the company's proposed penetration of the market?

International statistical systems

In most of the developed countries of the world information of this nature is available from governmental and trade sources. At the end of the Second World War agreements were reached among the world's principal trading nations designed to improve global economic relations in accordance with objectives set out in the charter of the United Nations. The result was the creation of a number of international treaty organizations, which include the General Agreement on Tariffs and Trade (GATT), the Articles of Association of the International Bank for Reconstruction and Development (IBRD), and the International Monetary Fund (IMF). Through these organizations and their various derivatives, the UN has established a variety of world-wide agencies, whose aims include the promotion of international trading opportunities, the provision of economic development assistance, and the regulation, by means of codes of conduct, of the trading policies of its member states.

During the past forty years the proliferation of international trading agreements has created a complex network of organizations and policies, to which must be added the emergence of regional economic communities. These seek to establish a common external tariff and the abolition of internal tariffs between member states. The European Economic Community, of which Britain is a member, is an example of a regional economic community, of which there are others in the Caribbean, in Central and in South America, in Central Africa and in South-East Asia. The basic aim of these blocs is the fostering of intra-regional trade and the expansion of the bloc's trade with other parts of the world.

A by-product of this global network of trading agreements is the regulated collection and dissemination of statistical information. Details of indigenous production, imports and exports, covering a wide range of commodities, are available in respect of individual countries throughout the developed world. The adoption of international trade classification systems also aids the researcher in pinpointing demand fluctuations. The United Nations publishes statistics on world trade, based on data submitted by some 120 countries, using the Standard International Trade Classification (SITC). This system employs five-digit code numbers to provide statistical values for all goods, subdivided into more than 40,000 items. Additionally, there is a four-digit nomenclature for customs tariffs, entitled Customs Co-operation Council Nomenclature (CCCN), covering all products of world trade, and classified in accordance with the type of raw material of which those products are composed. The relevant code numbers for the SITC and the CCCN are brought together in the SITC manual. Using this material, researchers can discover the relevant customs import duty for any product in any country.

These and other statistical systems simplify desk research into selected export markets. In most countries governmental agencies can supply such information at a nominal fee. In Britain the Department of Industry is a ready source of statistical data covering virtually every country in the developed and developing world.

As the result of this desk research, it should be possible to select a target market that offers the most promising opportunities for the company and its products. A visit should now be made to carry out a reconnaissance in depth of the selected country. Essentially one wants to get a feel for the country and some understanding of the business people who live and work in it. The visit needs advance preparation. Contact should be made with the commercial officers attached to one's own embassy in the targeted country, for they can provide marketing advice and will be able to arrange appointments with local business people likely to have an interest in the particular product or service you have to offer. If your visit can be timed to coincide with trade fairs or exhibitions relevant to your business, this will facilitate introductions and also provide the opportunity to assess some of the competition. Everything you can learn about the selected country – its history, its current affairs, traditions and customs – will be invaluable as a background to future decision-making.

Market research

Under this heading one should seek to establish the size, nature and future scope of the market for one's particular product, not forgetting the importance of establishing the strength of both indigenous and international competition. One should bear in mind what has already been said about the segmentation of markets. Overseas markets, too, consist of a number of segments, and research may disclose the fact that there are certain sectors of what appears to be a generally over-supplied market that have been left unsatisfied by one's competitors. In such circumstances close appraisal may reveal specific opportunities for the company's products. On the other hand, where research shows that a market is fully saturated with the supply of products virtually identical in quality and value to one's own, it could be wise to have second thoughts about entering it.

Product research

It is important to establish at the outset whether there is likely to be any local desire for one's product as it stands, or whether it will need to be modified. If alterations are necessary, then the likely demand must warrant the inconvenience cost such modifications will cost one's R & D and production departments. Apart from the design of the product, one must consider the design of the package. Local customs and taboos must be observed, and this could mean special packaging, which again will have a bearing on costs.

The price at which the product can be sold will depend largely on the price at which competitive products are sold in the same market. If one cannot afford, or wish to afford, to make, pack, ship and distribute one's product at this price, this market, on closer examination, may be less attractive to the company.

Distribution research

The pattern of distribution, the channels by means of which the product is brought to the right place at the right time, may differ from country to country. Before entering into any commitment, it is advisable to establish the existing pattern applicable to one's own type of merchandise, and to calculate the effect this distribution cost will have upon the selling price of the product. Sometimes it is possible to establish one's own distribution pattern at variance with the traditional methods of the market, but this can be hazardous and create resistance from potential customers. Innovation of this nature should not be attempted without considerable research and the canvassing of the views of customers in the targeted market.

Operational research

The maintenance of customer service is of paramount importance in export marketing. While it is obvious that the provision of satisfactory service plays its part in ensuring customer satisfaction and the receipt of repeat business in the home market, when one is competing in foreign markets, its effect upon the continuity of business can be decisive. The company's relation with overseas clients can seldom be quite as close as with firms at home. Competition for business abroad is international, and likely to be extremely fierce. Furthermore, the relative cost of acquiring and re-acquiring overseas business is often considerably higher than in one's domestic market. These factors emphasize the need for a continuing operational research to check that deliveries are made on time, that documentation is correct, that packing is adequate, and that after-sales service is maintained satisfactorily.

10.8 Representation in the export market

One of the first decisions that has to be made is how the company will represent itself to the target market. There are a number of ways in which to do this. The firm can sell through a local agent or distributor; it can decide to dispense with intermediaries and deal direct with the foreign customer; or it can sell its product through an export house, or a buying house based in the home country but acting on behalf of a foreign company.

For an organization with little previous experience and knowledge of the target market, appointment of a local agent or distributor is often the best course. The agent should be familiar with the peculiarities of the market and its needs, and versed in the intricacies of local trading legislation and practices. Based on the spot, he should be in a position to deal quickly with any customer problems that may arise. He will be talking to fellow-countrymen in a language they will understand and should have the advantage of quickly establishing that essential rapport between seller and buyer that oils the wheels of a good business relationship. Part of his function should be the provision of advice on how best to promote the product. He should also feed back to the company information on market trends and the continuing acceptability of the product, and advise on the need, should it arise, for product modification. A good agent will look after the company's interests in the foreign market because, to safeguard his commission earnings, it will be in his own interest to do so.

Depending on the nature of the product, it may be desirable to appoint an agent who will also act as the company's local distributor. This can be especially useful where the product is likely to be bought in relatively small lots by a large number of customers, and where direct shipment would be impractical and uneconomic.

Agents and agency agreements

Finding the right agent is often more than half the battle in exporting, so that the selection process should be undertaken with care. It will be necessary for the company to arrange a meeting with a prospective agent on his own ground. It is not only the personality of the individual one needs to assess. Account must also be taken of the facilities at his disposal, such as his business premises; the staff he employs; and, in the case of an agent/distributor, the suitability of his warehousing and transport arrangements. The overseas customer's perception of the quality of your company and, by inference, of your product and service, may be strongly influenced by the quality of the agent you have selected to represent you.

Suitable agents can be contacted either through advertisements published in the trade and national press in the target country or by writing to a short-list of firms culled from appropriate directories. Alternatively, enquiries can be made through home-country clearing banks or local chambers of commerce, which are likely to have a register of agents operating in the target market with experience of your type of product.

Having found the individual or company who will represent the company in the selected market, you must enter into a formal agency agreement. This should state the names and addresses of both parties, provide a description of the product, or products, subject to the agreement, and define without ambiguity the precise territory the agreement will cover. The date of commencement should be stated, together with arrangements for termination. If you discover subsequently that you have made a bad choice of agent, it could prove difficult to get rid of him. It would be wise to obtain legal advice, preferably within the target country, to ensure you know exactly how the agent's rights are protected.

The agreement should also set out the minimum performance levels to be achieved by the agent, the rates of commission he will receive, the method by which commission will be calculated, and the agreed method and time that payments will be made. There may be occasions when orders are placed by customers situated in the agent's territory direct with the principal firm. Suitable provision should be included in the agreement to cover this eventuality, and how such business will be treated for commission purposes. Other matters requiring inclusion in the agreement relate to any agreed responsibilities to be assumed by the agent for local advertising and promotion of the product, the delivery of goods to customers, and the collection of payment.

Once an agent has been appointed, it is vital that the company should give him full support. Your organization is unlikely to be the only principal for whom he acts, and, naturally, he will do his best for the principal who helps him in his work. The setting of mutually agreed sales targets, regularly monitored and reviewed, will assist motivation. So will regular up-dated information on all aspects of product development. He should be visited regularly, because personal contact with the company's managers will provide added stimulus. He should also be invited periodically to visit the company's headquarters to meet other personnel in the marketing, sales, production and research departments. The more he feels himself to be 'one of the family', the more concerned he is likely to be to safeguard this relationship by caring for the firm's interests within his territory.

There are other ways of conducting export business that do not necessarily call for the appointment of local agents. A company can opt to sell direct to customers in the target market, using its own staff for sales negotiations. In such areas as capital goods, and highly technical engineering products calling for special design and bespoke manufacture, the services of an agent may be considered unnecessary, because negotiation will need to be conducted by home-based sales technicians. In the case of consumer products, destined for sale in bulk quantities to supermarket and other large retailing organizations, the use of a local agent may be superfluous. Major deals are likely to be struck by senior company managers dealing directly with senior employees of the customers' buying agencies, who will not be interested in dealing through an agent.

For organizations inhibited by limited financial or management resources from setting up a company presence in a targeted foreign market, export houses, situated in the home country, may offer an alternative means of conducting export business. Export houses can fulfil the function of a company export department, or agent, by promoting the firm's products abroad, handling documentation and forwarding arrangements, and accepting the credit risk on all foreign transactions. Frequently they will also maintain an after-sales service. The benefit to the supply company is that it deals with the export house in the same way as it does with any other home-market customer, and frees itself entirely from the intricacies of exporting. The disadvantage is that it is divorced from the ultimate market and acquires no first-hand knowledge of the market's changing needs. In such circumstances the marketing concept goes by default.

The use of an export house can work very well for a firm in a comparatively small way of business, and where the nature of the product is such that personal communication with the overseas customer is not particularly important. However, by the nature of his business, the export merchant usually buys only those goods which he knows he can resell quickly. He takes the type of merchandise that he is confident will satisfy the immediate demand of his overseas clients, and will seldom seek to develop a market for a specific product. Because he is unlikely to have any long-term interest in any one product, information feedback is likely to be minimal.

Another means of avoiding, or at least minimizing, the possible trials and tribulations of exporting is to enter into some form of group trading agreement. This can be useful for a small organization, where the amount of export business is insufficient to warrant the expense of setting-up an export department. Sometimes a small firm will approach a larger company, producing related but non-competing lines, with the proposal that the major organization should export the small man's product along with its own. This so-called 'pick-a-back' method is often conducted on the basis of the payment of commission or a sharing of costs. The additional lines can assist the profitability of the larger firm's export operation by reducing its sales and distribution costs.

With a similar aim in view, several small firms whose interests do not clash sometimes get together and set up a special export company. This can produce problems, however, for the participants. Jealousies are liable to creep in, especially if it is suspected that the degree of effort being devoted to the sale of one man's lines is less than that given to another's.

10.9   The transaction of export business

Successful exporting is a demanding exercise. Any organization that seeks to move beyond its home market to offer goods or services abroad immediately faces world competition. The utmost professionalism is called for, not least in the order and despatch departments. Accuracy in documentation is vital if export objectives are to be achieved. The marketing department has a special responsibility to ensure that staff engaged to prepare export documents have received sufficient training for the task. Slipshod paperwork that might get by for the home market can create havoc in exporting. The goods may not travel or pass through customs if documents have not been correctly prepared. Serious payment delays can result from simple clerical errors. These hazards can be avoided by arranging for all export documents to be handled by an outside specialist agency – a useful option until such time as the company can recruit suitably experienced staff.

Some small firms are deterred from exporting, not only by the problems of documentation, but by those related to quotations and the securing of payment from foreign customers. Quotations may be expressed either in home currency or in the currency of the foreign market. In deciding which method to adopt, the simple answer may be to find out what the customer prefers, and oblige him accordingly. Alternatively, one can check the method used by competitors already established in the market and follow their lead. Payment terms vary from market to market, and, once again, the best policy is to adopt terms of account settlement that have been established by the competition. The payment record of customers abroad may not necessarily be much different from that of home-market customers. Obviously due care should be taken to establish the creditworthiness of every customer before credit facilities are granted. Here the appointment of an agent experienced in the particular trade or industry can be of assistance; he should be able to offer an opinion as to a customer's reputation that can be a useful adjunct to the formal taking-up of references.

There are, however, certain countries that have acquired a dubious reputation in matters of financial probity. Banks and other financial institutions in one's home country can often provide cautionary advice in this matter. But bad payers are not the only source of risk for the exporter. Major political upheaval, such as war or revolution, or sudden economic changes that result in the imposition of exchange controls in the foreign country, can disrupt payment, and credit insurance is an obvious precaution.

10.10　Sales promotion in export markets

Promotion, by means of press and broadcast advertisements, direct mail, cinema advertising and posters, and the use of PR, is just as important in overseas markets as it is at home. Indeed there is a particular aspect to overseas publicity that might be termed its 'commendation value'. Both the overseas industrialist who buys imported materials and components, and the overseas man in the street who buys imported consumer products, does so with greater confidence if he sees and hears the merchandise being advertised locally. Advertising, at home and abroad, lends distinction to the product, and commends the user's decision to purchase it.

It is important, however, to add the rider that sales promotion in export markets needs an entirely separate approach to such activity at home. Both the spoken and written word can have vastly different connotations from country to country. Apart from the obvious difficulty of language, there are major differences in idiom in various parts of the globe. Although a common language is spoken in Britain and the United States, it is well known that advertising 'copy' that is most effective in one country can fail completely when transported across the Atlantic.

There are other obstacles, apart from the language difficulty. In certain countries there are very strong religious and social taboos which must be respected. In addition, one must take notice of local regulations governing the use of advertisements and promotional material generally. It is advisable therefore to use the services of local advertising agencies wherever possible, to avoid the risk of committing 'howlers', or worse.

The media available to the exporter are generally the same as in the home market, but each will require special study if it is to be used effectively.

Press advertising

In most of the developed areas of the world there are newspapers, trade journals and technical publications. In some countries newspapers are produced in more than one language for a multi-lingual population. Some countries have Sunday newspapers, in others they are not permitted. There are countries where the daily newspaper appears in the morning. In others it is the evening papers that are most widely read.

The majority of newspapers published overseas have a political or religious bias. Different papers and magazines are produced for different sections of the community, usually divided by social class, sex, age, or special interests.

It must surely go without saying that all advertising matter should appear in the language native to its perceived audience. When producing illustrated advertisements, care should be taken to ensure that backgrounds conform to the environment of the readership concerned. Considerable 'howlers' can be committed in this respect, and vetting by one's local agent before the advertisement is published is a wise precaution.

Radio and television

In some of the most promising of export markets, such as parts of Africa and Asia, illiteracy remains a social problem. Here the impact of press advertising will be much less than that of the spoken word. The transistorized radio set has become a powerful medium of consumer product advertising in such areas, but once again local taboos must be watched.

Cinema advertising

Although in Britain the significance of cinema advertising has tended to decline with diminished audiences, in many other countries of the world the cinema enjoys great popular support. The promotion of consumer goods by means of short films which last, like television commercials, for a few minutes only is well worthwhile.

Sales literature

All sales literature designed for use overseas must of course be produced in the local language. Although English is widely spoken, it is not so frequently read – a factor many British publicists have failed to appreciate in the past. Technical specifications, too, should be presented in accordance with the systems that are employed locally if they are to be of any practical value to one's overseas clients.

Public relations

The importance of good PR in export markets cannot be over-stressed. Once again, those whose task it is to prepare 'hand-outs' for the press and other communications media should be fully acquainted with the way of life and the outlook of the local population. Announcements regarding the visits of company executives, or new products or services, can do an exceedingly useful back-up job to support the activities of a local agent or distributor.

Discussion questions

1 What are the main factors a firm should consider before deciding to enter the export market?
2 Describe the characteristics you would look for in appointing an export field sales manager for a company producing electronic equipment.
3 Describe the major factors to be considered in an initial examination of an export market and discuss their importance for the exporting company.
4 Adequate market research is vital to exporting success. By what means would you seek to obtain essential information about a targeted export market?
5 Give three examples of companies, each of which proposes to enter the export market with a different type of product and suggest appropriate methods by means of which each may present itself and its product to the selected market.

11
Pricing: policies and methods

We have already established that price is a major element of the marketing mix, together with product, place and promotion. It has an important job to do, both in the provision of benefits to satisfy consumers' needs and in the provision of revenue to satisfy the profitability requirements of the company.

Its first and most obvious task is to recover costs and create a profit. The problem that arises, however, is that costs are affected by the sales volume of the product, which itself is affected by price. Let us examine this dilemma:

1　Price is one of the elements that influence the attraction of the product for the consumer.
2　Therefore, in general terms, the lower the price, the greater will be that attraction and the greater will be the demand.
3　As demand rises, more units of the product will be produced to meet that demand.
4　In conditions of mass-production, the more units that are produced, the cheaper will be the cost of producing them.

The reason for this variation in the cost per unit of manufacturing the product can be seen if we now look closely at the composition of costs.

Firstly, there are regular costs in a business, regardless of the products it may be making. These include:

1　The management of the business.
2　Salaries and expenses of sales personnel.
3　Rent, telephone, lighting and heating of premises.
4　Research and development.
5　Office expenses.
6　Advertising and promotion.

These generally are described as the firm's overheads or fixed costs.

They constitute a fixed charge that the business must meet, regardless of fluctuations in the level of its manufacturing output.

Secondly, there are costs that are incurred as a result of production and sale of each of the company's products, such as:

1 Materials used directly in the production of the product.
2 Components incorporated in the product that are bought in from outside sources.
3 Labour directly employed in production of the product.
4 Fuel and power consumed directly in production of the product.
5 Carriage charges incurred in delivery of the product.
6 Packing materials used for the product.
7 Commission paid to sales representatives and agents in respect to orders obtained for the product.

Such costs obviously vary in total, according to the quantities in which individual units of the product are produced. For this reason such costs are known as *variable costs*.

Where a firm has a number of products, it is necessary to apportion the fixed costs – the general overheads of the organization – between each individual product. Failure to do so will give a very distorted and unreliable view of profitability. Variable costs of course are applied specifically to the product they concern.

When the product is offered to the market and orders are obtained, manufacture will commence. Revenue will flow into the organization as a result of the sales achieved. Once sales (and, in consequence, output) reach a volume where the total revenue equals the total of fixed costs and variable costs *at that volume*, a break-even point is reached (see Figure 11.1). Every sale beyond the break-even point produces profit.

The factors in the equation are therefore:

1 Fixed costs: a proportion of the general overheads of the firm.
2 Variable costs: relating to the production per unit of the product.
3 The number of units sold.
4 The price that has been set per unit.

Providing sales remain in excess of the break-even point and the fixed and variable costs remain unaltered, it will be seen that the profit figure will change either as the result of an increase or a decrease in demand or by an increase or a decrease in price.

The contribution that will be made by the sale of the product to the recovery of fixed costs and, subsequently, to the profits of the organization, is the difference between its selling price and the variable cost. From this it will be seen that there are occasions when making a sale at any price in excess of variable cost can be preferable

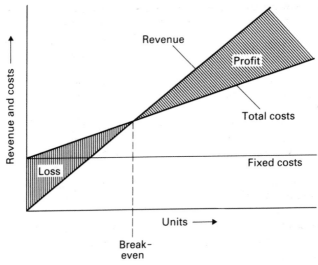

Figure 11.1 *A break-even chart*

to making no sale at all, in spite of the fact that an overall profit is not achieved. However, one could not run a profitable business on this basis; to do so would incur a net loss, although this loss would of course be smaller than if there had been no sales whatever.

Break-even analysis is a convenient means of relating the element of price to the achievement of profitability objectives, as we shall see later in this chapter. Before doing so, however, let us take a further look at costs in order to understand how these are calculated.

11.1 Cost control

To control its marketing operation effectively, a company should have the means of knowing the cost of every aspect of the selling and distribution processes relating to its products. Unfortunately it is not always easy to control such costs. There is less uniformity to the marketing operation than there is to the manufacturing function. Production generally is in a better position to exercise control over materials, plant and labour force than is marketing over distributors and consumers. While it is implicit in the adoption of a consumer-orientated policy that the needs of the consumer should be served, this must be kept within economic reason.

This is why a proper understanding of the nature of costing and cost control plays such an important part in the management of marketing. Means must be found to satisfy the consumer *and* to achieve the maximum profitable utilization of the company's resources. By the intelligent use of cost-accounting procedures, it should be possible to reconcile these potentially opposing factors.

Methods of cost accounting

Cost accounting utilizes two procedures:

1 *Historical costing.* This method makes comparisons between the costs incurred during different periods of time, different products or different sales areas.
2 *Standard costing.* In this case one establishes predetermined costs and subsequently makes a comparison between the actual costs incurred and the predetermined standard that has been set. The differences between the two sets of figures are known as variances, and denote the degree of inefficiency existing in the performance of the operations concerned.

The merits of cost accounting

It will be seen that by highlighting the variances which exist between prescription and performance, cost accounting provides management with a convenient method of exercising control over the selling and distribution processes of the marketing operation.

Whereas the unit cost of the manufacture of a product usually reduces as volume output increases, the cost of sales promotion tends to increase as sales grow. Therefore it is not unusual to find that the cost of attracting additional business is considerably greater than the unit cost of maintaining the current sales level.

The great merit of cost accounting in the control of the sales and distribution budget is that one is constantly required to review one's methods. It may be found that the cost of marketing certain products in certain markets makes the operation less profitable than one had previously imagined. Industrial-product manufacturers often discover that the cost of supplying certain customers with comparatively small quantities of a product, or 'tailor-made' versions of a product, makes the business uneconomic, and the company may be better off without these orders.

The principle of controlling one's *actual* costs by applying the yardstick of *standard* costs will immediately pinpoint any deviations in the performance of the marketing plan, and remedial action can be instituted. The benefits that can accrue may have wide application. Thus stockholding can be more effectively organized. Items of stock that are slow-moving will be spotted and means for their disposal arranged. Warehouse location can be planned with greater accuracy. In addition, the size of sales territories and the establishment of optimum calling frequencies for sales personnel can be organized far more effectively if one has the guidance of the statistical evidence cost accounting can provide.

Value-added costing

The theory of value-added costing takes the view that value is added to merchandise at every stage of its production and onward transmission through its various distribution channels. The value added by a manufacturer is the difference between the value of the product to the final consumer and the raw materials and consumable stores used in its production, plus purchases of light and power during the manufacturing process.

Some of this additional value will have been contributed by the sales and distribution departments. One of the merits claimed for this method of costing is that the money spent on selling and distributing the product is not necessarily regarded as wasted. Those activities that cause the product to be in the right place at the right time are said to give it an added value which may not be less important, from the economic standpoint, than the manufacturing processes by which it has been created.

Selling and distribution costs vary enormously between one type of product and another. Management should watch these costs to ensure that the profitability of the product is not being eroded by wastefulness in these sectors of the marketing operation.

Waste can be caused by a number of factors, of which the following are the most prevalent:

1   Market scatter causing inefficient use of transport facilities.
2   Average order size too small to be economically worthwhile.
3   Non-productive effort incurred in combating competition.

There are certain categories of merchandise for which transportation costs are proportionately high. Whether they are uneconomic will depend upon the ratio between the value of the goods and their bulk. Thus a large piece of computing equipment may be expensive to transport across country but its high value and the profit margin that it carries can absorb this cost very comfortably. On the other hand, the cost of providing a truck to carry a load of empty barrels the same distance could be completely uneconomic, because their considerable bulk will be out of all proportion to their value.

Some commodities have to be transported at a comparatively high cost, because they need special consideration. Perishable foods must be moved quickly, others may require the use of refrigerated vehicles, certain chemical products have to be transported in tankers or in special glass carboys, and there are goods that demand special protection in transit because of their fragility. All these factors result in a disproportionately high transportation cost.

High distribution costs can be incurred not only because of the type of product but because of the nature of the market that is to be supplied. Manufacturers of toys, for example, must often create stocks months before the Christmas trading season, thus incurring capital tie-up both in goods and storage premises. Certain classes of merchandise demand the provision of expert advice to assist the consumer, as, for example, central heating systems, business machines and industrial plant of all kinds. This service must be paid for, and represents part of the distribution costs of the product.

11.2   Profitability and marketing strategy

As with most aspects of business activity, there are various theories concerning the nature of profits. The first of these has been called the *increased net-worth theory*, which argues that the difference between the net worth or value of the business organization at the commencement and the completion of a specific period of trading represents the profit that has been achieved during that time. The figure will of course be adjusted to allow for any extra capital that may have been introduced and any drawings that have taken place. As a simple, rule-of-thumb approach, it has its uses, although it ignores the effect which has been achieved by forward planning by failing to differentiate between profit that has been deliberately engineered and profit that has occurred by chance – 'windfall profit'.

An alternative approach is that known as the *cost and revenue* theory. Here one takes the total revenue the business has earned during a specific period and deducts from that figure the total costs incurred. The result represents the profit gained. While this theory may be helpful in assessing the profitability of specific activities, it does create certain problems, such as how to deal with the question of items purchased during the period under review yet only partially used during that period, as well as the whole question of depreciation.

A more practical means of judging profitability is the adoption of the *return on capital employed* theory, which states that all the resources of the company have a value and that the profit achieved over a given period should relate to this value. From the long-term point of view this implies that every item of expenditure is an investment. Seen in this light, it is apparent that all management personnel who have authority to make investments have the ability to influence profits.

The area of investment over which marketing exerts the greatest influence is that of product strategy. Resources are invested in the product range with a view to maximizing the profit gained per unit of capital employed. There should therefore be an appraisal of the value to be derived from this investment, followed by a decision whether the strategy applied to each product is appropriate.

There are many businesses where 80 per cent of the sales turnover is being achieved by only 20 per cent of the product range. A reduction in the variety of products marketed may result in a considerable increase in profits. Of course there will be situations where it may be considered undesirable to reduce the number of one's products. In certain fields it is often necessary to offer a complete range of merchandise in order to remain competitive.

11.3 Pricing consumer products

Every trading organization depends for its revenue upon the prices that it charges for its products or services. A company's purchasing, manufacturing, sales and distribution costs, and its ultimate profits, are met from this revenue.

There are two different basic methods a firm may adopt for calculating its prices. One is the traditional cost-plus method, which is fairly easy to operate and orientated to meeting the needs of production. One calculates in advance what it is anticipated the product will cost to make and distribute and adds the margin of profit considered necessary to cover fixed costs and provide an acceptable return on capital.

The alternative method, known as the market approach, concerns itself at the outset with the price that the customer is likely to pay. From this, the costs of production and distribution are deducted. Providing the resultant figure, representing the gross profit, is considered satisfactory, the product can be offered to the market. If the profit figure is too low, one has two alternatives: production and distribution costs must be reduced, or, if this is not feasible, the product must be abandoned.

So far we have considered the effect price can have on the profit margin only in terms of revenue. In discussing the formulation of the marketing mix, however, we recognized that price was also one of the essential elements that influence buying decisions. In this context price affects profitability by influencing demand. Depending upon the nature of the product, in general terms high prices tend to deter demand, whereas low prices encourage it. This poses a dilemma. Should price be used to increase profit through its effect on revenue or should it increase market share by its effect on demand? The answer may lie in a consideration of the company's broader long-term objectives.

In a situation where an organization has a number of products, each at a different stage in its life cycle, it may be prudent to maintain a comparatively high profit level for a product that has passed the maturity stage and has only a limited life-expectancy. This could offset the comparative low price of another product, still in its growth stage, which has the potential to win increased market share. On the other hand, where a product has entered the maturity stage of its cycle, with the prospect of considerable longevity, price reduction to counter competition and retain its market share may prove the better option.

The theory that price reduction necessarily results in increased demand is not always valid. Sometimes a high price is used as a recommendation for the product. One finds that consumers, having no awareness of the true value of certain types of merchandise, believe that the higher the price, the better the quality. This applies particularly in the field of luxury products and services such as high-fashion clothing, cosmetics and the most exclusive restaurants. Among many professional buyers of industrial products and equipment the association of high price and technical supremacy is a concept that is deeply ingrained.

Generally speaking, producers do not favour the use of price as a competitive weapon. Experience has shown that in a competitive market no producer stands to gain from price warfare. There is nothing difficult about cutting one's prices to obtain a share of another firm's business, but competitors will not stand idly by, watching their business disappear. They are bound to react by cutting their own prices. Once the dust settles, it will be found that the relationship between everyone's price remains the same, except that now each producer will be selling at a considerably lower price than at the outset. In many instances it may be found that brands are being sold at below their full cost and no longer pay their way.

Enlightened managements prefer to counter the effect of competition by means of the adroit use of the marketing mix to offer customers a distinctive package of benefits that avoids direct comparison with competitive offerings. This achieves a dilution of the effect of price differentials in the customers' choice of the product they will buy.

In practice, when a producer enters a market, he will usually find that price levels have already been set by competitors, and he may have little option but to follow their lead. In most market segments it is one supplier who holds the lion's share of the business, and he is recognized as the market leader. His pre-eminent position is usually an indication that he has considerable experience of the market and has achieved a pricing policy that both satisfies his profitability requirements and is acceptable to a majority of customers.

Customers do in fact usually have an idea of what may be termed the 'going rate' for particular products and services within a fairly narrow band. Producers may, however, decide to deviate from this general acceptability band. Exclusivity in any form – and not simply in terms of intrinsic quality – may provide the opportunity to set a higher price. A new product or service that provides distinctive benefits, superior to anything the competition currently can offer, may be highly priced during the early stages of its life cycle, both to recoup rapidly the initial development costs and to limit demand. At a later stage, when production capacity has been increased and imitators enter the market, the price may be lowered to achieve greater market penetration and to counter competition.

Sometimes price-cutting is used aggressively as a tactical weapon. Where a producer occupies a dominant position in the market yet wishes to extend still further his market share, he may use savage price reduction to force small competitors to cut their prices below their break-even figure and thus drive them from the market. It is a brutal practice but one not infrequently adopted. Once he has the market virtually to himself, the large producer gradually can re-establish his price at a higher level without suffering any reduction in demand.

In the marketing of consumer goods, particularly, price considerations must take account of the distribution chain.

Pricing and distribution

Wholesalers and retailers will also need to recover costs and provide profit from their transactions. In setting distributor margins, producers once again have little option but to follow the market leader. However, the nature both of the product and the market is likely to affect marketing strategy. Products that require some element of personal selling on the part of the shopkeeper will often necessitate a higher margin than those that are 'demand goods', whose sale is largely promoted by heavy advertising campaigns. The more assistance the manufacturer requires from the dealer, the more he must enlist that support by offering an attractive profit margin.

The principle of resale price maintenance, by which manufacturers fixed the retail selling prices of their goods, may no longer be legally enforceable in the United Kingdom, but many firms still recommend the prices at which the retailer should sell their brands to the public. The general tendency today is for producers to fix ex-factory prices for their goods. Intermediaries at each stage of the chain add their own percentage (or mark-up) to provide their revenue. Thus a product leaving the manufacturer's premises at a price of £10 per item will be passed on by the wholesaler with, for example, a 10 per cent mark-up, at £11 per item to the retailer, who in turn will add his own mark-up of, say, 33 per cent, and sell to the consumer at £14.70.

Some producers offer quantity discounts to their distributors;

others do not. Market tradition is often the major factor. A discount for quantity ordered is usually justifiable from a cost point of view because a large order generally can be handled more cheaply than a small one. There is an obvious advantage in using a discount as an incentive to the dealer to place his order on a regular basis and in economical units. To use quantity discounts as a competitive weapon, however, is self-defeating, as in the case of price-cutting generally, because one producer's offer will quickly be countered by a similar offer from another.

One of the problems that may arise when a manufacturer is selling both to wholesalers and direct to certain large retail outlets is that a wholesaler may seek some special allowance as an inducement to carry the producer's brand. Providing the wholesaler's purchases are sufficiently large, the operation of a quantity discount scheme may be the answer. On the other hand, it is not uncommon to find some large retail establishments ordering quantities in excess of those placed by small wholesale firms. The dilemma very often is that one may wish to use the services of the wholesaler to distribute to small retail outlets, yet preclude him from offering one's goods to the large retailers, with whom it is considered expedient to deal direct. Some producers overcome this problem by issuing two price lists, one for wholesalers and the large retailers with a stated minimum order size, and another for the smaller retail outlets.

An alternative use of quantity discounts occurs where a manufacturer has no nominated dealers for his products and will supply to anyone. The price then varies according to the quantity that is purchased and takes account of the additional costs of administration and transport caused by small-lot despatches. It is a method adopted frequently by producers of high-technology industrial items, who prefer to be in direct contact with customers to gain feedback on the performance of their products and to provide technical support when necessary.

11.4 Pricing industrial products

The pricing methods employed in the consumer field are generally not appropriate in the marketing of industrial products. Whereas demand for consumer goods may be induced by means of large-scale advertising and promotional schemes, such as premium offers, it will be obvious that the buyers of raw materials, components or capital equipment do not respond to appeals of this nature.

Both the consumer-product manufacturer and the producer of industrial goods have one thing in common: a preference to sell on factors other than price. Whereas consumer marketing seeks to exploit the distinctive features of a brand image and a unique selling proposition as alternatives to price competition, in the industrial sphere the emphasis is generally placed on the attainment of technical distinction. In all the multifarious markets for industrial products there is a continuous demand for technological innovation and improvement. Thus a product which offers better value to the user can usually command a better price.

Cost-plus pricing

In the industrial sector the use of cost-plus pricing has been traditional. It establishes a price sufficient to cover the costs of production, distribution, overheads and a margin of profit. It must also take account of what the user expects to pay. One must remember that price is only one of the many factors that influence the decision to purchase industrial products. Of equal importance are such aspects as the ease of processing a material, its delivery time, or, in the case of equipment, the frequency and amount of servicing that is necessary.

It will be seen that the worth of a product to the user is the decisive factor. Certain products will be worth more to him than others, because their combination of desirable properties will have a greater value. Some products will have greater worth for some users than others. The needs of industrial customers vary widely, and it is an essential part of industrial product marketing to segment markets with extreme care.

One of the major problems facing the industrial-product producer is that his product range is often very complex. So diverse can be the needs of the market that he may well have to provide a considerable number of different qualities of materials or sizes of components. Furthermore, industrial buyers expect to receive quantity discounts. All of this tends to make the pricing of industrial goods very complicated. For a firm manufacturing a large number of engineering components, many of which may be made especially to customers' specifications, the task of formulating and implementing a consistent pricing policy is often formidable.

The normal procedure followed in firms which use the cost-plus system of pricing is for the estimating department to establish the anticipated cost of materials, tooling and labour. In a large organization reference can often be made to standard costs, but generally this offers little more than a guide to the actual cost of the production of special items. Smaller firms, lacking the resources to carry out time and motion studies, seldom have a system of standard costing upon which they can rely. Many companies therefore use historical costs as a guide to their current costing, making allowances for known variations in the price of materials and labour. For short-run work this method will often prove satisfactory, but on longer runs the effect of volume upon historical costs is often difficult to ascertain.

Product analysis pricing

In an attempt to find a new approach to the problem of pricing for firms that have wide product ranges and a high proportion of short-run production, a system known as product analysis pricing was devised some years ago. Whereas, in traditional costing methods, an analysis of materials and labour is carried out, PAP examines the finished product. It attempts to equate the market value of the product with its main properties.

For companies making a large variety of products of a non-standard nature, it is necessary to delegate the pricing function, and means must be found to meet two essential needs:

1 That those to whom pricing is delegated are implementing the company policy.
2 That the prices quoted are market-orientated.

The difficulty with cost-based pricing is that it is production-orientated. But the manufacturer's costing system means nothing to the buyer. In a market where he has a choice of suppliers he has no interest in the fact that the firm with whom he is dealing finds certain processes easier and therefore cheaper to perform than others. He could not care less that, because it has undertaken fixed-price purchasing contracts, the same firm finds that it is paying too much for certain raw materials. The value of the product to the buyer does not vary with the vagaries of his supplier's costing system. The fact that his supplier has a particular cost situation does not give the buyer grounds for paying more. He will pay only for what is of benefit to *him*.

PAP endeavours to recognize this fact by relating the price directly to those properties of the product for which the buyer is prepared to pay. The first question it asks therefore is how much value does the market put upon each of the properties of the product?

The procedure followed in product analysis pricing is that senior management establishes, initially, the significant properties of the product and sets sample target prices. A basic formula is then prepared by a pricing analyst. Management also prescribes policies that take account of competition and other variable commercial factors. Pricing standards personnel are responsible for *ad hoc* pricing, which they do by analysing the properties of the product, applying the prescribed formula and either adding or subtracting what is called the 'market percentage' (the set policy covering the commercial factors of the market situation). Account is then taken of certain variable calculations based on the current cost of materials and components and also of variations in order quantity. The result-ant calculation, which is passed to the sales division, is capable of final adjustment within a discretionary limit allowed to the sales manager.

At first glance the procedure appears complicated. Certainly extensive preparation is necessary at the outset. Once in operation, however, the PAP method is claimed to be relatively simple.

The advantages of this system are:

1 Quotations can be provided promptly.
2 Consultation with production staff is eliminated, owing to the separation of the pricing system from operating costs.
3 The technical description of the product is the basis upon which the price is determined.
4 The sales department can use discretion by adjusting the price in the light of market conditions.

The main disadvantages are:

1 Failure to link pricing with operating costs.
2 Danger of over-emphasis upon the initial judgements by which the properties of the product have been evaluated.

It is claimed for product analysis pricing that the system meets the need for both stability and flexibility. The value of the basic properties of the product can be identified always within the total sales price, which ensures a degree of stability; and flexibility is obtained by means of the discretion the system allows both to the senior management, in setting property values, and to the sales department to make a final adjustment to the price quoted to the customer.

Pricing methods, in company with many other aspects of business practice, require constant reappraisal. PAP and its potential variants may not be a complete answer, but the kind of thinking from which they have developed is very much in harmony with modern marketing concepts.

Discussion questions

1 Describe circumstances where price, as an element of the marketing mix, may be used to assist the achievement of marketing objectives.
2 To what extent should a company be influenced by the prices of competitors when deciding price levels for its own products?
3 Explain the meaning of fixed and variable costs and the use to which break-even analysis may be put.

12
Caring for the customer

12.1   What is customer care?

A recent addition to the range of marketing strategies, and one that is receiving a lot of attention, is customer care. Stated briefly, its objective is to achieve a positive commitment on the part of every member of an organization, from the board of directors downwards, to the provision of quality products and services.

The pressure of competition in the developed world has created a remarkable improvement in product design and a uniformity of quality in recent years. Generally speaking, however, this has not been accompanied by a corresponding improvement in the service provided for the customer. In many respects care and consideration for customers have declined. Somewhat belatedly, manufacturers have realized that an unacceptably high proportion of prospective customers are deterred from purchasing their products, and too many of their existing customers are lost, simply because of the poor standard of service that is being provided.

Customer-care policies are intended to redress this situation by the encouragement of greater staff interest in the objectives and progress of the organization, increased motivation and a sense of corporate pride.

There is of course nothing very new in this. In many respects it is little more than a restatement of the marketing concept. What is perhaps novel about customer-care strategies is that they are directed specifically to the improvement of workforce awareness and performance in the interests of customer satisfaction. Their increasing implementation in all spheres of product and service marketing underlines the changed consumer attitude of recent years.

12.2   The revolution of rising expectations

Today's consumer is cast in a very different mould to that of previous generations. In most advanced countries greater personal affluence and improved living standards have created a revolution of rising expectations. Standards of product reliability and quality of service accepted by their parents frequently are rejected as simply not good enough by the present generation.

Businesses that have recognized this change in consumer attitude and done something about it stand to gain a vital competitive edge over rivals. We must beware the trap, however, of believing that a mere cosmetic retouching of the company's image can achieve the benefits that a genuine customer-care strategy has to offer. Meaningless slogans, such as 'We put the customer first', have no impact on a marketplace that is increasingly sophisticated and demanding.

There is no doubt about the need for improved customer care and consideration. The early pioneers of the Industrial Revolution tarnished the image of capitalism by their exploitation and abuse of labour. In our own times we must ensure that we do not blemish the face of marketing by the exploitation and abuse of the consumer. The increasing acceptance of the concept of the market economy in many parts of the developing world, and notably in the countries of Eastern Europe, depends upon it.

There is a hoary joke coined frequently in commercial circles that says the conduct of business would be immensely simplified if it was not for the customer and the nuisance he/she causes. Unfortunately the jest is not entirely spurious. It continues to condition much management thinking about the role of the consumer in the economy.

Too often the consumer is convinced he *is* being exploited. Products once sold singly become available only in multiple packs, and in order to acquire the one item he needs, he is compelled to buy three. Too many electrical goods manufacturers fail to attach the essential plug, so that the appliance is not ready for immediate use and cannot be tested before purchase. Too many supermarket checkouts fail to provide assistants to pack the housewife's groceries. She is left to tackle the task herself. What is more, if she asks for a carrier bag, she will be charged for one that is emblazoned with the store's logo, to ensure that she will provide the firm with free advertising as she carries her purchases home! Too often one sees a company delivery vehicle using its size and power on the motorway to hustle and intimidate other road-users, while displaying the slogan 'We are the company that cares'.

Customer care is not of course a philanthropic concept. It is part of the marketing mix and has one aim: to assist the generation of profits by satisfying the customer's needs and expectations. It carries a cost, and can be expensive to operate. Yet it makes no economic sense to invest in customer-care programmes while uncaring behaviour towards customers on the part of company personnel is allowed to persist.

Marketing has a role to play here, because the avoidance of customer dissatisfaction is what customer care really is all about. Before any useful strategy can be devised to deal with the problem, research must discover what it is about the company, its products and its service that causes complaint.

12.3   The value of complaints

It is a recognized human weakness that while we are often quick to criticize others, few of us wish to admit to our own guilt. Whenever a complaint is made against the products or service of any organization, those personnel responsible for receiving it feel threatened. Frequently they do not want to accept responsibility, the customer is frustrated and, however the matter is finally settled, harm has been done.

In the majority of firms complaints that are received are recorded and at intervals senior managers examine the figures to check whether the incidence of complaints is on the increase or the decrease. If it is on the increase, alarm bells are sounded. If the figures show a decrease, there are smiles of satisfaction. The attitude of mind that is passed down to all levels within the organization is that many complaints comprise bad news and few complaints good news. The logical inference presumably must be that nil complaints means perfection.

It means nothing of the kind. There is not a thing created by human hand or mind that has been perceived as perfect by everybody for evermore. Everything we create has some imperfection for some people at some time. Grasp this truth and it is obvious that a degree of dissatisfaction will exist for some consumers in respect to every product or service that they purchase.

We shall never arrive at a precise figure for dissatisfaction, because large numbers of dissatisfied customers *seldom* make a complaint, and an even larger number *never* do so. What is important for marketing is to assess the *degree* of dissatisfaction.

The first thing to get over to personnel is that a complaint is not something one should necessarily be ashamed of. Human failure has to be regarded in much the same light as mechanical failure. A well-designed and maintained machine may, on occasion, break down or perform erratically. No one 'eats their heart out'! Engineers find out what has caused the malfunction and try to correct it. The machine, however complex, is purpose-designed to perform a limited number of operations, but no human being is purpose-designed for the infinite variety of functions he or she must perform during the daily round. If the machine fails continuously to perform properly, we accept that it either needs repair or it is being used for the wrong purpose. Similarly, when an employee is not performing correctly, we must conclude that there are factors affecting the person's concentration or he/she is miscast in the role to which he/she has been assigned. In other words, in this instance we should apply a similar scientific approach to the human resource as we would to a mechanical resource, and remove, as far as it is possible to do so, emotional considerations from the reception of complaints.

The tip of the iceberg

Once this emotional barrier to complaints has been breached, it should be possible to approach customer dissatisfaction realistically. It will be seen that complaints should always be welcome to any business. The pity is that we cannot begin to make any sensible assessment of customer dissatisfaction if we rely solely upon the record of complaints actually made by customers. We know this is merely the tip of the iceberg.

It is, however, a starting point. To obtain the greatest value from specific complaints, procedures should be initiated to ensure:

1 That all personnel whose duties bring them into contact with customers receive training in the handling of complaints.
2 That every complaint is duly recorded and examined.
3 That every complaint subsequently is classified and analysed.

Training in the handling of complaints is essential for all customer-contact personnel. They should be encouraged to adopt a positive response, with an understanding of the likely feelings of the person making the complaint. Few people enjoy having to complain. Often they are tense, and this shows itself in what can appear to be an aggressive attitude. The need to listen carefully to what is being said should be stressed. It is important to offer an apology; this confirms that the statement by the customer alleging failure has been accepted and that there is regret that the customer has been inconvenienced. Attempts to shift the blame on to third parties – to suppliers in the case of a retail shop, or to the kitchen in the case of a restaurant, for example – will only exacerbate the customer's annoyance. Arguing with the customer should be avoided at all costs.

The next stage is to find out what the customer wants done about the situation and, wherever possible, to do it quickly and pleasantly. If remedial action cannot be taken at once, the customer should be told the reason, with an assurance that he or she will be contacted within a specified time either by telephone or letter. Staff should be urged to show the customer their personal concern that standards have slipped on this occasion, and to give an assurance that something positive will be done to rectify the matter. Once the problem has been solved, effort must be made to ensure that the customer is fully satisfied with the solution.

All complaints should be recorded on a single-sheet complaint form. Heads of departments should be responsible for ensuring that each complaint has been dealt with to the customer's satisfaction, and that appropriate action has been, or will be, taken to learn from the incident and avoid a repetition. Completed forms should be passed to a central collection point in the organization, where they can be classified and analysed by nature of complaint, responsible department, seasonality or any other variables pertinent to the product or the company.

Complaint analyses should be distributed to all departments of the organization on a regular basis, with summaries to senior management.

In many organizations staff dealing directly with customers are allowed little or no discretion in settling complaints. Management should review this situation with a view to providing those at the customer interface with sufficient authority to deal swiftly with minor problems. Where a systematized complaints procedure operates, it should be possible to monitor optimum discretionary levels for such staff and to modify them as necessary in the light of experience.

12.4   Systematic satisfaction checks

As we have noted, the problem for marketing is not so much with those customers who complain but with those who may be equally disenchanted with product or service and merely shrug their shoulders and in future go elsewhere. If they do voice their complaints, it is not to the shop or the restaurant or the garage: it is to their friends, neighbours and anyone who will listen. The damage this can do to a firm's image is likely to be out of all proportion to the defect that has caused the complaint. Marketing has to take a serious view of such character assassination by gossip. This means that positive action must be taken to assess the opinion held by the silent majority regarding all aspects of the company's products and service.

Many large organizations have well-established methods to deal with the problem. A major car manufacturer sends questionnaires to all customers following their purchase of a vehicle, and repeats the exercise one or two years later. A company supplying exhaust systems conducts a telephone survey of 100 customers every month. Some firms have installed 'hot lines' by means of which customers can telephone a special department that is ready to deal with their complaints. Some retailing groups employ so-called 'mystery shoppers', who visit each store within the group periodically and report back on various matters that include the behaviour of sales and other staff. A more controversial ploy to find weaknesses in the organization is to employ persons from specialist agencies to pose as customers. They telephone various departments within the company to make enquiries, and conversations are taped for subsequent play-back to the hapless staff members who have erred in their responses.

These are all positive programmes designed to pinpoint areas of possible customer discontent. Their effectiveness depends on how the researched information is used.

12.5 The need for total commitment

We are all customers, and know how it feels to be on the receiving end of indifferent service. Sometimes it is the result of bad organization but more frequently its cause is ignorance on the part of a company's personnel. The fact that customer care has become a sufficiently important aspect of modern marketing as to warrant a leading place in staff-training programmes could be seen as an indictment not merely of the business community but of society generally. When adults have to be taught to show courtesy to their fellow men and women, who incidentally happen to be customers, it is not unreasonable to wonder if there is not something serious-ly wrong with our world. Business cannot arrest the decline in behavioural standards; within all stratas of society that is now largely endemic among many nations of the Western world. All it can hope to do is to instil into its workforce at all levels an awareness of the need for professional behaviour in the conduct of its professional duties.

If a customer-care strategy is to have any meaning, it has to be a total commitment entered into by every member of the organization, regardless of whether the individual is employed at the customer interface or not. Consideration for others is a virtue that cannot be nurtured in isolation. It must be seen to exist at all levels of the company and between all departments.

Attitude to suppliers

Modern business consists of a chain of linked processes. At each process stage there is a supplier and a customer. Some of these suppliers and customers are external to the company, others internal. The point to be grasped is that the degree of consideration and cooperation existing at each link in the chain will influence the quality of service and consideration extended to the final customer, the consumer.

So the principle of consideration must begin with the firm's treat-ment of its external suppliers, the first link in the chain. Many large organizations buy-in components and services from small businesses, and there are some that use their purchasing power to bully such suppliers, sometimes unmercifully. For example, credit abuse by large concerns in times of business recession has not infrequently destroyed small firms dependent upon them. This is not the behaviour of a company that can claim to be a caring organization. There are large companies whose senior management metaphorically shrugs its shoulders when accused of harsh treatment of their smaller suppliers. But marketing should not ignore the results of such an attitude if the company aspires to win public recognition as a caring company.

Interdepartmental attitudes

Similarly the attitude that exists between internal supplier and internal customer departments has an effect upon ultimate customer care. The goods-inwards and warehouse sections are suppliers to the production department, which, in its turn, is the supplier to the sales and despatch departments. The quality of the personal relations between personnel in all these interlinked sections of the firm can have a profound effect on efficiency and productivity. Internal co-operation can achieve important savings in time and the avoidance of expensive wastage of materials and labour. Such is human nature, and the clannish attitude that frequently develops between one group of people and another, that none of these blessings will come about by chance. They have to be promoted, nurtured and encouraged by management at all levels. The only thing that will bring people together and harmonize their efforts is the perception of a common purpose.

This sense of common purpose lies at the heart of the customer-care concept. But petty jealousies between different groups of employees are not dispelled by the managing director calling for team spirit at the firm's annual dinner–dance. A common purpose can only be achieved when it relates to a principle that is seen to be relevant to the interests of all concerned.

The single principle that might be seen to be relevant in a commercial organization is the satisfaction of the customer, because it is the customer who is the source of the employee's income. When dealing with people, there must unfortunately be a loss-or-gain inducement to create a common purpose. Once the shop-floor worker is convinced that outwitting the management is self-defeating and that customer satisfaction alone creates and maintains jobs, once the personnel of one department accept that they rely upon the cooperation of those in another in order to retain the customers who keep them in work, you have the beginnings of a sense of common purpose.

It does not stop there. Satisfying the customer to ensure the survival of one's current employer and one's current job does not have any emotional pull. In most developed countries employment levels rise and fall in accordance with trading cycles, but there are comparatively few economies where the spectre of long-term unemployment haunts the modern worker. Motivating customer care has to go beyond the negative threat of saying 'Our jobs depend on it', even when this may be true.

Caring for and showing consideration to customers demands a positive attitude. It requires the sublimation of selfish instincts into the sense of pride that being part of a highly regarded, achieving group can impart. The appeal must have an emotive quality, because it is essentially an emotive response that is needed. Personnel will only show care and consideration for customers on a consistent basis *if they want to do so*. The reasons why they should want to do so have to be provided by management.

12.6   The internal image of the company

Many factors play their part in supplying these reasons. The first is the company itself and the way in which it behaves in all its corporate dealings. If the company is not perceived by its workforce to be fair-minded in relation to its suppliers, its employees and its customers, customer-care policies are meaningless. Obviously employees will base their quality assessment of the company largely on its record as an employer and, in today's climate, this transcends such basic benefits as pension schemes, health-care and holiday entitlement, which are largely uniform among major industrial and commercial organizations. Influencing factors are likely to be more personal: the attitude of managers towards their staff, the openness with which policies and practices are explained and discussed, the willingness of the management to listen to staff problems and suggestions. To these should be added a further important factor: recognition of individual effort and achievement.

Above all, the door must close on the outmoded idea that going to work is a penance. Managements anxious to promote a true customer-care policy need to devise work schedules that create and sustain employee interest in the tasks that have to be performed. This starts with the premise that many, if not most, operations are capable of being performed more efficiently, and therefore more effectively, which can be achieved by the implementation of training programmes that need not be restricted to specific skills instruction but can cover the wider spectrum of the company's current activities and future objectives. The effect upon the individual employee will be to broaden his horizon and enable him to discover the significance and value that his own contribution makes to the common effort. The acquisition of improved skills and performance ability has greater meaning and creates a greater sense of self-worth when it can be related to the common purpose.

12.7   Internal marketing

Customer care starts with care for the employee in its widest sense. A technique known as internal marketing has been practised in recent years, mainly in service industries, to address the principles and practices of marketing to the problem of employee motivation.

Internal marketing begins with the premise that employees have an understandable reluctance to recommend to customers that which they find unacceptable themselves. It follows that staff acceptance of, and enthusiasm for, the company and its products or services is an essential preliminary to their acceptance by customers. Therefore employees must be seen as internal customers, and their jobs as internal products that need to be designed in such a manner as to meet the needs of these internal customers.

Looked at in this light, the aim of the company should be to regard the jobs of its employees in the same way as it regards the manufactured goods or the services that it offers to the marketplace. To gain and sustain employee satisfaction, the job must exhibit certain qualities that offer employee benefits in the same way as a product must offer benefits suited to the needs of the customers.

An interesting survey carried out recently among workers in British companies showed that pride in the firm and its reputation was a bigger morale booster than benefits such as high wages and 'perks'. Researchers found that the crucial factor in determining a firm's ability to survive was the degree of staff motivation. The most effective motivating influence was said to come from managers who made staff feel proud of the image the company had with customers, shareholders and suppliers.

Job security came a close second: the most successful firms in the survey valued long service and offered employees a significantly more secure future than the less successful. Strong management was considered the next most important factor in staff motivation. Executives of successful organizations were seen by their subordinates as more competent, credible, trustworthy and accessible than they were seen in the less successful. This was followed by company identification. Workers in the best firms felt a stronger sense of pride in association with their employers than did workers in other firms. Workers in the best firms were said to be more likely to recommend the company as a good place in which to work and were less likely to be thinking of leaving it themselves. Pay, 'perks' and other benefits came only fifth on the list of motivating factors.

Once the concept of internal marketing is understood and accepted, its implementation can follow similar lines to that of external marketing. There will be an initial need for research into current employee attitudes to the company, its management and organization. What is the perceived company image? On what is this perception based? What is it that employees like or dislike about the company? How do they view the way the firm is organized? What improvements would they like to see? What changes, if any, can they suggest for the improvement of their own working conditions and performance?

The object of this internal research should be to discover the perceived strengths and weaknesses of the company on the part of its employees. Its findings will provide an 'employee impressions' audit that will contain a number of elements suitable for inclusion in an internal marketing mix:

1 *Company image*: successful, responsible, respected, ethical, progressive.
2 *Management image*: competent, fair-minded, communicative, accessible.
3 *Working conditions*: organization, responsibilities, training, working environment.
4 *Job quality*: employee rights, remuneration, other benefits, wage review, promotion opportunities, status.

The promotional element for the internal marketing mix will include many of the techniques employed in the external marketing of products or services. Because the audience is a captive one, it can be reached easily. Internal advertising, for example, can take the form of a company magazine or simply periodical bulletins that keep employees informed of the firm's current activities and focus their attention on new products or new services to be offered to the external customer. Internal presentations to groups of employees by members of the sales or marketing departments offer another promotional channel.

12.8   Motivation by job appreciation

We have seen that if customer care is to mean something more than the expression of meaningless platitudes, it requires a positive commitment on the part of every member of the organization. In order to achieve this commitment, there has to be motivation. The concept of job satisfaction, aimed at ensuring the general well-being of the employee by means of suitable remuneration, job security and various fringe benefits, coupled with a favourable working environment, was at one time considered to have a strong motivating influence. In practice, however, it has proved insufficient to achieve full commitment.

What is needed is job appreciation: establishing an appreciation that the job itself brings benefits over and above the provision of an acceptable standard of living. It means valuing the job for its own sake, with all the problem-facing challenges this entails. It means enjoying the pressures and being glad to accept situations where frequently one must be resourceful and display initiative. Above all, it means taking pride in doing a difficult job successfully.

Looked at in this light, the job itself is the motivator. It provides much more than mere satisfaction. It elevates the individual to a higher plane of personal pride and confidence, so that the workload, with all its attendant frustrations, acquires its own fascination.

The cynic of course may consider such a suggestion to be high-falutin nonsense, in view of the attitude of many wage-earners in commerce and industry. What belies the criticism, however, is the undoubted enthusiasm with which so many of these wage-earners engage voluntarily in their leisure-time pursuits of do-it-yourself home improvements, or the energy with which they compete to raise vast sums of money for charitable causes. They enjoy the experience of stretching themselves to achieve new skills.

The starting point of motivation, as we have seen, is the company and its perceived image. Pride by association is a very strong motivator in all aspects of life. But a belief in the company image must be genuinely held at all levels. Nothing can be so demoralizing to a workforce than loose talk by managers that implies contention at the top, creating muddled thinking and flawed policies. Managers should be aware that it is they who are paid to manage. Staff should not be burdened with management problems not within their power to resolve.

Managers should also recognize that they are conspicuous figures in the working environment. They may expect their performance to be monitored by their superiors, but they may not be so acutely aware of how keenly they are observed by those who work for them. Their attitude, work-related or personal, necessarily affects their subordinates, becomes a prime topic of office or works gossip, and can have a considerable influence on morale.

The manager's personality inevitably imprints itself on the entire team, but it is in his or her relationship with individual members of the team that motivation may be especially enhanced. Each will have some self-doubts. Everybody may need reassurance, some more than others. When accolades are to be handed out, the subtle-minded manager considers primarily the motivational needs of individual members of the team. Wherever credit is due to an individual, it should be given freely, because one success, duly recognized, encourages the performance of another.

The role of management – and particularly middle management – in fostering and maintaining the concept of customer care by means of a highly motivated workforce is therefore vital. Once it is accepted, there is a reasonable chance that it will influence the personal attitude of staff in their relationship with customers, and thus greatly enhance the caring image of the company.

Discussion questions

1   Why is the development of customer care policies considered important for business firms?
2   Describe how an effective complaints procedure can be adopted in: (a) a company manufacturing domestic appliances; (b) a retail department store.
3   What are the likely factors that will influence employee attitudes towards: (a) inter-departmental cooperation; (b) the company image?
4   Discuss methods for the improvement of employee morale and the care and consideration of customers.

13
Marketing and the small business

As the result of acquisitions and mergers, the size and power of business organizations has grown enormously during the past two decades. Not only has the retail trade of the High Street become dominated by large combines, but in industry, too, the amalgamation of manufacturing firms has advanced to an extent where most industrial activity is also dominated by a comparatively small number of very powerful corporations. Despite this trend, however, the popular urge to operate an independent enterprise remains as strong as ever, and every year the number of such independent firms increases.

In recent years there has been growing concern about the situation of the small firm, coupled with a realization of its importance in the industrial and commercial scene. Politicians sing the praises of the small manufacturer and entrepreneur, pointing out his/her essential role in the free-enterprise system.

It is appropriate therefore to consider the situation of the small firm in the modern business world, and to discover how far the principles of marketing can be of assistance to the small producer or distributor.

13.1 Motivations of small-business proprietors

What motivates individuals to set up in business on their own account? It is an important question, because motivation often provides the key to the subsequent success or failure of the enterprise.

Probably the strongest motive of most self-employed people is the desire to achieve and maintain independence. They dislike working for others or being in any way subservient to them. They seek freedom, and, having once gained it, will often refuse to give it up. It does not matter to them that they might earn more money, work easier hours and have more congenial conditions if they were employed.

Some people decide to start their own business after a long period of unemployment, or because they have become redundant in their employed occupation. Redundancy payments and 'golden handshakes' sometimes provide the modest capital that starts the business.

For others, it is a means of escaping the frustration of working for a large organization, where their ideas and abilities are denied sufficient scope. The only way they feel they can fulfil themselves is to break away and operate independently. This is often the case with designers, development engineers, and salespeople, whose work is of a creative nature.

Those whose prime aim is to achieve independence or to gain the chance to develop a product or service that is their 'brainchild' may find that they can keep their business small and still satisfy their ambitions. But the business created by a man or woman whose overriding aim is to make money is unlikely to remain small. The quest for wealth will always be the spur to do bigger and better things. Continual expansion will be the theme.

Because the underlying motives of those who set up in business on their own varies so widely, the question of what is, or is not, a successful business is difficult to answer. For many small shopkeepers and owners of modest manufacturing firms, their ability, year after year, to pay their way and keep their heads above water is enough. Their personal satisfaction comes from their high degree of independence or their freedom to develop their personal skills and ideas. If they are satisfied with their own progress and they contribute, however modestly, to the well-being of the community, who shall say they are not successful?

But if the business aim is to make money, there is a yardstick by which success can be measured. No success can be claimed if the profits of the business are less than could be achieved by the owner investing his capital in a good security and his time and talents working for someone else.

13.2   Opportunities for the small business

Whatever the motives that impel individuals to strike out on their own, the business climate in which they must operate has become increasingly hostile. Giant enterprises dominate the economic landscape, seemingly denying opportunity to the small firm.

The survival of these giants, with their huge overheads, depends, as we have seen, on mass-production and mass-trading. Products of uniform quality consisting of uniform components are sold by uniform methods of advertising and promotion. Because of this uniformity, production and distribution costs are kept to a minimum. It is almost impossible for the small workshop or the small retailer to compete against these giants.

But this uniformity of manufacture and distribution by big firms does give the small firm its opportunity. Production lines geared to produce nothing less than hundreds of thousands of standard components cannot turn out short runs of special items economically. Nor can the chain stores and supermarkets economically stock a wide range of speciality goods. When it comes to providing personal service, everyone has had experience of the inability of the large organization to meet the particular needs of the individual. Here is where small firms find their opportunities: providing the goods and services that the giants are no longer capable of supplying.

13.3   Strengths of the small business

What are the strengths of the small firm compared to those of large corporations?

1 *Flexibility*. It is simpler for the small workshop to undertake something special than it is for the large organization. It can change its production programme in the time it takes the production committee of the major manufacturer to sit down to have a meeting on the subject. It can tailor-make a product to meet a specific need without undue cost, because of its small batch methods. The big firm, with mass-production techniques, cannot match this service.

2 *The personal touch*. The proprietor of a small firm often knows his customers personally, just as he personally knows his suppliers of raw materials and components, and usually the people who work for him. Because of his first-hand knowledge of all aspects of his business, he can make quick decisions when needed.

3 *Improvisation*. Another distinct advantage that the small firm has over bigger rivals is the comparative ease with which it can improvise in an emergency.

These three factors – flexibility, the personal touch, leading to speed of decision, and the ability to improvise – give the small manufacturing business a distinct edge over larger competitors.

It is not always appreciated how important these facilities are to potential customers. Domestic-appliance and electrical-goods manufacturers, to take just one example, frequently contract out the production of short runs of vital components to small firms in their locality. They do so because they will get a keener price and will most certainly get better service than if they tried to make them themselves or put the work out to larger component manufacturers.

As far as the small retail shop is concerned, the same qualities of speed, service and speciality apply. The retailer who specializes in a type of goods not readily available from large stores and multiples, and who provides a speedy personal service to his customers, can operate profitably despite the apparent attractions of the High Street giants, simply because he is not in competition with them. The ladies' fashion shop specializing in garments that appeal to a minority section of the local community, or the specialist photographic shop that carries a wide range of cameras and photographic equipment, offer exclusivity that the department stores do not wish to match.

Every new business venture needs to be based on an exploitable idea. Here are some examples of exploitable conditions and circumstances that have put many small enterprises on the road to success:

1 The possession of some special skill, knowledge or interest that is connected with a certain type of commodity or service.
2 The discovery of a particular need for certain types of goods or services that is not being fulfilled adequately by existing producers or traders.
3 The recognition of a better way to satisfy a particular need for certain goods or services.
4 The recognition of a better way to promote the sale of certain types of goods or services.

The needs of the public are changing, slightly but constantly, every year. Popular tastes and interests fluctuate. Every minor change in the way of life of the community creates a need for new or modified products. This means that there is always scope for the small manufacturer to bring to the market something that is new, even though its novelty may be no more than a modified design that gives the product greater appeal to the eye, greater usefulness, or enables it to be sold more cheaply.

The small producer, with his facility for improvisation, his flexibility, his ability to produce special short-runs economically, often has far greater scope than his bigger rivals to innovate. The proof of this statement lies in the experience of the past twenty years, because most of the new product ideas developed during that period were originated by small manufacturing firms. Innovation is one of the most important features of the small business, and the reason why a thriving small business community is so vital to the industrial health of the nation.

13.4 Weaknesses of the small business

There is, however, another side to the coin. Small firms are extremely vulnerable to a host of outside influences and factors:

1 *Limited finance.* This imposes restrictions on everything the small firm tries to do. Management often is acutely aware of the need for plant re-equipment, product and market research, and better

company and product promotion, but is unable to escape the straitjacket of critical cashflow and lack of financial reserves.

2 *Limited management capacity*. Many small firms are run by individuals or partners. The day-to-day operation of the business very largely depends upon their availability. Fully occupied with the current workload and its attendant problems, they have little time to consider future objectives and strategies.

3 *Limited market*. With a limited spread of customers and a restricted market, owing to the need for specialization of product or service, the small firm has difficulty in diversifying its activities, which makes it extremely vulnerable in times of trade recession.

These three factors of limited finance, management capacity and market are all interlinked. The lack of financial resources of the small business prevents the recruitment of professional management skills, which in turn could improve its marketing capability, and that improvement might result in the achievement of a strengthened financial position.

Before looking to see how marketing principles and practice can assist small business, let us examine in greater detail some of the weaknesses categorized above.

Small-firm finance

The majority of small enterprises are funded at the outset with a relatively modest introduction of capital by the founders, supported by a loan from one of the clearing banks or some similar financial institution. Overdraft facilities may also be provided to take care of likely fluctuations in the firm's cashflow. From the experience of a considerable number of small businesses set up during the last decade, it has become obvious that one of the basic faults that has been made is under-funding. Insufficient allowance has been made for the inevitable mistakes a new firm will make within its early months of trading, when it is still finding its way into its market. Factors well beyond the control of its management can have an unpredictable effect upon its financial standing.

The most serious of these factors is credit abuse. In the industrial sector the majority of small firms inevitably find themselves sandwiched between large company suppliers of materials or components, on the one hand, and large company customers, on the other. If they wish to conduct business, they are compelled to grant credit to their customers and, where their capital is restricted or already invested in setting up the business, they need to take credit from their suppliers. The arrangement works satisfactorily while money is reasonably plentiful and cheap. When the cost of money rises, however, the tendency is for their customers to delay payment while their suppliers insist upon prompt account settlement before further supplies are made available.

Bearing in mind the cyclical pattern of trade and of interest rates in recent years, you will see it is perhaps no coincidence that a considerable number of new small businesses have failed within three years of their foundation. Many such firms have not run short of work, they have run short of money. Such is the vigour of these small entrepreneurs that the majority contrive to start up again, and on their second attempt prove successful. Nonetheless the economy must inevitably be weakened by the comparatively high incidence of small-company failures and the wastage this entails.

Small-firm management

The lack of adequate management knowledge and experience that typifies the majority of small firms also contributes to their vulnerability. Most such businesses are started by individuals or partners who have some exploitable knowledge or skill either in production or marketing. Depending upon the area of their skill, the business will be either production- or sales-orientated. Unless the two skills are combined in a partnership, there will be an immediate weakness in the area where one of these skills is lacking.

The day-to-day operation of many small firms is virtually dependent upon the availability of the principals, which means there is minimal time in which management can turn its mind from current problems to consider and plan for the future. The cliché questions 'Where are we now? In what direction should we be heading? How shall we get there?' seldom get answered, because small business proprietors are often convinced that unless they devote all their time and energy to today's problems, there *will* be no tomorrow. In such circumstances tomorrow has to look after itself, which of course it rarely does.

The small firm and its market

Inevitably a small firm is compelled to specialize in whatever area of product or service provision it undertakes. With limited resources at its disposal, it can cater only for a limited number of customers. This element of specialized production means that the market in which it operates will also be specialized. Not altogether unwisely, many independent operators decide to concentrate upon doing what they are good at. They see this as the means to build their reputation for quality and consistency. The inherent danger, however, is that this makes their business extremely vulnerable in times of trade recession.

With perhaps only a handful of regular customers, small industrial firms rely heavily on the demand they receive from companies mostly in the same industrial sector. Any sudden trading recession within that sector will affect all their customers and have a domino effect upon themselves.

Where a small manufacturing firm is heavily dependent upon the business it receives from a single customer, its freedom of action is very restricted. As the requirements of the larger organization change, continuation of business may depend upon the small firm undertaking additional commitments, such as re-equipment or entering into new processes for which it has not budgeted. Unless future utilization of such new equipment is assured by the customer's continuing demand, the small producer may find himself crippled with the burden of repayment for plant and machinery he can no longer use.

13.5   How marketing can assist the small business

One of the most important benefits that the concept of marketing brings to any business is the structured methods by which its principles are put into practice. These structures impose discipline that is lacking in the management of many small firms. Most proprietors of small businesses are individualistic in outlook, which in the majority of cases is the reason why they are running small enterprises. Many are conditioned to *ad hoc* decision-making, because of the circumstances in which they find themselves. As we have already noted, large numbers of such operators possess specific production or sales skills. Few may have had formal professional management training, and those who have may have practised professional management only within the environment of large organizations, and in situations totally different from those that apply to a small business.

There can, however, be no logical argument for rejecting the principles and practice of marketing in even the smallest commercial enterprise. The notion that structured programming calls for an unnecessary use of limited time is false, because, once in place, it will save management time in the future. Time is wasted when proprietors or partners repeatedly have to contend with recurrent problems that forward planning would have eliminated.

The first stage in applying marketing practices to a small business is to carry out the firm audit. One does this by considering all the resources of the business, in terms of available finance, available borrowing facilities, existing plant and equipment, existing personnel, including the firm's management and its knowledge and skills, the reputation the firm has acquired with its customers and its suppliers, and any other plus factors that can be thought of. These are the firm's assets or strengths. One next considers its weaknesses: the things it would like to have but lacks. These include the limitation of its equipment, knowledge or abilities appropriate to its products and markets that its management and workforce does not possess, and past events that may inhibit the firm in future dealings with certain suppliers or customers.

At the end of a soul-searching session of this kind the owners of the small business will have a very much clearer idea of what the firm can and cannot do. Perhaps, even more important, they will realize what it must do and what it must not do. The reason why some of its recent activities have been successful while others have been a failure may also become more apparent.

Armed with the information this internal audit has provided, management now can review the firm's present situation. Are the firm's resources immutable or can they be improved? If they cannot be improved, are we making the best use of what we have got? Are we making the right products and are we in the right market in view of the resources at our disposal? Should we make a fundamental change and use the resources we have got to better advantage doing something different?

The next stage is to look at the market, or markets, to which the firm is currently supplying its products or services. How much is known about the market? Are the customers we currently supply the best customers for us in our situation? In the industrial field large customers placing large orders may, on the surface, seem attractive. But what sort of demands do they place on the small firm? How disruptive are such demands to the economic – and therefore profitable – use of the firm's resources? Are their payments prompt and reliable? Or does payment-chasing occupy a disproportionate amount of management time? Can we get equally attractive business from potential customers without such uneconomic aggravation?

A more important question to be asked, following consideration of the market, is how sound that market appears to be? Will it remain buoyant or are there things happening out there in the wide world that could change the market? If changes do occur, where will they leave us? Should we perhaps be thinking about insuring against future market downturn by looking at alternative markets for our products?

This kind of thinking must inevitably lead to a better understanding not only of the firm itself but of its future if it continues to pursue its present course. It may suggest that concentration upon current activities remains the best option, or it may indicate the need for a change of direction. Whatever course is decided upon, objectives, some fairly immediate and others long-term, will have entered the discussion. If such objectives are ever to move beyond the discussion stage, a plan will need to be put into operation.

13.6   Tackling the problems of the small business

On a previous page some of the specific difficulties faced by many small businesses were highlighted. Many of these can be eased, if not entirely overcome, if appropriate action is taken at the right time. The relative financial weakness of the small firm is largely endemic but the problem of credit abuse is one that management can do something about.

Factoring of accounts

The basis of factoring is that a firm sells to a factoring company its trade debts and the company provides in return a debtor accounting and administration service. The routine activity of sending out invoices to customers, followed by statements and possible further reminders, is undertaken by the company, which will advance to the firm up to 80 per cent of the cash due from customers at a date earlier than that at which it would receive the money from the customers.

The benefit to the small business is that it frees management from the task of debt collection, allowing it to concentrate its attention on other important aspects of the commercial or industrial operation. Expert guidance is given by the factoring company on all aspects of the firm's credit control, the firm's cashflow is improved and it is protected against bad debts. During times of financial stringency, when late payment from large customers can endanger the solvency of a small business, factoring may prove very helpful.

Depending upon the amount of work to be done, factoring companies charge in the region of ½ per cent to 3½ per cent of turnover. The firm can draw up to 80 per cent of the invoice value in advance, and will receive the residue after the customer has settled his account with the factoring company.

The use of consultants

With the growth in the service sector of the economy, there is now a proliferation of consultants and advisory agencies to whom the small business proprietor can turn for advice and assistance covering virtually every aspect of commercial activity. The inherent weakness of the small firm that results from the limited knowledge and experience of its management is now capable of correction by the use of such services.

Advice is available on such diverse subjects as marketing, product design, quality control, manufacturing, and finance, as well as product promotion by means of advertising, exhibiting and sponsorship. Guidance on the selection and use of computer systems is also readily available. There are consultants and agencies that assist small firms seeking to enter the export market, and they will undertake much of the essential research work and provide introductions to overseas agents and distributors.

The better the service provided, the more it will cost and, until recently, this has deterred many small businesses from using consultants. In Britain, however, the Department of Trade and Industry has recently introduced its Enterprise Initiative scheme with the intention of making the use of consultancy advice more easily available to smaller businesses. Under the scheme an independent business counsellor engaged by the Department reviews the situation of the small firm to assess problems and identify opportunities. Specialist assistance is subsequently arranged to deal with specific projects, with the DTI paying up to two-thirds of the cost.

Recognition of the need for expansion

The principles of marketing discussed earlier in connection with larger enterprises apply equally to the small business, and not the least important of these is the need for expansion. We have seen that a fundamental weakness of the small firm is its dependence upon a limited market that is always liable to fluctuation and possibly to decline. It is for this reason that no business, large or small, can afford to stand still.

A firm's customers and the world in which they live is changing constantly, and any proprietor who is content to sit back and let business 'tick over' will soon find that it is running downhill. But it will not be enough in a competitive climate merely to make changes as the need arises. Change must be anticipated, and every effort must be made to increase volume, because it is inevitable that, year by year, some existing customers will be eroded away. Overhead costs will mount increasingly, owing to inflation, and better ways to run the business must be found to offset these rising costs and to ensure future continuation. There are no soft options, and the only way the small proprietor can keep his or her business alive is to expand its activities.

Expansion can take a number of forms for the large and for the small firm:

1 By increasing sales of the existing range of goods or services.
2 By selling more high value goods, thus achieving a higher monetary turnover at the same percentage of profit.
3 By bringing additional products into the range, so that existing customers may be encouraged to purchase more of their requirements from the firm.

4   By extending the size of the firm's market, e.g. opening another shop in a different neighbourhood, or introducing a different category of products that will attract a different and additional section of customers from those currently supplied.

Expansion of profits, as distinct from expansion of turnover, may be achieved by reducing costs. This means running the business more efficiently without loss of effectiveness. The management of small businesses are usually highly cost-conscious, which is one of their strengths. But sometimes the attitude to costs is a narrow one, resulting often in penny-wise, pound-foolishness. Cost economy can best be achieved by investment in mechanization to replace labour-intensive activities.

Finally, in seeking that elusive unique selling proposition with which to expand the business, the small operator should remember one priceless asset totally lost to the giant combines: his or her own personality. It is an asset that, in this day of so many faceless organizations, should be exploited to the full in advertising and publicity, as well as day-to-day correspondence and contact with customers. Too often one finds small, somewhat insignificant firms trying desperately to ape the impersonal image pattern set by the majors in a vain attempt to disguise their smallness. What folly when, as is so often the case, personal attention is what so many customers are seeking!

Discussion questions

1   State the principal strengths and weaknesses of small firms and discuss the reasons why these conditions apply.
2   Describe ways in which a small engineering company can expand its activities.
3   The importance of the small business sector is frequently stressed. Name three major contributions that small firms make to the betterment of the economy.

Glossary of marketing terms

Barb research. A method of television audience research conducted in the United Kingdom by Broadcaster's Audience Research Board (BARB), in which the receivers in a representative sample of households are electronically metered to record the number of hours per day the television set is on, and to which transmitting channel it is tuned. Subscribers to the service receive a weekly analysis of the total audience and of its composition for all programmes transmitted.

Benefit. A feature or property associated with a product or service that is intended to satisfy a specific customer need.

Brainstorming. A method of product-idea creation in which a group of people attend a totally informal meeting for an uninhibited exchange of ideas.

Cognitive dissonance. A psychological condition experienced by customers who suffer tension as the result of anxiety and doubt following a major purchase. They may require reassurance that they have acted wisely, and that they were justified in the expenditure they have incurred. Such doubts may usually be dispelled if the salesman reaffirms the benefits provided by the item and commends the customer's decision to purchase.

Consumer panels. Recruited for the purposes of market research, members of panels are permanent samples representing the *universe* or sub-section of the total population being investigated. They usually undertake to keep special diaries, issued by the research organization, in which they record their purchases of branded items.

Deal-in. A term used to describe an offer made by a product manufacturer to a retailer of a price reduction for a specified period, usually conditional upon the retailer accepting an agreed minimum supply of the product.

Deal-out. A special attraction offered by a product manufacturer to the consumer. It may take the form of a kitchen utensil, a toy or a gadget that the housewife can purchase at a reduced price upon presentation to the retailer of labels or wrappers from the manufacturer's branded product. Other attractions offered may be the chance to enter a competition or just the opportunity to buy the product at a specially reduced price during a limited period.

Decision-making units (DMUs). Major purchasing decisions, especially in industrial markets, are frequently influenced by the views of groups of people, including production managers, technical and design staff, and financial directors. This underlines the need for salesmen to establish the composition of the decision-making unit within a targeted company before negotiating the sale of industrial raw materials, components and capital equipment.

Diversification. The engagement in products, industries, technologies and markets new to an organization for the better utilization of its resources. Principal methods include (1) specialization and the extension of markets, (2) acquisition of other firms, and (3) introduction of a new product range.

Feature. Any distinguishing property of a product or service that potentially offers advantage to the user. Features do not, however, become *benefits* unless they satisfy a specific customer need.

Four Ps. *Product*, *price*, *place* and *promotion* are the four predominant elements of the marketing mix, formulated to produce a specific blend of benefits to match the needs of a targeted market segment (also termed the *core strategy*).

Franchising. A channel for retail distribution that combines the expert management strength of the large organization with the flexibility, enthusiasm and motivation strengths of the independent operator. The franchisor legally empowers the franchisee to use his brand name and his idea in the pursuit of his business, subject to the franchisee conducting his business strictly in accordance with policies and methods prescribed by the franchisor. The franchisee must provide the bulk of the financial investment from his own resources.

Invisible earnings. Defined by the British Invisible Exports Council as earnings from the provision of services, in direct contrast to 'visible' exports, derived from the sale of tangible goods. Invisible earnings include interest, profits or dividends from investments in foreign enterprises, and currency earned by British individuals and companies in the provision of services to foreigners.

Market segment. A section of a market composed of customers whose needs are closely similar and can be distinguished from the needs of those of other sections.

Market share. A firm's sales by volume to a market expressed as a percentage of the total volume of sales made to the market.

Marketing mix. A conceptual mix or blend of perceived benefits by means of which the needs of specific customer groups may be satisfied.

Objective. A future goal of an organization, considered attainable within a specified time-scale, subject to the availability of quantified resources, in terms of finance, technology and personnel.

Merchandising. A term used in marketing to denote all those sales-promotion activities that aim to generate the customer's interest in the product or service other than conventional press and television advertising or the use of public relations. Many large producers have teams of *merchandisers* attached to their sales departments and their specialist function is to create promotions and displays in retailers' premises to boost the sale of their brands.

Pareto effect. Also commonly referred to as the 80/20 rule, it is a phenomenon characteristic of most commercial firms that some 80 per cent of business comes from about 20 per cent of customers. Of the 80 per cent of customers who account for only 20 per cent of sales, some may possibly be of potentially greater value to the company in the future. Despite the considerable additional costs the company must bear in servicing these small customers, their aggregate contribution to sales volume and to recovery of overheads may be significant.

Penetration pricing. A marketing technique whose purpose is to achieve maximum market penetration for a product by means of a special low price, taking advantage of the economies of scale that high production levels may offer. Such action also reduces the penetration opportunity of competitors during the period of the low price offer.

Physical distribution. A comprehensive term for all activities that make services and products available to customers, including order-processing, stock control, warehousing and transportation. Together with the *distribution channel*, it forms part of the place element of the marketing mix.

Planning. The means by which a course of action is determined as the result of assumptions based upon indicators of a future pattern of events.

Positioning. Finding the segment of the market where customers' needs can be matched most closely by the benefits offered by a specific product or service.

Primary data. Information required to be gathered by marketing research from primary sources, usually by means of special surveys. These include personal interviewing of selected samples of the universe (groups of specific consumers), postal questionnaires, panels or discussion groups.

Product life cycle. A graphic representation of the stages by which the sales revenue of a product is affected over a period of time: introduction, growth, maturity, market saturation, and decline.

Product portfolio matrix. Developed by the Boston Consulting Group, the matrix is a graphic device to assist the balancing of a portfolio of products with a view to achieving the best alternative use of company resources.

Resources. A term that encompasses the totality of human skills, knowledge and experience, together with the technical and financial capabilities by means of which a company can confront a problem or exploit an opportunity.

Retail audit. A market-research technique that uses panels of retail outlets to establish brand shares and sales from shops to customers by volume. Trained auditors visit each sample shop at frequent intervals and stock-take for all their clients' brands. By adding the previous stock figure to subsequent purchases and deducting the current stock, they calculate the sales of the subject brands during the given period.

Secondary data. Information required for marketing-research purposes that is available from existing sources. Such sources may be internal, such as company records, or external, such as governmental statistics, trade association publications, the reports of professional bodies, or articles and reports published in newspapers and trade and technical journals.

Sponsorship. A method of sales promotion in which an organization invests money to support cultural or sporting activities. The object is to enhance public goodwill for the company by means of the contribution it is seen to be making to popular causes, and to achieve repeated public recognition and mention of its brand name in media coverage of the sponsored activities.

SWOT analysis. A summarized version of a company's situational analysis. The firm's *strengths* and *weaknesses* are related to trends in its external environment, including customer needs, competitive activities, the economic climate and governmental policies, to identify possible *opportunities* and possible *threats* to the organization.

Target. The end to which a marketing strategy is aimed, e.g. a market or market segment, in order to achieve a specific objective.

Triangle clause. Used by market research, it consists of three related questions inserted within a questionnaire, each of which approaches the same subject from a slightly different angle. If it is found that one answer contradicts another, it is assumed that the answer given to the third question decides the issue.

Unique selling proposition. A product or service offering, consisting of a package of benefits designed to appeal to a specific market segment, which is unique to the supplier organization and consequently not matched by competitors (also known as *differential advantage*).

Universe (or *population*). This refers to the sub-section of the actual population investigated in the course of market research. A universe may be the total number of schoolteachers or the total number of families with two or more cars.

Further reading

Belson, William A., *The Design and Understanding of Survey Questions*, Gower, 1981

Branch, *Elements of Export Practice,* Chapman and Hall, 1985

Burton, Graham, *Effective Marketing Logistics*, Macmillan, 1975

Chisnall, Peter, *Marketing: A Behavioural Analysis*, McGraw Hill, 1975

Drucker, Peter F. *Managing For Results*, Butterworth-Heinemann, 1967

Foxall, G. R., *Consumer Behaviour: A Practical Guide*, Croom Helm, 1984

Hibbert, E. P., *The Principles and Practice of Export Marketing*, Butterworth-Heinemann, 1985

Kotler, P., *Marketing Management: Analysis, Planning and Control*, Prentice Hall International, 1984

Lloyd, Herbert, *Teach Yourself PR*, English Universities Press, 1973

McDonald, Malcolm H. B., *Marketing Plans*, Butterworth-Heinemann, 1984

Maclean, Ian, *Handbook of Industrial Marketing & Research*, Duncan Publishing, 1985

Piercy, Nigel, *Export Strategy: Markets and Competition*, Allen and Unwin, 1982

Walsh, L., *International Marketing*, Macdonald and Evans, 1976

Willsmer, R. L., *Directing the Marketing Effort*, Pan, 1975

Wilmshurst, John, *The Fundamentals and Practice of Marketing*, Butterworth-Heinemann, 1984

Index